Nicolas Rothwell is a journaovel-
ist. He has spent years worki       and
the US. He lives in the North

# Wings of the Kite-Hawk

## Nicolas Rothwell

**PICADOR**
Pan Macmillan Australia

First published 2003 in Picador by Pan Macmillan Australia Pty Limited
St Martins Tower, 31 Market Street, Sydney

National Library of Australia
cataloguing-in-publication data:

Rothwell, Nicolas.
Wings of the kite-hawk.

ISBN 0 330 36402 2.

1. Rothwell, Nicolas – Journeys – Australia. 2. Australia – Description and travel.
3. Australia – Social life and customs. 4. Australia – History. I. Title.

919.404

Typeset in 12/16 pt Granjon by Post Pre-press Group, Brisbane
Printed in Australia by McPherson's Printing Group

*For My Mother*
*Tu fui, ego eris*

# CONTENTS

# One Leichhardt

# I

On May 21st 1845, after weeks of searching through the ranges of Cape York, the explorer Ludwig Leichhardt came upon a steep-banked, westward-flowing river system, unseen by European eyes. This discovery, made eight months after his expedition's departure from the settled country of the Darling Downs, opened the way for his passage across the Great Divide, towards the Gulf of Carpentaria, and towards his far-off goal, the military outpost at Port Essington, on the north coast of Arnhem Land.

In the explorer's *Journal of an Overland Expedition in Australia*, which is largely composed of austere botanical and geological observations, a brief sunshine of emotion bathes the entries for these days. The country becomes romantic, the plant life lush. Leichhardt describes the eagerness, and the ease, with which he and his riding-companion on that sortie, the Aboriginal Harry Brown, hastened back to their main camp, through valleys full of trees and flowers still unknown to science. Like most of Australia's early explorers,

Leichhardt regarded the landscape as a sounding-board of his heart, and he named this river, accordingly, after his close friend, the gloomy and hypochondriacal Sydney barrack-master, Robert Lynd.

Theirs was a curious connection, formal yet intimate, like several others in the explorer's life. Lynd put Leichhardt up soon after his arrival in the colony. He tried to speak with his guest in German, though Leichhardt had long since attained a perfect mastery of English. The two men discussed science and plant collections, and read poetry together. Leichhardt even copied some of Lynd's poems into his notebook. When Leichhardt was first presumed lost in the desert, Lynd wrote a dirge in his memory.

With this solid name attached to the evanescent water-course before him – the Lynd was, in fact, at that point in its passage, a standard Cape York creek, all overspilling pools, wide sand-beds and abrupt, deep-bored flood channels – Leichhardt returned to camp and gathered up his men. They pressed on, following the river-bed, across rocky bars, through high gorges, between sheer walls of basalt and porphyry, where Leichhardt observed tell-tale signs of mineralisation, and where, within half a century, stepped open-cuts, deep shafts and gold-rush shanty-towns would punctuate the bush.

Leichhardt's descriptions of the upper Lynd oddly conjure up the scenery of the Sächsische Schweiz, a wild region south-west of the town of Cottbus, where he had attended boarding school two decades earlier: '*The country was broken by low ranges of various extent, formed by exceedingly rocky hills and peaks, which lifted their rugged crests above the open forests that covered their slopes.*' But it is at this stage in his narrative that one first begins to sense the potency of the Australian Outback. The landscape stamps itself on Leichhardt's mind. Its sounds, scents and rhythms enter him; he struggles to remake his language, and himself. A few weeks before, on a lone ride from the expedition's camp on the Boyd River,

Leichhardt had come upon a valley ringed by high sandstone rocks, *'fissured and broken like pillars and walls and the high gates of the ruined castles of Germany.'* Now the tree-clustered summits high above his party's route called forth a different, less conventional image: they resembled *'the lifted crest of an irritated cockatoo.'*

With renewed concentration, Leichhardt turned his gaze upon the plants before him, upon the cliff-faces and the receding ranges, even on the changing winds, the temperatures and the weather patterns, as if somewhere he might find a clue to the transformations within him: *'During the early part of our journey,'* he writes, *'I had been carried back in my dreams to scenes of recent date, and into the society of men with whom I had lived shortly before my expedition. As I proceeded on my journey, events of earlier date returned into my mind, with all the fantastic associations of a dream; and scenes of England, France and Italy passed successively. Then came the recollections of my university life, of my parents and the members of my family; and, at last, the days of boyhood and of school. At the latter part of the journey I had, as it were, retraced the whole course of my life, and I was now, in my dreams, almost invariably in Sydney, canvassing for support, and imagining that, although I had left my camp, yet that I should return with new resources to carry us through the remainder of our journey.'*

By this stage in his life, Leichhardt was almost wholly a self-created man. He felt himself to be a driven spirit, inspired by the force of his own imaginings ever onward into new lands. Cities, civilisations, rock formations, scientific disciplines – he hurled himself upon them as if seeking to measure and prove his capacities. He had been born in Trebatsch in Prussian Brandenburg into a large family from which he was almost immediately thrust out to receive an arduous schooling. His mother, Sophie Straehlow, was a peasant woman, very likely of Slav descent; his father, Christian, a peat-workings inspector, divorced her when Leichhardt was fifteen. Early in his student career, Leichhardt's protean talents became evident: so, too, did his fierce love of the horizon, his need to push beyond the confines of a familiar life. But even as he fled from whatever was known and sure around him, he showed a longing for close, deeply-realised friendship, for soul brotherhood. This kind of tie became the true expression of his sentimental character.

While reading philosophy at Göttingen, Leichhardt fell in with a rich, gifted English medical student, John Nicholson, whose influence helped persuade him to take up the natural sciences. On returning to Berlin University around Michaelmas of 1835, he encountered and became fast friends with John's engaging younger brother, William Alleyne Nicholson. Leichhardt's exploration paths across Australia are the fruit of this protracted relationship. Within days of their meeting, William was a guest at the Leichhardt family home in Trebatsch; within weeks the pair occupied the same Berlin lodgings. A tenderness, a sense of shared endeavour, of joint embarkation on some tremendous project, is plain in Leichhardt's letters from this time, as he seeks to build and strengthen their association.

*'I am getting on better and better with William,'* he confided to his father early in the friendship. *'We have got to know each other, and have learned to adjust ourselves to each other. I have nothing but praise for his keenness and steady devotion to scientific knowledge, and for his affectionate behaviour towards me . . . Little things that happened by chance, in which I saved him from embarrassment, brought him nearer and nearer, and he gradually became more and more confidential with me. This was what I wanted, so I in my turn converted the quiet courtesy with which I had been treating him into kindly attentiveness, so that we grew more and more attached to one another. Perhaps I'll stay here as long as he stays in Berlin, after which I may go away with him. But*

*far be it for me to say definitively what I think may happen in the future.'*

Plans, though, were already crystallising in Leichhardt's mind. The two young men persuaded each other into a grand dream: they would become scientific travellers, creative students of the natural world. In keeping with the scientific and literary fashions of the time, they set out on rambles, cultural and geological, funded by William's fortune and spurred by Leichhardt's curiosity. After long spells in the Harz Mountains, London and the English West Country, they arrived in Paris for a further chapter of intellectual adventuring. William had come into his inheritance, and named Leichhardt his heir. They were like twin brothers: *'We're in complete accord,'* wrote Leichhardt. *'If we both sometimes feel dejected, we console ourselves by behaving like two dogs howling together when the bells are ringing.'*

With a view to their future travels, William put aside his slow-maturing thesis 'on the particular forms of death' and instead took up draftsmanship. Leichhardt walked the wards of the Charité, and haunted the lecture halls of the Musée d'Histoire Naturelle. Close by, at their rooms in the Rue des Fossées St-Victor, another destination came abruptly into view. One of William's brothers was about to emigrate to New Holland, an uncharted scientific province:

*'The fascination of the unknown, the possibility of achieving something on a grand scale aroused our ambition. We formed and confirmed the resolution to seek the fairer skies of Australia. There, if it please God, we shall follow our avocation and become "Interpretes Naturae".'*

The mapping of the new continent would be a fitting keystone to their scientific partnership. There was only one aspect of their education still left uncompleted: the two men planned a last tour of the civilisation they were leaving behind, the itinerary modified to fit Leichhardt's obsessive interest in volcanism, to provincial France and the Italian art capitals. Just before the date of their departure from Paris, William was summoned home for a 'family council'.

When he rejoined Leichhardt a month later all was changed. Gradually, hesitantly, he confessed that he would no longer be going to New Holland, then pleaded with Leichhardt to remain in Europe as well: *'But since I'm wedded in complete earnest to a grand plan,'* wrote Leichhardt to his brother-in-law, who would for the rest of his life serve as his main correspondent, *'I'm not going to be seduced from it by the comfort of an English fireside. We had to agree that our separation was inevitable.'*

The two brother-spirits climbed the Mont D'Or, they reached Marseille, took ship for Genoa, saw Naples, Vesuvius, Rome. But their paths were now diverging. William left for Florence by coach, Leichhardt on foot, the better to inspect the geology of the terrain. From then on, for the remainder of the journey, they were apart almost as much as they were together.

Shortly before William's departure to Paris, they travelled by steamer down Lake Zürich, watching the snow-clad peaks receding, reflected in the water, while Leichhardt contemplated the dissolution of his dreams and amused himself by replaying in his mind a familiar set of ideas. There was something in his nature that kept driving him forward, yes, he knew, but it was not the mere self-seeking ambition William thought it was, and going without William had its good and its bad sides:

*'It suits me better to be able to act according to my own views and leanings by myself, than to have to consider those of somebody who differs from me in nearly all respects. William is the child of wealthy parents, used to comfort, used to servants, and he has curious, refined notions of what is fit and proper. I grew up in very straitened circumstances, and have always striven to be regarded as somebody able to endure hardship. Neither to my own appearance nor to the opinions of others about my behaviour have I ever paid much attention. Even if two people of different physique, different habits, different ideas, do manage to live happily alongside each other, they*

*can't deal with each other satisfactorily. The recollections of nearly six years attach me to William. We have had our ups and downs together. Nevertheless, he's more interested in his own family than anything else, and towards all my activities he's become indifferent. And indifference blunts the edge of one's keenness even more than does opposition.'*

Such were the memories 'of England, France, and Italy' that passed through the explorer's mind, at his first encampment on the Lynd, as he marked the birthday of Queen Victoria and munched the flour and suet fat-cake prepared on such occasions, and sipped his sugared tea. The sights he had seen on his last journey passed before him: Rome's ruins; the Pope in St. Peter's, moving with solemn splendour, clothed like a pagan idol; Venice, that place of extraordinary silence, where many of the citizens had never seen live horses, and gondolas like coffins plied the canals; the smoking cone of Vesuvius, and Pompeii, with its uncovered amphitheatre, and its bright-walled houses, and the skeletons found buried by the ancient rain of ashes. These visions had flooded more insistently in his dreams during the earlier stages of the journey. He had become a creature of the present. If he thought of the friends and the experiences of his youth at all that day it was because he had compelled himself to summon up their images, and then at once he found his mind jumping to 'his enterprise', his 'favourite object', and the idea – awful, yet oddly glamorous – that he might by now be presumed dead or unsuccessful in his voyage.

Over time, his European companions, and above all William, had become less vivid, at least to his conscious, directed thoughts. In the three years since his arrival in Sydney the written contact between the men had frayed. At first, Leichhardt sent letters to his friend with urgency: *'The thought of those left behind, memories of home, gnaw at the vitals, like the eagle tearing at the liver of Prometheus chained down on a rock in the Caucasus.'*

He goes on to lament his sharpest loss: *'As for you, my dear friend, I find myself doing just what I used to do about girls who had made a deeper impression on me . . .'* Once he had idealised their charms, he would stay true to his vision for years; his heart would be full, his feelings have direction. Renouncing the hope of ultimate possession would be harrowing. But those times were brief, for *'it seems to be true that the human heart cannot live without love.'* And just as the memory of one girl kept him from courting others, so, continued Leichhardt, *'my recollections of you, my friend, are making it hard for me to cultivate new friendship here. I've come to know several young men very well, but even here in Sydney you are the only person who can follow the innermost workings of my mind. Your portrait is hanging in a handsome frame above my work-table, and after every excursion I come back laden with tributes of the finest and fullest efflorescences of the native plants. At the moment, you're standing under the heavy shadows cast by drooping Casuarinas, acacias, the big yellow cylindrical blossoms of Banksias . . .'*

In the wake of this heartfelt declaration, the tone of Leichhardt's letters, and their substance, changes. They become less frequent, dashed off between geological and botanical forays. Their pages are full of descriptions of nature and of scientific speculations, with only the rarest references to the two men's shared continental journeys and their student days. Some six months before setting off on his Port Essington expedition, Leichhardt wrote his last surviving letter to William, posted at Durandur station, south-west of the Glasshouse Mountains. It returns briefly to the vexed fields of love and marriage, and counterposes their delights to the summons of scientific exploration: *'Could I be doing anything better in this trivial existence,'* he asks, *'than to devote myself to the study of Nature and of mankind?'*

This farewell message, which has an Olympian coolness and clarity of perspective, ends with a Latin salutation: *'Vive, vale, memento esto mei.'*

Since the writing of that letter another year had been devoted to Leichhardt's campaign of self-mastery when at last he secured his route across Cape York. By a process of sublimation so thorough its extent already eluded him, Leichhardt had taken all his hope, his desire, his longing, and turned it into something else: it flowed out in the pace of his onward progress; it breathed in his evocations of the landscape, the rocks, the plants and eucalypts. Love and soul-brotherhood had become tangled up in him with the romance of exploration. His passage through the ranges, westwards, towards the secret inland, was both a memorial and an effacement of what he had once felt – a cure, you could say, by movement. His present condition – loneliness, even in the midst of his men – was something he now viewed as almost a natural state of affairs:

*'Amongst foreign peoples I have done my best to understand their ways, and have tried to make myself feel at home in whichever country I have happened to be. Yet every day I am more aware of the difficulty – yes, perhaps the hopelessness, of such a struggle. I have always felt myself to be alone, isolated; and the surroundings, which have to do instead of a father, mother, brothers and sisters, reflect nothing whatever but my own voice, like an echo. People have been very kind to me, but their range of feeling has been so different from my own that they don't understand me nor I them, and we become a trial to each other.'*

Such were his reflections on human friendship, on the day in Paris when his hopes of joint scientific inquiry with William in New Holland were dashed. It was logical for a man who made this analysis of his own character to sink himself in an expedition, and to sculpt the journey as a succession of solitary rides, a kind of courtship, a search for the one true road into the heart of the continent.

*'He who is thus occupied is in a continued state of excitement, now buoyant with hope, as he urges on his horse towards some distant range or blue mountain, or as he follows the favourable bend of the*

*river; now all despairing and miserable, as he approaches the front of*
*the range without finding water from which he could start again*
*with renewed strength, or as the river turns in an unfavourable*
*direction, and slips out of his course.'*

Bright hopes; deep miseries – but only dealt out by the hand of
nature. Why, then, as this composed being rides on, do we so often
feel another's presence beside him? Why does he seem always to
write with one eye looking over his shoulder?

The Lynd valley is all but deserted now, and Leichhardt's route
across the Cape neither marked nor remembered. Vast cattle stations occupy the landscape. Their homesteads lie on high ground,
each beside its airstrip, connected only by rough dirt roads which
wind down towards the river valley and sometimes, by chance,
bisect the expedition's vanished track. It requires an effort to reach
this country, and even more to picture Leichhardt there, or to summon up the scene which he records: a profusion of plants, birds,
flowers, instead of the green wilderness of gums that greets the eye
from every look-out, and the half-wild herds of beasts stampeding
aimlessly between artificial water-points.

But some who have spent their lives in the bush believe that
purely by retracing the path of a traveller you can tune in to him,
recapture his feelings and his thoughts in each place he passed on his
journey. This idea, which I regarded as absurd when I first encountered it, seems to have hovered, half-formed, in Leichhardt's mind,
so carefully does he record and correlate his own reflections – as if
for the benefit of those who might come after him – with the ever-
changing patterns of the landscape.

He believed, too, as he tells us, that the elements of nature *'enter*
*into the composition of our souls'*. One night, moved by this intuition,
he woke his companions at four in the morning so they could

admire the constellation of the Great Bear, which had just risen above them for the first time on the journey. '*The absence of the stars gives us painful longings, the nature of which we frequently do not understand, but which we call homesickness – and their sudden re-appearance touches us like magic, and fills us with delight.*'

Of such reveries was this stage of the expedition, for all Leichhardt's intellectual purpose, made. We are shown the explorer in one further cameo: the scene unfolds some way downstream, along the same branching, intermittent watercourse, at a camp-site close by a chain of shallow lagoons. He stands to one side from his men. They have just enjoyed a 'good dinner' – six whistling ducks and four teal. Their talk is of the nearness of the Gulf: they had found, for the first time, broken sea-shells scattered in the river-bed. Leichhardt looks down at three of his companions, who are plaiting palm-leaves to make a hat, and occasionally he joins in their conversation, while 'musing near their fireplace'. Those were the brief moments of his triumph. He had won through; the ocean was at hand; his dreams of serene scientific exploration were still intact. That same evening, Aborigines stormed the camp, spearing one of the party to death, gravely wounding two others, and throwing into ruin all his plans.

Only at this moment do those who have followed Leichhardt's footsteps see how thickly foreboding has come to choke his *Journal*. The bush has changed its complexion: from a dull monotony of tree and scrub, it is now a chain of secret signs. Creatures of ill-omen are everywhere. The black cockatoo is seen more frequently; the ring-tailed opossum sends up its 'somewhat wailing cry'. The natives, whose presence before has been remote, almost mechanical, like the action of the wind, are suddenly of central importance. Their families are glimpsed upon the hills, hunting; they burn the country; whole mountainsides are engulfed by fire. There are repeated encounters between the members of the exploration party and

Aboriginal groups. Native camps are disturbed, and plundered, with odd, token payments left behind. The bloodwood trees have burst into flower; burial platforms line the riverbanks; the explorer's favourite pony goes missing, and is found at last on the sands of the Lynd, bleeding to death from its nostrils.

*'Accidents of this kind,'* writes Leichhardt, *'were well calculated to impress us with the conviction of our dependence on Providence, which had hitherto been so kind and merciful'.* At the same time nature was conspiring to lull and calm him, for *'the mornings and evenings were very beautiful, and are surpassed by no climate that I have ever lived in. It was delightful to watch the fading and changing tints of the western sky after sunset, and to contemplate, in the refreshing coolness of the advancing night, the stars as they successively appeared, and entered on their nightly course.'*

One sign, above all, troubled him, and even as he tries to make light of it, it leaps out from his narrative. For some days already the party had been moving through terrain patrolled by kite-hawks, those strangely human-seeming birds, which soar endlessly upon the thermal draughts of northern skies, or gather in their thousands to swoop and dart between the flame-fronts of bushfires. The kites made a strong impression upon Leichhardt, as they did upon many of the first European explorers, who had never before encountered wild creatures so fearless and bold. At meal-times, the birds *'perched around us on the branches of overhanging trees, and pounced down even upon our plates, although held in our hands, to rob us of our dinners.'* With a kind of wary fascination, Leichhardt returns to the theme, and tells the story of a kite's theft from him of a bush turkey gizzard: *'The idea of the fat dainty bit made my mouth water – but alas! whilst holding it in my hand, a kite pounced down, and carried it off'.*

'Not quite so bad, perhaps, as the Harpies in the Aeneid,' he jokes of the lurking predators in the trees above, but uneasily, for one of the kites had snatched a virtual emblem of the cause of scientific exploration – a skinned specimen 'of a new species of honeysucker' – right from the tin case of the ornithologist, John Gilbert, who would be killed a day later by an Aboriginal spear, who had hated and conspired against Leichhardt, and whom Leichhardt had deeply, guiltily disliked. The kites had seen him; they had marked him down. They were arbiters: fatal birds. How daring they were, and how relentless! Thieves of, but symbols, too, of man's desire, all one struggled against, and all one struggled for – love; freedom; knowledge. Leichhardt would look up to the sky as he rode, and see the kite-hawks soaring, and glimpse in them the dark reflection of his own character.

# II

A few years ago, after a long absence from Australia, I began a journey of my own across Cape York, towards the Northern Territory and Arnhem Land, acting on the idea that prolonged immersion in the country might make it seem less foreign to my eyes. I set off one morning from Cairns, with only the vaguest plans or conception of where I was going, and quickly found myself struck by the speed of the changes in the landscape as I drove. Within half a day I had passed through tropical suburbs, the rainforest flanks of the Dividing Range and the neatly-cultivated Tablelands. I knew, or remembered, at that time, next to nothing about the early explorers – even the most famous of them, Leichhardt, was a blur to me, as were the details of his route, which I was to cross repeatedly in the days ahead, although by chance I had with me and planned to look through a reprint of his *Journal of an Overland Expedition*, which an Aboriginal friend of mine had just given me: 'I hope it will assist you in your investigations of country,' she had written, perhaps a touch sardonically, inside the front cover.

After several detours, I found myself, just as the light began to soften, approaching a town which advertised itself along the roadway as 'Queensland's highest', Ravenshoe. The main street was broad and empty, and lined by closed, shuttered shops and second-hand stores, several of them in various stages of subsidence or decay. Dominating the prospect was the two-storey Ravenshoe–Tully Falls Hotel, brightly-painted, with a mournfully attentive air about it, as though its true purpose as a building had been somehow suspended long ago. This impression seemed confirmed at once when I glanced inside. For beyond the public bar, which was unusually cramped and narrow, I found a corridor, leading round a corner to a dark, silent guest drawing-room. This, much to my surprise, appeared to be a North Queensland version of the Amber Chamber, that strange, ambiguous gift, sent in the early eighteenth century by Friedrich Wilhelm of Prussia as a token of his eternal friendship to Peter the Great. I paced around, gazing at the unusual decorations: gleaming, polished hardwood; cedar, mahogany and ironbark, for every surface had been hewn from local timbers – the walls and door and window frames, the chairs, the tables and the fittings, even the fireplace mount, the drinks coasters and the ashtrays. Upon one wall, a large axe and a two-handled timber saw were hung across each other, in imitation of an armorial crest. Filtered light from the corridor seeped through the doorway, and glinted on the blades, which, picked out so faintly, seemed almost to resemble sacred objects rather than instruments of destruction.

Within a small frame, beneath glass, was a paper 'scroll' bearing an account of the hotel's, and the town's, history. After a bright beginning to its timber industry in the 1920s, when three sawmills and a number of little 'sleeper' mills were open around Ravenshoe, all was transformed by the outbreak of the Second World War. The country of Cape York proved to be the only suitable training ground in Australia for jungle combat. Accordingly, in much the same way that tropical North Queensland serves nowadays as a stage-set for movie recreations of the Pacific theatre, or even of Vietnam, soldiers were rotated through Ravenshoe for familiarisation with the rain-forest, before being dispatched to the New Guinea battlefront. At one point, 40,000 troops and two generals were based in the area. The hotel itself became an Officers' Club.

When peacetime came round again, tree-felling was once more the hope of all the communities clustered on the crest of the Divide. Its development, so the legend continued, had been much advanced by Austrian refugees, among them a barrister, Harry Miexner, who married into the Rosenfeld family. Arnold Rosenfeld, a second son of this line, had conducted 'many experiments in timber preservation'. Like tidings from some vanished world, these few sentences – all they included, and all they left out – seemed only to deepen the hotel's gloomy atmosphere, despite the scroll's upbeat sign-off: 'May both the hotel and the township continue to prosper . . . cheers.'

As I was leaving the building, I cast a quick look into the bar, but a look, given its lay-out, was enough to thrust me into the centre of its social exchange. The barmaid was talking to a young couple in lacklustre tones about a 'body beautiful' contest scheduled for the week ahead at Herberton; the radio was giving a race-call; and a lone man, bearded, wearing jeans and a heavy, dark-brown, fur-collared jacket, though the day was still warm, sat, staring round at me.

'Do you know,' said he, 'where you are?'

A line of little shot glasses, I now noticed, six in all, containing a deep-red liquid, was laid out before him on the surface of the bar. He began to drain them, each in turn from left to right, while the barmaid produced their parent bottle of Benedictine, and, with a smooth, continuous motion, keeping pace, refilled them.

'I mean,' he said between swallows, 'really know? This is Ravenshoe – a timber town, or used to be – but not any longer, thanks to that World Bloody Heritage, and the Greens, and the Do-Gooders.'

He paused, but that paralysing silence that steals over one at the most inopportune times had seized hold of me.

'So – you curious about what happens here now? Not too much of anything. I'm getting quietly drunk. I always drink here,' the man went on, confidentially, leaning forward, inspecting me with reddened eyes. 'Wouldn't drink down the road. I don't go in there. It's full of Aborigines. They smell, they shout. They're not even human beings. They're subhuman, that's what.'

He left another gap for me, and smiled, and shrugged.

'You know what I think we should do about the Aboriginal problem? We should round them up, stick them all in a pit, and burn them, burn them together on one great pyre. Did you know – when fire's breaking down the body, and the fats pour down, and the juices of the vital organs too, you can tell from the colour of the flames what part's actually burning. In black men, especially in alcoholics, which means most of them, when the liver burns, it makes a purple colour. You wouldn't forget that if you'd seen it.' He shook his head for emphasis. 'Call me prejudiced? No! It's a rational solution' – and a complex theory did then follow, for several minutes, before the monologue swirled off into more abstract terrain, how drunkenness made you pit yourself against yourself; how there was an unknown darkness to the world, and its centre was the Hotel Tully Falls. He waved a hand, almost seigneurially.

'And so – did you like that? I'm not an idiot, you know – I understand what's going on. I can tell what you think you're seeing. The other side. And have you found it yet – what you're looking for – your own mirror?'

All the while he was speaking, the sounds in the bar, the talk and radio hum continued, as if this was the most familiar of subjects for late afternoon discussion. Still without having said a word, I backed away from him, and began to edge outside into the street, where dark was falling.

'What's the matter with you?' he barked out after me, in an anguished voice. 'Don't you get it? Silence means nothing. Even by listening, you talk.'

The next morning, still troubled by this episode, which a night's fitful sleep had only made more vivid inside me, I left Ravenshoe early, just as the mid-year dawn was breaking, and turned onto the developmental road that runs across the Cape. I drove on for some while, scarcely taking in the little townships and the abandoned homesteads along the way. My head was full of confused, conflicting thoughts, and I was left wondering at my silence in the hotel bar, and all the other silences that came to the forefront of my mind. Full of self-reproach, I hurtled on, as if through blank terrain, seeing nothing.

How different, I realise for the first time now, as I try to recapture my reactions of that morning – which seems somehow beyond the range of my experience, although its sights and sounds are still clear to me – how different were my thoughts then from the moods that take hold of me today, on journeys through the inland, or the Cape; moods of lightness, of emptiness, moods that seem dictated solely by the landscape. Their seed must have been alive in me even on that voyage out from Ravenshoe: for, as soon as the sun had risen above the line of the trees and hills, I became aware of an unfamiliar rhythm, a pattern to the brightness and the shadows, a pattern unlike anything I had ever seen.

Perhaps this intuition was not wholly my own, but was strengthened by another element: the music I was listening to that day, the only music I had with me on that journey, even though I had been told by my more experienced colleagues that music was a central aspect of all inland travel and one should choose one's sound-track with the utmost care. There were the advocates of old back-country tradition, who said one should play only compilation cassettes picked up from the sale-bins of run-down, isolated roadhouses. There were voices that spoke in favour of American highway blues, or an exclusive diet of Motown. And there was even one veteran of North Queensland travel I knew, a photographer, who had spent months searching for the Night Parrot in the hills around Dajarra, who was sure that leaving without Slim Dusty's greatest hits would be to court disaster – tyre blow-out, roll-over, engine failure – and so it must often prove.

But on this trip, all my efforts to find the right supplies in Cairns had been unavailing: I had with me a single tape, of austere cello music, the Unaccompanied Suites of Johann Sebastian Bach, the composer I listened to most often in those days, and whose works I most loved, yet whose personality remained then, as it does now, wholly elusive to me. It was these grave, joyful pieces, which many of their performers interpret as sketches of the various emotions, that sent their sounds through me, mingled with the wind's race and the roar of the diesel engine. It was the Suites, their agreement with the bush, that made me first look out at the country, and concentrate upon it, in exactly the way that a novel or a painting which a woman we love finds beautiful becomes beautiful at once to our own eyes. And so throughout that journey the creek-beds, the paperbarks, the yellow plains and purple hills were transformed into a single resonating chamber, an extension of the cello's sounding-box: everything I saw called up rich associations. I pressed on, as the sun's glare beat down through the windscreen, and signs giving grim place-names – Massacre Creek, and Dead Horse Gully – went flashing by.

———

It was late, towards nightfall, when I reached my next stop, Normanton, the second-oldest township in the north. I had heard it spoken of as the last example of a disappearing world: the old Gulf, which once was crowded with ports and cattle stations and short-lived mining settlements. For several days I stayed there, exploring the country and the coastline, searching for old-timers who remembered the town in its heyday, and who might be willing to describe it to me. Quickly, the landmarks fell into place. The Normanton Hotel had been painted purple, although in the sunset it fluoresced reddish-pink. The main road led by a cemetery, where vast conch-shells served as grave decorations, and by a rubbish dump. The bridge over the mud-brown River Norman was flanked by disused wharf piers and large stone buildings from the nineteenth century. Grandest of all was the railway station, drenched in flowers, the terminus of a line conceived as an artery between the Gulflands and the wider world, but laid only as far as the nearest ghost-town, one hundred kilometres of track, down which, unless wet season floods intervened, a slow train would shuttle back and forth as touristic demand required.

On my first morning there, I saw the brown kites that infest the town. They were perched on fence-posts and on telephone poles, gazing downwards with their large blue eyes, tilting their heads, or launching into the air, where they would hang, their forked tails moving with the breeze as they hovered above each passer-by, paying special attention to the environs of a low-slung building in the centre of the town. What could it be? I walked across to investigate, opened the door, and found myself inside a bakery, where enormous cream-buns were almost the sole item offered for sale. A war of attrition was being waged between its clientele – throngs of Aboriginal children and an occasional white housewife – and these aerial scavengers. The moment a satisfied customer emerged from the premises, munching, perhaps, a breakfast roll that dribbled cream and jam, the kites would descend, and flap above them, comically, yet with an air of menace, until the purchaser broke off a bit of the roll and threw it as far into the air as possible, at which point the kites would break away to retrieve their morsel and fight amongst themselves. So institutionalised, so much a part of Normanton, had this conflict become that specially modified rubbish containers had been placed along the roadway near the bakery, and each bore a stern notice instructing the townspeople not to yield to the pressure of the kites but to discard any unwanted scraps in the bird-proof receptacles provided.

After a series of fruitless conversations with the Normanton establishment, I found my way to Stella McNab. Stella was a slight woman; she wore a short flower-print dress and old-fashioned gymshoes.

'I'm not as good as I used to be,' she told me, wringing her hands, once I had paid an obligatory visit to the cage that housed her ill-tempered pets, a Blue Mountains lorikeet and a galah that was engaged in plucking out its last remaining breast-feathers. Stella's eyes were china-blue, and beautiful; her chin was as firm and tight as a young girl's; she had strong, protuberant collar-bones. She was the town's sole surviving life-long resident: I would have guessed she was in her mid-fifties, but it soon became clear she was much older, though she was, in fact, uncertain exactly when she had been born, even if she could describe the event itself with unnerving precision.

'My father's family came over from Scotland,' she said. 'They were strict people. I can't quite remember from where.'

They had lived, she, her mother and father, and her two brothers and her sister-in-law, just over from the Christian Centre, in a neat house screened by mango trees. 'He was a saddler and a taxi-driver, my Dad. And he was a coach-builder, as well, and other things – I've got his stamp, and his boot-last.'

She produced this token of past time from an arrangement of household objects on a mantleshelf. It was small and bright green; she gripped it in both hands.

'Normanton,' she sighed. 'Nearly all the old people have passed on, or left, and there's a lot of new people here now. We used to have a Supreme Court, a hospital, a School of Arts. We didn't have bitumen streets, but we had good race meetings, and eight nights dancing in August – then, in the forties, there was three days' races and a day's rodeo, and in October they'd have the Diggers' meeting too. I used to go there. They had a picture theatre, and they used to print the *Normanton Chronicle*, before my time. There was quite a number of hotels – just as well they're not here today! They didn't drink like that in old times. They were more sociable.'

'And did you ever go to the hotels yourself?' I asked, peering not so much at Stella, perched on her little chair before me, her legs crossed, the pale skin tight across her knees, but at the picture she was painting, at this blur of recollections, thinking as I did so that the time she was describing was the last time that would find safety in the past, in silence, beyond the reach of film and sound recordings and digital archives. It all belonged to Stella now. It was hers, to shape, or cast aside – she could plunge into its murk and bring new treasures to the surface, and hold them up before me; they would glitter, and sink back into oblivion as soon as I reached out to hold them.

'The hotels? Of course not. And I never went out to work. We were brought up strict. I stayed at home, with my people, I went to church, and did a lot of fancy needlework. There used to be more hotels in those days: one at the wharf, one at the six-mile, and the Leichhardt, too, but that burned down in 1923.'

'The Leichhardt,' I echoed.

'He was German. He came along here – but I don't know about him. He stopped out along the road to Burketown, I think, but I've never been there.'

She dabbed at her eyes, where tears had formed.

'I can see it again,' she said. 'All the goods used to come on the boats – there was no bridge across the river, and the trains used to meet the ships at Market Street and Jane. Croydon was the gold-mining town then, you see. Mother always reckoned there was plenty of gold in Croydon: she came from there.'

With each new prompt, and question, Stella became more upset, until I could no longer bear what I was doing. I stood up to go. For a second, she held on to my hand.

'I can see how red the roads were then; and I can see the old town drinking-well – they used to have a hurricane lantern for lighting it. The Aboriginal reserve was just over there, up on that hill. You know, I was just looking at some cards before you came.'

She gestured to a sheaf of letters and half-sorted photos, on a little table, and a pile of tiny paper fragments, torn into neat squares, to one side of her feet.

For some days, I felt myself under the shadow of this conversation: I stayed in Normanton, trying to look with Stella's eyes, to picture the streets full of mid-century cars, to hear them alive with the noise of station-hands. I could see the busy shop-fronts. I could look down on children playing along the river-banks.

Only a week later, after I had reached the port of Karumba, where the temptations of the past were absent, did I begin making the sorties into the bush that I had planned. Daily, I set out down back roads and tracks that led up the west coast of the Cape, towards far-off places with inviting names – and each night, as I drove back down the thin, straight highway, or as I lay awake in my motel room, with the colours and the cloud-shapes still unfolding on the screen of my eyelids, I found myself taken over more and more by what I had seen.

Suspiciously, I waited for this reaction to fade: how could empty landscape be captivating? But with each new journey I found barriers of reserve and disinterest inside me giving way. Such, I imagined, was the feeling that comes to a mathematician who stumbles on unforeseen worlds of order and symmetry – and, pleased by this metaphor, I would head out almost at random, pausing at rivers, shade-trees, and disused stock-wells to record my impressions, taking great care to avoid encounters with other travellers, for fear human contact might destroy the spell.

It was in this mood that I first opened the *Journal of an Overland Expedition*, and flicked through its pages, at first listlessly, for the heat at night-time seemed more intrusive, and reading, after such days, a pointless occupation for the eyes, while the text itself was mannered and prolix. Yet I was swept up in it.

It was not the charm of the entries for Leichhardt's passage through the Gulf country, for this section of his journey, which followed close upon the spearing of Gilbert, is dourly described, nor did the personality of the explorer shine through in those pages: indeed, they bear the unmistakable stamp of Leichhardt's well-meaning, interventionist editor, the hero of Australian coastal mapping, Captain Phillip Parker King, and are full, too, of reflections on the party's melancholy spirits, interspersed with accounts of river-courses and the unchanging forest-scrub. This bleakness itself was, after a while, oddly compelling. One paragraph I glanced at, and returned to, was Leichhardt's account of his resolve to abandon all his horse-shoes and spare equipment.

'*The natives will probably find them,*' he surmised, '*and, if preserved, they will be a lasting testimonial of our visit.*'

Where, though, in the Gulf, was Leichhardt's trail? Where the memorials to his passage? After many unsuccessful inquiries in Normanton, I found a well-informed attendant at the Shell garage, who directed me up the Burketown road.

'It's the loneliest place in the world,' he said, gravely. 'You can't miss the signpost: Camp 119.'

'Really – I didn't know any of his camps had been discovered.'

'Too right they have – and you'll have the place to yourself, no worries. One tour group a week round this time of year: the "Outback Discovery". Apart from that, nothing.'

I went in search of this landmark, which lay some distance down a track of corrugations and creek-crossings, across flat plains of box-wood trees where dust-columns danced and whirled. At last I turned off, along a well-worn route, and soon found myself in the middle of a heavily-labelled historic site, devoted to the memory not of Leichhardt, as I very quickly grasped, but of a rather different enterprise – the expedition led by Burke and Wills, whose party had reached this spot, their furthest north, in February 1861. Here, for the first time, they had tasted brackish water in the river they were following, and realised they were close to their goal, the Gulf. Short of supplies, they turned back towards their Depot at Cooper's Creek: a blazed boxwood tree, almost collapsed from old age, was the proof of their passage. Their tribulations were described in solemn prose upon a plaque installed at the site by the Royal Geographical Society in 1986. Next to this was a memorial slab erected by the Normanton Lions Club and a rusting iron pole that bore a strong resemblance to a decapitated nineteenth century street lamp. Thick tyre-tracks had been carved in the sandy soil all round this spot. Stray Winfield cigarette butts and bits of orange peel lay freshly discarded close by. A few steps away, the Little Bynoe River trickled past, its banks guarded by a platoon of cattle, while yet another signpost, this one boasting vivid graphics, announced the presence in the vicinity of saltwater crocodiles. A burst of raucous coughing came from a pair of kookaburras in the river-gums along the channel. The heat and light poured down. After I had spent sev-eral minutes taking in this landscape, which was coming to seem like the country of some inescapable dream, a deep-red cloud became visible on the horizon. It resolved itself into the dust-plume of an adventure tour four-wheel drive, and I watched this vehicle, in mounting vexation, as it neared the turn-off, slowed, then lurched onto the side-track and clattered to a halt only inches from the blazed tree-trunk. Its driver emerged and nodded in my direction.

'Good day for it,' he called out, then before I could answer turned away, slid back the main door of his vehicle, and, with movements of great gentleness, began guiding his passengers down from their seats, taking each of them by the hand, speaking to them softly, as though they were children, lost in strange terrain – and I realised his charges were holding canes in their hands, they wore dark glasses, and each last one of them was blind.


The next day – for by this stage I was running short of time to com-plete my trip – I left Normanton on the quickest route to the Territory, through Mount Isa, which I had long wanted to visit, and where I had several appointments to keep. I approached the town by dusk, at speed, straining to catch a glimpse of its tall smelter chimneys against the last streaks of sunset, but all I could make out when I drove in was the red lights that flash constantly upon the smoke-stacks in the night. It was only in the morning, when I checked out of my motel room, that at last I saw the town stretched out before me, and, high on the hillside above it, the smelter buildings and their can-tilevers, the tailings dumps and ore stock-piles, the exhaust-plumes spreading in the sky. There was something about the shape and curve of the hill, about the picturesque confusion of its buildings, that was familiar to me in a distant way. Not until I was walking up the main street, navigating the town's thickly-clustered system of roundabouts, did I place the memory. It was of one particular castle: Hunedoara, in Romanian Transylvania, the stronghold of Janos Hunyadi, set amidst rich, ore-bearing mountains, where the communist authorities had built a metallurgical complex I visited once, a kingdom of green, billowing toxic clouds, deep excavation pits and funicular ore-transports that passed like chairlifts just above the castle's courtyards and crenellated walls.

So dear was this fortress to the romantic intelligentsia of neighbouring Hungary, for whom it represented the spirit of their eastern provinces, that it was recreated in scale replica in the main park of Budapest, amidst duck ponds and ornamental gardens, so that passing strollers would be reminded of their heritage as they made their way towards Heroes' Terrace and the Museum of Fine Arts. I allowed myself a little inward smile at this memory: I could be confident, I decided, as I sat down in the only coffee-shop I found open so early in the morning, that no one had drawn that comparison before.

After some minutes a middle-aged man with a distinct Central European accent came to take my order. He had been born and brought up, he told me, in Deva, an obscure Transylvanian town. Repelled and drawn at the same time by the force of coincidence in life, I could not refrain from asking him if he had ever been reminded of his homeland by Mount Isa; of Hunedoara itself, for example, which I was careful to give its Magyar name.

'I have made the parallel often in my mind,' he answered. 'And perhaps now, with all my family gone, that is the reason why I stay on here.'

Almost at once he returned, bearing a plate of toast and a cup of coffee, which he laid in front of me in ceremonious fashion before sitting down, folding his arms, and giving a sigh: 'If I tell you something of my story now, it is not because I flatter myself at all that it may be of some vivid interest to you – or that it will remain with you in your memory for its own sake – but because, in a place like this, stories need to be told, and told again. They need to stake their claim on life, you could say, otherwise what do we have? My name is Szelenyi Sandor' – he showed me a laminated business card, and this, indeed, was the name that figured on it in italic type – 'I come, as I mentioned to you, from Deva, it is true, but my background was mixed. My mother was a Romanian woman, and my father was Hungarian by nationality. Communism was living its triumphant years when I grew up there. My father was a party member, and I was in the youth brigade. We young aristocrats of the working class were escorted on journeys all around the country, to the mines, and to the construction camps where the railways and the roads were being built, so we could be filled with consciousness of the labours undertaken on our behalf, and the splendours of the future awaiting us. One result of this indoctrination is that I know my country well. But I am unsure whether I should speak of it that way. It was not from there, you see, that I came to Australia. I had made a visit to my father's relatives in Budapest – this was early in 1956, when I was not quite fifteen years old. I stayed in their family apartment, high up in a grand building on Castle Hill; there were long, dark corridors; the rooms were panelled, and from them there was a view across the river; you could see the long barges making their way up and down. All through the uprising I remained in the city, and afterwards as well, although my father sent me urgent messages to come home, but he had not the faintest notion of the things I had seen: the massed crowds in the streets, young men shot down, their skulls smashed in; faces that were known to me. I can still hear the echo from the gunshots ringing out around our block. I can see the bullet-holes – see them as they were being made, exploding in straight lines, like sewing stitches – and that experience is one that has stayed with me through the years. Whenever they blast, here, today, deep undergound, I can feel those bullets. I feel the pulse go through me, I feel it in the soles of my feet – just the way they say the Kalkadoon people who once lived here could feel the coming of a stranger far distant from where they stood. So if you ask me whether I remember the scenes of my childhood, and the castle, and those mines, my answer is that there are other memories that have come to fill my thoughts. Not that these things prey upon me: but I said to myself when I came to this country that I would never go back home. You have to choose your ground . . . but please . . .'

His voice, which had been low and even, took on a note of concern; his face became solicitous.

'You won't have any . . . ?'

While giving this account of himself, he had contrived to eat his way through most of my breakfast; a lone piece of half-charred buttered toast remained, and when I shook my head he pounced on this last survivor and it too vanished, stage by stage, into the corner of his mouth.

'An unusual tale for the morning in Outback Queensland,' I said.

'But there are hundreds of us, you know, refugees of 1956, scattered throughout the bush. I can give you addresses – in Quilpie, in Newman, or Broken Hill. Come back tomorrow and I may even tell you the story of how I reached Australia.'

As he left me, he extended towards me a folded slip of paper.

'Three dollars and sixty cents' he had written out at the foot of the itemised account, which was signed with a little flourish: 'Szelenyi S., Prop.'


I set off from town to find the Mayor of Burke Shire, 'Honest John' Molony, a man whose sphere of influence included much of the Gulf of Carpentaria's muddy, oppressive coastline, as well as a large bush clothing and outfitters business that stood on the main east route towards Cloncurry, its presence announced by the effigy of a horse, moulded from fibreglass, realistically painted, poised like a votive temple god above the entrance.

In the doorway, arms folded, frowning, waiting, was the Mayor, a square-faced, rangy man. He was wearing shorts, work-boots, a checked shirt and sunglasses. For several minutes he engaged me in urgent conversation as the highway traffic thundered by.

'The fabric of the Shire's in tatters,' he announced. 'I've got great-grandparents buried in Burketown, but I've sold up my pastoral holdings now and I can tell you: despair is setting in.'

Rarely had I met someone with a less despairing manner. I would have liked to reply, but he swept on: 'I'm flat as a tack. You want to talk, you'll have to come round to the back entrance and help me load the truck.'

'The truck?'

'Yes – it's not a public holiday, you know.'

Through his shop, which was almost impassable, so thickly was it filled with boots, jeans, bridles, shirts, all the costly impedimenta of bush existence, we went, single file, the Mayor pushing ahead, stroking and smoothing stray items from his path, waving off attempts by his sales assistants to catch his eye. At last we were in a storage area, it, too, choked with piles of clothes and little pyramids of cardboard boxes. He resumed: 'Burke Shire's the perfect place in Australia for rainfall. It's where I'll spend the rest of my life, and I want it to go ahead. When we get serious about Australia, we'll develop it. But first,' he went on, looking at me accusingly, 'first – we have to deal with this dreamtime mythology.'

'This what?'

'We've got our own past. We've got a history of our own in Burke Shire as well. We've got to go out into this new millennium, laptops in our hands, memory in our hearts. If you don't remember your history, you never transcend it. We should be following the example of the pioneers, the overlanders.'

'Who do you mean, exactly?'

'I mean everyone. Everyone passed this way. I mean the Duracks,

I mean Leichhardt. Leichhardt went through Burke Shire, you know. I sometimes think it was dead before he came here, and he brought it to life.'

'Like one of the Aboriginal creator heroes, in fact?'

'Perhaps. He was the first white man to see it. If you ever want to know Australia – really know it – that's the way: following in his tracks, looking with his eyes. I know: I drive his route in my truck all the time, out through Hell's Gate and Calvert Hills and Seven Emu, to Borroloola.'

'Really?'

'Would I mislead you? About that? I can show you where he camped along the way; where he killed his bullock; where he first saw the native carvings; Beame's Brook station, which he said was the most beautiful place on earth – I've still got livestock on it today, in fact.'

'So you would know his *Journal*?'

'Inside out. I feel like I've got to know him very well, and the more I've studied him, the more admiration I have for him. There's not many Australians today who could do what he did with his men. He was an innovator. He's an inspiration; he adapted – and we're innovators too. Look at this!'

He retrieved from the clutter around him a compact, round-formed object, the function of which I could not imagine.

'I got the idea from a children's cartoon. See – it's a donkey-collar mirror. That's the kind of thing we like. Things that are new and different. We like style. Fashion fades, style's eternal. When you've got it, you've got it. Why don't you come out with me into Leichhardt country, if you're so interested? I'm leaving right now. You could ride behind me.'

'But don't you have to stay in one place if you're the Mayor?'

'There's only five hundred people in Burke Shire,' he answered, rather testily. 'It's not like being Mayor of Brisbane. I combine it with my business. I take it on the road, right out to my customers – my constituents. See, that's what I'm talking about. There are three kinds of people: those who watch things happen, those who make things happen, and those who wonder what happened. The problem with a lot of people in rural areas is very simple: their life is the past; they're living in a dream. There were no good old days. These are good days: better food and grog, nicer women, faster cars, better clothing. You've got to be an achiever, make it happen. Not just have a go, but pick it up, succeed!'

He broke off, jumping into his truck, and started the engine, then leaned out of the window and banged the door with the side of his hand.

'You sure you don't want to come with me?' he called out. 'You'd have a good ride. It's a Super-hawk – fastest on the road.'

'And what do you have in there?' I parried.

'Everything! I spend a third of my life on the road. Just take a look.'

He threw the back door open. Inside, arranged in an elaborate system of hanging racks and cupboards, was the merchandise – but also a large bed, a cooking bay, a little table and a lounging chair.

'The worth of a man,' came the Mayor's voice, from just behind me, 'manifests itself in the vision which perceives an opportunity and the address which knows how to seize it.'

'What?'

'In 800 BC Homer said: "Always to be best, and distinguished above the rest".'

I glanced around. The Mayor had begun quoting, long, sub-clause-ridden profundities: Napoleon, Franklin Roosevelt, Alexander the Great. He patted his chest pocket which I noticed was bulging with index cards. He pulled out several and brandished them in front of me.

'Words are very important,' he said. 'I left school at thirteen. It

WINGS OF THE KITE-HAWK    34

didn't do me any harm. I've got stuff in here that would blow your head apart. Good words, strong words. There are some I don't like. Weak words, words like community – I prefer neighbourhood; it's a better, finer word. I like words like tenacity, staunchness, motivation. Those are the things that speak to me.'

'But where do you get the time to read?'

'I read in the truck.'

'While you're driving?'

'Yes – half a line at a time – always drink water – you don't get tired.'

The loading, which had punctuated this conversation, accentuating its spasmodic quality, was now complete.

'There's one last thing,' said the Mayor, and he flicked one fingertip against the canvas sun-hat I was holding in my hands.

'If you're going into the bush, I mean really going, then you need a good hat – wide-brimmed, well-balanced.'

He picked one up from the pile inside the truck, and waved it with a sinuous motion before my eyes: 'A hat like this one. Now this is my own design – the "Honest John" – the swagman's friend. Best hat there is in the world.'

I inspected it as he held it out, and a ghost of suspicion was born inside me.

'Your design?'

'You may not know it,' he went on, 'but bushmen are very particular about their hats. That colour – that brown – is what we call tan-bark. It's very popular with head stockmen on the big stations. The man at Wave Hill buys them from me. I have them specially made up, by Akubra. You'll see them everywhere. You can tell them by the bright feather in the hat-band. And they've got my name inside them too in gold letters.'

I knew, at that moment, knew for certain he was having me on. I laughed, put on a knowing expression, and flipped the hat over as he held it. And there it was – 'Akubra – Honest John' – in stamped gold capitals inside the crown.

Perhaps an hour later, after several circuits of the town's main streets, and inquiries in its hotels and newsagencies, I came upon the office block that I was looking for: more by good fortune than by design, so well concealed was the headquarters of MITEZ – The Mount Isa to Townsville Economic Zone – although, I thought to myself as I made my way into a blank, mirror-windowed building, there was something appropriate to its facade, the prime characteristic of the thousand-kilometre corridor between Mount Isa and Townsville being the complete absence of economic activity of any kind.

A young woman was seated at the front desk, alone, surrounded by a maze of glass-walled offices.

'Your Executive Director?' I began, unsure quite what to expect, so much had I been told of Darcy Redman, the dynamo of North-Central Queensland, the Voltaire of the Selwyn Ranges.

'He's hiding,' said the young woman.

I digested this news.

'But,' she whispered, leaning forward, 'if you go down this corridor, and into the back room, you might find him.'

There, seated at a desk, with a row of mobile phones of different makes in front of him, and a huge waste-paper basket at his side, was a man with greyish, wavy hair, his face obscured by a handkerchief which he was clutching with both hands. He blew his nose with great violence, and then in answer to my prompts and questions embarked on a conversational display of the most sustained, inventive brilliance – although it was not without its comical side, being constantly interrupted by trumpeting nasal blows, for Darcy had just undergone a devastating sinus operation.

The future of the region, the charm of the bush, the nobility of Mount Isa's rock systems – I rested back in my chair, listening, half closing my eyes as he jumped, gazelle-like, between gleaming peaks of metaphor. Though I have since that day had several further talks with Darcy, a man deeply reluctant to engage in written communications, as if from fear they might somehow freeze his imaginative flights, never have I heard him recapture in words the wild, desolate splendour of that morning, when time was short, and I was urging him onwards with my eyes, and blood was oozing forth from his nostrils onto his handkerchief. I blew my nose, in sympathy.

'You too?' said he, and offered me a Kleenex. 'Rubbish-bin here, of course' – and on he rushed, pausing, between breaths, to glance at a panoramic nocturnal photograph of Mount Isa, the mining-plant illuminated, the smoke-stacks belching skywards.

'How do we regard the country?' he asked me.

With one hand, he made a gesture to indicate the elusiveness of the question, and the lack of any need for me to answer.

'Rural – romantic – many-layered? Language itself becomes a problem.'

Delighted to find that we were in the territory of theory, I opened a notebook, the way one moves slowly to avoid disturbing a timid animal, and began to jot down Darcy's words but even as I did so I realised they would seem in recollection contrived, or arch, or too emphatic, just as all the reported conversations and witticisms caught in histories or memoirs down the ages lie entombed upon the page. While I wrote Darcy gave a little frown, that seemed to come from the periphery of his awareness, as he registered this betrayal. He was telling me about his own journeyings closer towards the heart of inland Australia: how he had been brought up on the Darling Downs, where his father was a relief pastoral manager who dragged the entire family with him across the face of Queensland; how his wife had been named principal of the Mount Isa School of the Air, which covered fully one-third of the state, from Birdsville to the Gulf, from across the Northern Territory border as far east as Richmond; how he himself in recent years had developed the habit of making fishing expeditions deep into the swampy lowlands of the Limmen Bight, where the land and water became one.

'Throughout our life,' he now said, in the grand manner of some ancient bard, rising to his feet, declaiming a final stanza, and simultaneously lowering the handkerchief to reveal a thin, sharp-featured face – the face, one might have said, of a late Roman emperor, tense, strained, active, 'throughout our life, we recount ourselves by our adventures – and life in these parts carries sufficient of the real model of adventure.'

He began to gather up his mobile phones, for he had lost himself in words, and was late for his rendezvous with the Minister for Mines and Energy.

I followed him out to the street, questions forming inside me about the landscape, about the mine's discovery, about the links between past and present. Almost with reluctance I mentioned the *Journal* I was reading, and my first explorations within it.

Darcy stopped. He stared at me, and his stare was something close to a challenge. His eyes were grey and narrow in the sun.

'Leichhardt,' he repeated. 'As a man, I find him totally underexposed. If you go out there you will find him. I have gone out there – and I have.'

# III

A year later, during a period of prolonged uncertainty in my life, I set out once more by road from Cairns into the back country of Cape York, this time with a clear destination in mind – the near-deserted mining town of Chillagoe, which lies set in a landscape of jagged limestone towers almost one-third of the distance from the Pacific coastline to the Gulf. Though I still remembered the discussions from my first journey, and all the details of Leichhardt's westward progress along the river valleys of the Cape, I was following a different lead: that of the artist Ray Crooke, who had long been captivated by the bare scrub country surrounding Chillagoe.

Just before I left, I went to visit Ray and his wife June at their house in Edge Hill, and in the darkened study I listened while he told me the story of his experiences as a young man during World War II, when he had been stationed in the north and had seen for the first time the small, dusty towns and settlements of the Palmer River goldfields.

Sitting at his desk, and looking down at his hands, which were never still, Ray furrowed his brow, as if trying against all odds to remember something impossibly deep-buried – although the ghost-towns of the Cape formed the subject of all the paintings that hung round us in that room.

He had been based in Townsville, as I knew, and had gone north in the first military expedition group that laid in the dirt road to the tip of Cape York.

'We had engineers putting bridges over creeks as we went, and we'd camp at old forgotten places, like Laura, Coen, Chillagoe – the buildings were just crumbling away – and this all made a big impact on me. I was very much attracted to that landscape. I've never been able to get very excited about rainforest, but once you get out into dry, scrubby country – well! I'm taken over by the character of the trees, the light.

'Of all the places I went to, Chillagoe was the most significant to me: it had been completely forgotten by the outside world. There were three hotels, and an old smelting works in the most beautiful disrepair. Geographically it was once a coral reef, so the country's quite different from elsewhere on the Cape. Those sculpted outcrops!

The colours, that scruffy, silent landscape. Black rock, low trees – monotonous, reptilian – but I quickly found that a miraculous light came over it as the afternoon wore on.

'It was the human occupation of the place, though – or the remnants of that occupation – that most interested me at first. Being there was like being in a living Drysdale painting, except he's all Venetian reds, whereas Chillagoe's all browns. I stayed at the Burns Imperial Hotel, which was run by three sisters who had never married. They carried on as if they were still in the 1890s – roast beef and polished silver and starched tablecloths in one hundred degree temperatures. They were always impeccably dressed, even though the hotel itself was falling to bits, and looking out from the rooms you could see that great brooding brick chimney.

'All round you there were the beautiful old buildings and decaying machinery and bits of broken equipment. It was like a dream to me; I did this painting of it a long time ago – look – do you see: the sisters – the way they used to dress. There's the chimney in the background, and a few Aboriginal people who worked there – and on the bar, that's the mineral collection that belonged to one of the sisters. I shouldn't think anyone who's in that picture is still living now.'

He drummed his fingers on the desk.

'For a long time,' he continued, 'I lived quite happily in the north, in the years after the war, painting away, without too much contact with my contemporaries. I didn't really know how they went about painting Australia. In my mind I was just an odd bod.

'It was only when I went to Europe that I realised what I'd been doing and seeing in Chillagoe; how I'd been painting there. I realised that my contemporaries are the old masters – all the artists whose works I'd studied so long in reproductions, without really knowing them. Botticelli, and Piero della Francesca, of course, Piero above all. But when I actually went to Italy I must confess it was a real struggle to see the paintings I'd been so fond of.'

'A struggle?'

But he fell silent, and it was only on that drive out, as I passed through Dimbulah with its odd main street monument in the form of an elevated tractor, and Almaden, where the road was choked with grazing Brahman cattle, that I began to imagine his thoughts as he tried to bring his two worlds into balance.

'I was getting all this wonderful material, you see – all this wonderful barren awful country, unlike anything I'd ever seen.'

'Foreign to your eyes?'

'Of course,' he said, softly, as if lapsing back into a dream from which he had emerged only briefly in order to show his guest a proof of courtesy.

'But painting is a contrivance – and our presence here is a contrivance. I admire the Aboriginal artists, who work here more naturally; in some way, they say more about this country and its spirit than we do. Myself, though, I'm interested in the European experience – in what I find in the past of those old towns. I mean that sense of stillness, of surrender – and the constant flow of time.

'But I don't know there's any point in going up there any more. There's a group in Cairns, the Arts Society – they asked me to take them on a painting trip – to Chillagoe. We went up for the weekend, some months back. It had changed completely. New buildings are never as attractive as the old. The smelting works has been turned into some kind of heritage site. I got the feeling it was like everything: human beings are just spreading out.'


When I reached Chillagoe, all was silent. It was midday. The houses, separated by wide scrub tracts, and lying along thin, potholed roads, showed no sign of life. The horizon was ringed by peaks of weathered limestone. Across a line of gum-trees where the town creek ran, the smelter chimneys rose into the blue sky. A little wooden church; a fibro motel backed by an empty caravan park; a phone-box, broken, on the corner; a post-office, closed; a general store, from which the faint sound of easy listening could be heard – Chillagoe had all the conveniences of a bush community, as well as the trademark attractions with which such places seek to stave off oblivion: a heritage precinct, a historical plaque, a Museum and Information Centre perched upon a hill-side.

After some agonising, I spurned the hotel and its offer of 'shuddering cold beer', and drove instead into a flower-glutted enclave on the outskirts of the town, where at once I noticed a tall, well-built man wearing a dark green uniform.

He was standing before a desk inside a mesh-netted enclosure, which seemed at first sight very like a cage: indeed, it was a cage, I soon realised, although within its confines were a computer system, a telephone console and all the associated clutter of an up-to-the-minute small business office. At the rear of this screened and shaded area were various mounts and perches and feeding bowls, and in one corner, eyeing me gravely, was a large black cockatoo, which now screeched at piercing volume, drowning out some words of welcome from the man in green. A woman, blonde, lean and suntanned, appeared.

This couple, Gary and Carolyn Bondeson, invigorators of the township, internet visionaries, samaritans of the region's wildlife, took me in.

'We were fascinated by this place,' said Gary, 'by its beauty, its grandeur; the marble-pits, the cave-tunnels, the mine-shafts and the limestone towers – the world above ground, and the world below. I suppose you know Chillagoe's only here because Atherton was an amateur fossicker: those are his diggings, just over there. It had a population of ten thousand at one time, and two hundred of them on the smelter. We've only been here a short while: in fact, we got married here, on the first of May a year ago. We were the very first couple to be married at the Chillagoe church.'

'The first couple?'

'That's right. The church was built in Wolfram, down the road, in 1906 – it was only moved here a few years ago, and more people die in Chillagoe than get hitched. But we're happy enough here, in our little bird haven.'

'I'd noticed the birds,' I said.

'That's the General,' said Carolyn, 'the big cockatoo – and you can see the others, the nightjars and the frogmouths – or maybe you don't?'

Alongside the cockatoo were a handful of other creatures, more like brownish blurs than living things, each of them frozen in its own pose of immobility.

I went over, and inspected the cage with greater care.

'We rescue them,' said Carolyn. 'We're like a foster home for the injured and abused. The cockatoo came from an owner near Cooktown who was feeding her Weet-bix. Isn't she beautiful? Can you imagine – they used to think black cockatoos were birds of ill-omen! Now we're slowly introducing her to gum-nuts and pandanus fruits.'

'And you're going to release her?'

'No,' said Gary. 'She's hand-raised: she'd be very unhappy. But that's the aim, of course, the ideal, isn't it? Freedom, for everyone.'

He looked at his wife with admiration: 'We had a blue-winged kookaburra come in, paralysed. Carolyn had to give him physio-therapy every hour for two months.'

I picked up a thin pamphlet with a black and white photo of limestone formations on its cover.

'That's the famous "Tower Karst",' said Gary. 'It's put out every year by the Chillagoe Caving Club: Karst means limestone.'

'A good publication,' declared a voice at my shoulder. We had been joined by a grey-haired, bespectacled man. The Bondesons smiled at him uncertainly.

'I think you're looking for me,' said the newcomer, glancing in my direction with an air of triumph.

'I am?'

'Yes – Roly Mackay. Your truck stopped outside my Museum.'

Mr Mackay, a new arrival in the microcosm of Chillagoe, and an individual of convinced opinions, plainly disliked being on the margins of any social exchange. Without delay, he made himself the centre of the conversation, which veered at once into unusual territory: fly-fishing, animal aggression, his recent purchase of the Chillagoe Information Centre, which he planned to turn into the base camp for a pan-continental wildlife survey.

It became, though, increasingly hard to follow his words, so loud was the chatter of apostle birds in the trees and the cries of Carolyn's grandchildren in the swimming-pool and the pulse of water from the garden hose.

After a decent interval I made some excuse and retreated to a cabin, where I started leafing through my copy of the lavish, endlessly discursive bible of Cape York mining history, *Northmost Australia*, published in 1922 by the impetuous Robert Logan Jack: but Chillagoe had failed to impress the book's pioneering hero, James Venture Mulligan, who was bored 'to incoherence' by the landscape when he passed through, and formed a very dim opinion of the Walsh River catchment adjoining the town: '*In all my travels I never saw such rough country as today: all porphyry, intermixed with sandstone. I cannot see to what earthly use it can be turned – too rough and stony, destitute of grass, not even enough for a kangaroo.*'

Once the sun had dropped close to the horizon, I slipped away from the property for a walk round town. Behind me, Roly and the Bondesons were still locked in their discussion, amidst an ever-rising cacophony of cockatoo shrieks and cries.

In the centre of Chillagoe, along a back corridor of the top hotel, I found a working public phone, and made some calls that had long been preying on my mind; then, on some impulse, I rang the number I had in Mount Isa for Darcy Redman.

Some months had gone by since our last talk; in those days I had been on the verge of a little expedition to the stone country of Arnhem Land.

'And where are you now?' asked Darcy.

'In Chillagoe.'

He laughed.

'Back on the Leichhardt trail – just like when we first met.'

'Not really.'

'But you are – he went close by. North of you is the spot where Gilbert was killed: up past Stirling station, on the road towards Van Rook. And there's someone you should meet while you're in Chillagoe – a friend of mine, an extremely enjoyable man; his field is biological systematics.'

'Not Roly Mackay?'

'He's already there, then, with his six thousand books and his van-load of samples. He knows the country like the back of his hand. You should go and talk to him before you head out: but be careful you control the conversation, otherwise you'll never get away: they'll drag out your skeleton in years to come.'


I edged onto the shaded front verandah of the Chillagoe Museum. The light outside was softening, the heat was easing, but in the furthest corner of this antechamber, leaning forward across a counter display of postcards, fridge magnets and basic guides to fossicking, Roly Mackay had caught the attention of a young family from Brisbane and was lecturing them on Chillagoe's unusual geology.

My appearance distracted him a moment. He glanced towards

me – the spell was broken; his victims, with a dazed air, prised themselves away.

'I'm closing up now,' said Roly, curtly, indeed almost accusingly, as if he blamed me for this escape. 'But I suppose you can stay – if you want to help with the unpacking.'

'Unpacking? It looks like everything's here already.'

'My samples; my collections.'

He nodded towards the next room, where rows of drums and boxes had been arranged in neat lines: 'Rock specimens – and spiders.'

'Spiders?' I echoed.

'Didn't I mention? My scientific specialty is spiders: wolf-spiders. I'm interested in the history of the bush and its settlement, of course, but my big thing' – he paused, rather proudly – 'is the multiplicity of life, and the preservation of its diversity.'

He held up a shiny slab of rock, and looked at me.

I shrugged.

'Galena! The glinting lead – you have to know them all, the rock types, if you're moving through these back-blocks. The bush varies, endlessly and subtly. When I can't tell the difference between two tracts of desert, when I think they're identical, the distribution of the spiders tells me otherwise.

'The truth, though – the scandal, really – is that most of the spiders of Australia, the great bulk of them in fact, are still undescribed! No one knows much about them. Too few people do this kind of work; students prefer what they imagine to be the cutting edge of science. But science, of course, is nothing – nothing at all – without secure foundations.'

By this time Roly was hunched over an open cardboard box, from which he began fishing out small glass test-tubes, each one wrapped in its own protective film.

'Preserving fluid,' he announced. 'My little elongated tombs.'

He held them up, and the liquid glowed in the last sunlight.

'The higher organisms we pay so much attention to aren't in control at all, you know. It's the lower organisms: bacteria and viruses. You can find bacteria in every conceivable place – even six kilometres under the earth's surface. Bacteria exploit everything.'

'So why don't you study them, instead of the wolf-spiders?'

'Wolf-spiders are extremely important micro-predators,' said Roly, with indignation in his voice. 'A very cosmopolitan group of spiders, in fact. We can learn a lot from them – they're very much in tune with their food sources. To some extent they're even cannibalistic, so they control their own numbers. The children of a single spider, if they meet each other in later times, it's quite true, will sometimes attack and eat each other, but if there's abundant prey, well – then the wolf-spider will never attack his fellow.

'They do a wonderful job. They're everywhere: under rocks, burrowed deep into pure salt on salt-pans, but they're commonest, of course, in the dry areas. They like to pounce on their prey' – he mimed a spider lurching forward – 'that's why they favour sparsely-wooded habitats. I've named forty or fifty species myself . . . is there something wrong?'

All through this exposition I had been moving warily about the museum's display room, a long chamber illuminated by a single ceiling-light. There was a school-desk at one end, as if some phantom class were listening to this lesson, and empty glass cases stood waiting to receive their spider exhibits.

My attention by this time was scarcely on the wolf-spiders and their life and times at all, so intently was I watching, and fending off, the mosquitoes that had gathered as dusk fell, dancing around me in ever closer circles.

'They don't seem to like you,' I said. 'Maybe you've become an honorary spider.'

'Oh, I don't think so, but after forty years working on them, I'm now quite in tune with them, you could say. My questions to them are of a higher order: the crucial diagnostic difference, of course, is in the genitalia. I've looked at five hundred or a thousand types of spider under that microscope over there; these drums are all full of specimens. Most of my work up until today has appeared only in the Memoirs of the Queensland Museum, but now, at last, I'm writing a book, the book of my life, you could say: *Wolf-spiders of Australia – Family Lycosidae*. That's one reason I've come up here.'

'And who's going to publish it?'

Roly sighed.

'In these times not too many people are interested in wolf-spiders. There are plenty of men and women who study butterflies, which are assumed to be beautiful, and so worthwhile, but when you're talking about mites or nematodes, or . . .'

He held up a phial to the light:

'*Lycosa Gibsoni*! One of my discoveries. I called it Gibsoni for Alf Gibson, who got lost in the desert, just the way I did, on a journey to Lake Dora, out in the Great Sandy, when I was following the river-course – and I thought of poor old Gibson, the first white man to die in that desert.

'I've named my spiders after scientists, and people who've made a contribution to systematics. I've even given them Aboriginal names, sometimes: there's *Lycosa Yulkara*, the desert spirit.

'Often, though, I prefer to name them after the explorers who aren't well-known: Hann, for instance, and Jardine, not that I admire them, for all their bushcraft. They were sometimes a bit too gung-ho. I've named one after Giles, a truly competent explorer, and of course Leichhardt, who came this way. I think he went much further than people believe on his last expedition. I think he penetrated deep into the Simpson desert – it's such easy terrain to become lost in, it wasn't the kind of country the Aborigines went into, even. At least he has his spider now, like the others.'

'Do you think that would have consoled him – or the spider?'

'He was an individual who expended great thought and feeling on his journeys through Australia. Death, of course, as we all agree, is everything . . .'

Roly waved a hand at the line of opened plastic drums, from each of which scores of glass tubes protruded, gleaming like distant galaxies.

'But if anything survives out there, perhaps it would be his kind of consciousness – systematic, observant, dispersed among all the creatures he saw, and classified. Perhaps – in some sense – to disappear is not wholly to die.'

In the morning, after breakfasting to the sound of bird calls, Gary Bondeson and I set off for the abandoned shafts and open-cuts around the town.

'At first,' he said, 'I felt I needed to know about the bush, the history of the place. I've put all that up on my web-site: who, when, how. These days, though, when I come out here, it's with a kind of reverence for what the old-timers achieved. I could take you out to Redcap, to Ruddigore – there are holes in the ground so deep that when you shine down your torch you can't even see the bottom; shafts where you can feel the wind's updraught flooding past you, and it seems to be coming from the centre of the earth.'

He turned his truck off the dirt road, down a rough track which went winding between limestone pinnacles, crossing and recrossing a broken rail-line until we reached a pile of tumbled bricks and struts and cantilevers.

'Zilmanton,' said Gary with an air of pride. 'The very first settlement. See?'

We bent down at the edge of a square pit full of black water.

'Once this was the end of the longest private railway in all Australia. It ran right from Port Douglas. They used the remains of the old Story Bridge to build it. Everything gets turned over out here, and recycled, and comes back for another stab at life. You see that limestone tower there: that's the Suicide Tower' – we drove on – 'and that's the Haunted Tower; and in that one there's six and a half kilometres of cave passages that have been explored. Think how many more to be found, or to be left alone.

'I've heard all the comparisons: cathedrals, temples in Central America. To me they're just part of the rhythm of the landscape. Once you're inside them, though, it's like a separate creation down there: all the different chambers with their marble and their stalag-mites; the shawls and folds; the rimstone.

'Sometimes I've been down there in the hot months, and there are hidden amphitheatres, so thickly filled with butterflies that you can hardly move. But this is what I wanted to show you.'

We lurched to a stop. Gary walked over to a white-painted bar-rier and held open a neat wire-mesh gate.

'Mungana cemetery.'

His voice was low.

'Do you see?' he murmured, pointing. 'Almost all the tomb-mounds are losing their distinctness; they're vanishing back into the soil. Walk through: have a look for yourself.'

He followed close behind me.

I knelt down beside the first grave with an upright head-stone. I read out: 'Sacred to the memory of Sarah, beloved wife of Thomas Stewart. Died 31 December 1912, Aged 67 years.'

'Go on,' said Gary.

There were morning glory leaves of marble, carved around an epitaph:

*We watched her suffer night and day.*
*It caused us bitter grief*
*To see her slowly pine away*
*And could not give relief.'*

'They didn't have much in those days,' he went on. 'It seems to have been common to use iron bedsteads as a kind of restraining fence around the grave. If you look at the different cemeteries here, hidden away in the karst like this one, you'll find that people died very close to each other in time – but whether they fell sick together, or died of broken hearts, I don't know.'

He crouched down and ran his hands along the rusted iron-work that ringed the grave. We were facing each other.

I said quietly: 'Why exactly are you doing all this?'

There was a rustle in the bush alongside us as I asked this question; then, from behind a stand of gum-trees, a brumby stallion, white, with a broad face, emerged, followed by a deferential pack of mares. He paused, gazing at us both for several seconds, then gave a lunging nod to his concubines, who retreated, and he too turned and trotted off, tail held high in the air.

Gary smiled at me and twisted a grass-stem round his fingers, and looked away an instant.

'Isn't it all about this?' he said. 'About finding a place, and role, in life? Why here? Why Chillagoe? A little spot of nothing, nowhere, lost in the back-blocks? Because we can be here. Carolyn and I, we haven't known each other that long: five years, maybe. We wanted to really have a world together, to start life anew. And I feel by coming up here, by listening to the landscape, moving through it, caring for it, thinking about the people who used to be here all those years ago – I think that's a good way to spend my life. Isn't that what you're doing out here, looking for something, someone? Aren't you trying to find the answer to some question, even if you don't quite know what the question is? It wasn't just some accident that made you stop at Chillagoe, was it?'

His voice, which at first had been gentle, became richer, stronger, as he spoke: 'No – and I don't think I found my way here by chance, either. I had a very different life before, in Townsville. But you come up here, into this heat, and light, when you're ready for it – when all the wordlessness in life has built up and up. Don't you reckon, in the end, that's what the gold prospectors and the pioneers were really searching for?'

And at this, it was my turn to look away, so questioningly did he glance up at me.

At the end of the afternoon we made our way back to Chillagoe, and found it full of life.

A French couple from Noumea, a relief nurse, an air-conditioning repairman and a light plane pilot had all been stranded in the town, and somehow had found their way to Carolyn, who was giving them a quick introduction to the aviary's residents as we drove up.

'And this is our third frogmouth owl in the last three months,' she was saying, pointing to a mottled shape frozen on a perch above the telephone. 'They like lizards, mice, day-old chicks – anything with feathers, fur or bones. And this little creature there, he only came in a few days ago. He's an owlet nightjar – one of the locals found him in a hollow log. He's very particular about his diet, too: ox or lamb heart, he has to have, dipped insect meal, and maybe the odd moth. I know they're all around us, but I've only been able to catch one all day.'

With a theatrical flourish, she produced the moth, and dangled it above the tiny bird, which remained unmoving, blinking each time the creature's hairy wings were passed before its eyes.

'Only one,' repeated Carolyn, 'and he won't even eat that . . . Still,' – her manner brightened – 'there's a bush barbecue for tea, and a special treat in store as well. The children have something to show you – at least, I think they do.'

And she was right: an hour later, once the night had fallen, as her guests munched through their steak and chips, talking in low voices, Carolyn's two grand-daughters stepped forward wearing bikini tops and grass skirts, with frangipani blossom wreaths about their shoulders. Shyly, they edged into the glare of a waver-ing spotlight, switched on a cassette player, and placed it on the ground before them. After a delay of several seconds dance-music began to play, and the two girls, both of whom were graced with an unsettling, adolescent beauty, embarked on a brief Hawaiian dance routine as clouds of moths and insects wheeled giddily around their heads.

A day or two more, and the charms of Chillagoe had begun to pall. After several evenings lost in the lush prose of *Northmost Australia* I decided the time had come to take the north-west road, a dirt track that runs across the creek, beyond the smelter reserve, past disused mining camps, towards the turn-off for Palmerville, until it curves, almost doubling back upon itself and swinging south towards the coast-line of the Gulf.

Before leaving I called in for fuel at the BP garage just off the air-port road. But even as I drove in I realised petrol and diesel sales were very much a secondary aspect of the garage's business, for all around the forecourt, under green awnings or shade-covers of cor-rugated iron, I could see brightly-polished vintage cars, each with its own neat-stencilled label displayed upon the bonnet.

A short man with striking facial lines strolled out, hands in pock-ets, towards me, glanced at me, and glanced again: 'Morning, young brother,' he said after a while, his mouth pulled back into an uneven grimace, exposing the crooked top row of his teeth. 'Going to be a hot day again.'

And without a word more being spoken, I knew we were indeed brothers, in the club whose membership is assigned at birth, of those with harelip and cleft palate, who travel through the world for years on end without striking another of their kind, who know at once each other's trials, who have in common a bond deeper than language. These encounters follow a strict pattern: the thing shared is never mentioned; the conversation is brief, perfunctory, but a tender feeling seems to fill the air – it is as if, for a few minutes, the rules of human contact vanish.

'Morning,' I said in reply, gently, and the man before me stared at my lips and mouth, and smiled at this greeting, as if he had heard the most beautiful sound in the world.

With abrupt enthusiasm, he shook my hand.

'Tommy Prior,' he said, perspiring from the effort as he tried to catch the consonants. 'You here for fuel? Take a look at the cars. Best collection of Fords in Far North Queensland.'

His gaze wandered over the silver badge of my Landcruiser. 'You're not a Ford man?'

'It's a hire car,' I said, apologetically.

'It has to be Ford, for me,' announced Tommy, with unflinching sternness. 'Don't mention Holdens here. Older Fords never die – they just come out here to revive.'

The evidence for this claim was all around us: piled behind the display of vehicles were engine parts and fragments, gear-boxes, axles, wheels and shafts and air compressors, while beyond the garage buildings a row of ancient trucks in various stages of decay or reinvention stretched into the scrub.

'I'll show you,' said Tommy, and he plucked at my elbow, pointing. 'Look. Ford Blitz, 1940 – they used to call it the Desert Blitz. That's Old Ben, with the machine-gun barrel. And that's a 1942 Dodge four by four weapon carrier.'

There were many others, and he described each one, its year of manufacture and its special characteristics. We came to the pride of the collection, housed in its own special quarters.

'Can you imagine that, in 1946, coming out of the showroom?'

'What is it?'

'That? The V8 Super Deluxe Coupe Utility; the first into

production after World War II, in Australia and the USA. Look at the engine – and the wooden dash and fascia – and this – see?'

He opened a little panel.

'Isn't it perfect? A concealed tool-box! That's all the car we needed, in those days, when we drove out to Mungana on the dirt. You could take them anywhere. We used to have water over the bonnet crossing the river sometimes. Fords! You had to have one in Australia in the fifties. I'd get a hundred thousand dollars, easy, for this in the US. But I'm not selling: I get more joy from this car than I would from fifty or a hundred grand. And this Ford Freighter 1952: fifty grand, guaranteed. But if I sold him I couldn't enter him in the Ford Retro Run, could I? And where you headed?'

I told him.

'What you doing up there? There's nothing there.'

He gazed at me, his face completely open.

I looked back, and all my familiar answers – that I liked driving alone in the Outback, I had time on my hands, the road was new to me – all my answers seemed to vanish.

'I don't know I have a reply for you,' I said.

'Try – go on.'

I had the sudden wish to leave something of myself behind; to mark the day.

'What would you think,' I said, uncertainly, with the odd sensation that I was discovering something even as I described it out loud, 'if I told you that last time I drove up through this country, into the Cape, I was looking for something – someone, whose route I once wanted to follow – but that was years ago.'

'You mean Leichhardt,' said Tommy, completing the ceremonial filling of the sub fuel tank and screwing the cap back on.

'That's right. He went up the Lynd, just south of here, then west. I must have followed all his expedition's track by now except this stretch, from Chillagoe out towards the Gulf –'

'There's really only one question,' interrupted Tommy, nodding repeatedly and wiping his hands. 'Would he have been a Ford driver?'

'Well – it was a long while back, but he always wanted to have the best-designed equipment, and the simplest – the most reliable – and he loved beautiful things, too.'

'There's no doubt, then,' said Tommy. 'No doubt at all: he was a Ford man.'

And he walked back to his cluttered office, turning at the door to give me a quick, complicit wave.

I drove up through bush thickly wooded with young, pale-leaved eucalypts, by the marble quarries and rusting machinery dumps, over the Walsh crossing, into a landscape of steep broken hills – and as I drove, my thoughts returned to the explorer whose steps I was dogging, to the gift of his *Journal* just before my first trip from Cairns, and the effect his words had made on me then.

At first there was a dawn of interest, nothing more, much like the beginnings of a friendship. It was only over time, in bleak hotels and roadhouses, as I pursued my project and read through his writings in the landscape where they were first set down on paper, that I gained some sense of Leichhardt's resolve: how he fought to bring his loves and dreams into the Outback with him; to raise new realms in exile; to overcome not just his surroundings, but all that he had been, and it was this desire that guided him along the Cape York rivers, across the swamplands of the Gulf, through Hell's Gate, onward, into Arnhem Land.

Figures from the past are free, of course, to float between the realms of truth and legend in our minds – but the further I travelled through the Cape's back country the more I imagined his presence beside me, forever suspended between triumphs and disasters, forever bound towards unseen horizons, much as he was bound, in the early

June of 1845, along the Lynd, through the low, drab country where Wrotham Park station now stands, its airstrip and white buildings visible, like the outhouses of some great, half-ruined mansion, from far away.

Porphyry-quartz and feldspar; sienite and granite: in his narrative, the explorer makes plain how tired he had grown of that confining valley system.

When three of his men told him that the Lynd joined a broader water-course ahead, he altered the expedition's heading and made camp that night on the west bank of a long lagoon. With a certain whimsy, Leichhardt named the new river 'after Sir Thomas Mitchell, the talented surveyor of New South Wales'. As if by way of explanation, in his *Journal*, he continues:

*'The bed of the Mitchell was very broad, sandy, and quite bare of vegetation; shewing the more frequent recurrence of floods. A small stream meandered through the sheet of sand, and from time to time expanded into large water-holes: the river was also much more tortuous in its course than the Lynd.'*

Mitchell, indeed, was everything that the amiable, supportive Lynd was not: a scholar and a bureaucrat; a skirmisher and a politician; a much-praised cartographic artist; a translator of Camoens. When Leichhardt first arrived in New South Wales he came laden with letters of recommendation to the Surveyor-General, and was keen to travel on Mitchell's official expedition of discovery into the inland.

Mitchell, though, quickly came to dislike and fear Leichhardt, whose literary and scientific learning and desire to unveil the hidden secrets of Australia so plainly rivalled his own. Leichhardt's attempts to plead his case with the Surveyor-General came to nothing: just before he set off on his journey towards Port Essington, a voyage few in the colony believed he had any chance of completing, he called on Mitchell in Sydney, twice, but failed to find him at home.

In a letter to the Surveyor-General, he expressed the hope that, since they had not crossed paths in town, they might meet *'in the Interior, which I consider my home, as I have no other one.'*

Mitchell, he went on, could *'bear down by the force of your equipment'*, but he, Leichhardt, would come through only by patience and perseverance. *'I shall not do it brilliantly,'* he ended, *'but I shall show by my unremitting efforts, how great my desire is, to investigate the nature of this continent, to which I have consecrated my life.'*

Mitchell, whose journals bear an uncanny tonal resemblance to Leichhardt's, was already in the field, bound for his 'scientific ladylove', the land of Carpentaria, when news of Leichhardt's successful passage to Port Essington reached him. His own elaborately prepared and equipped party failed to penetrate far beyond the Tropic of Capricorn. On a rest day, close to his furthest north, while protected from the sun's rays by a blanket, Mitchell penned a brief epitaph for all his hopes and yearnings: *'Are not beauty and gold as dust in the balance, when weighed in lofty minds against glory or immortality? When the shadow he pursues is worth more, and is more enduring than the substance, well might it be said that "Man is but a shadow, and life a dream".'*

Such was the enemy for whom Leichhardt named the broad watercourse that would lead him towards the shoreline of the Gulf; an enemy whose eclipse as an explorer of tropical Australia was all but guaranteed by the fall of that river; an enemy who would condemn Leichhardt's expedition *Journal* in time as the writings of a 'damned foreign coaster'; an enemy whose name alone was enough to bring misfortune, for it was down the Mitchell, christened by Leichhardt with such rare and secret irony, that attack and disaster lay.

The ambush took place just after seven in the evening. Leichhardt and his men had crossed a lightly timbered plateau, and halted near a quiet pool, whose whereabouts is unknown today, although a local Aboriginal tradition holds that Gilbert's body was buried close to a waterhole still visible on one of the furthest reaches of Rutland Plains.

Leichhardt, as if to downplay the impact of the fatal event, gives only the briefest account of Gilbert's death, which he did not see, for it was dark, he was dozing, and he always slept at some distance from his men. '*The body was still warm,*' he writes, when he came on the scene, '*and I opened the veins of both arms, as well as the temporal artery, but in vain; the stream of life had stopped, and he was numbered with the dead.*'

Who could have done more? And who could have led the survivors with more skill, or care, through the new chapters of their journey, over thousands of trackless kilometres, for half a year of onward exploration, until they reached the waters of Mountnorris Bay?

That moment of reflection, near the junction of the Lynd and the new river, was an end as much as a beginning. When Leichhardt threw down his oblique challenge to Mitchell's name, the plan of systematic exploration, the project of his long-protracted student life, in Berlin, Paris and London, gave place to something more raw and primal: a struggle to blaze the trail and live on in memory. Between the Mitchell and Port Essington, the dream of knowledge fell away. At the Limmen Bight, Leichhardt was forced to leave behind his rock collection. Just beyond the Roper Bar, where several of his packhorses met their death, he jettisoned his botanical samples, the pride of his heart, which he had intended to give to the Museum of Natural History in Berlin. His next, brief journey was a scientific fiasco. On his last expedition, as is well known, he vanished into the Outback, with all his equipment, animals and men.


At least I seemed favoured with an easier passage. By midday I was far beyond the Cape's ranges, and the peaks of Palmerville, like hazy pyramids, had disappeared from sight. Then, abruptly, the road, which had been wide and featureless for many kilometres, swept into a series of tight bends and dropped down to a river crossing. I drove over this narrow causeway, through the stagnant pools that marked its lowest point, up the far bank, past a sign. 'River Lynd', it said, and nothing more.

I pulled off the road at once, and switched off the engine. The stillness of the bush, pure and uncaring, descended. Some way downstream from where I had stopped the river broadened and the high banks fell away. In the distance, running across its course almost at right angles, a wide, sandy, reed-choked channel could just be seen: it was the Mitchell, as the maps told me, and by chance as much as by intent I was standing close by where Leichhardt had stood in the same season a century and a half before.

Slowly, with a sense of sentimental reverence growing inside me, I made my way down to the Lynd – or what was left of it. In the shade of some flowering grevilleas and ancient paperbarks I lay down on the thick sand, which had been churned up everywhere by cattle-hooves. Great dragonflies, with shimmering wings, hovered in pairs before me. There were a few signs of civilisation in the riverbed: scoured and flattened aluminium cans, a shard or two of dark brown bottle-glass, and in the undergrowth close by a discarded cigarette pack, lying beside a new-spun spider's web. Along the causeway, ribbed iron side-struts had been laid down to strengthen the concrete against the force of wet season floods – but these had long since been twisted out of shape. Upon the far bank, a herd of Brahman wandered listlessly; at a bend in the river, a half-rotted bullock carcass was outstretched.

I was turning, disconsolately, to climb the bank, when I had the sense of someone watching me – or so I imagined for an instant. I shook my head – all day, all through that drive in vacant country, when I should have been most at peace and free from thought, I had been uneasy, on some edge inside myself.

It was then that I heard a mewing call from one of the highest gum-trees above the river: a quick, falling scale of notes, and a kite-hawk soared above my head into the sky. Doubtless, I decided at once, it was a descendant, many generations distant, of the birds that had followed Leichhardt, and that were ever-present as the harpies of his imagination. How, though, to make true contact with the thoughts of those, like him, who have gone before us, whom we have lost, and those still living, those passing from our lives, as all passes – ideas, impressions, memories – until no solid thing remains? It was on the Lynd, as I liked to read the story, that Leichhardt had gone through his own stage of crisis and decision: had staked his life, right there upon the river where I stood, in return for fame, for glory, and intimations of the inland.

And what would I have wagered in his place, I wondered, as the kite-hawk flew above me, then came to rest again, and gave its whistling, yelping cries. What would have been dear enough to me for me to give my life?

I heard the bird's calls, in their sharp, repeated pattern – a soft note, and a series of falling cries, always three or four of them. Then, at once, as if the landscape had just confessed its deepest secret to me, I knew: I knew the wager, the game that the explorer played, a game with the kite-hawk, of life and death. Three calls from the fatal bird meant No to one's desire; and four, Yes. Three calls, and he would throw himself down; four, and he would live. He had made his pledge, then listened for the kite-hawk: and the bird called out those four cries, and cast its boundless shadow over him.

Even as these intuitions were running through my head, I had climbed my way up the Lynd's bank to the crest of a sand-cliff, where I paused, with a steep drop to the rocks and pools below me, to catch my breath. My heart was pounding; sweat dropped from my eyebrows; I was dazzled by the sunshine, dazed from the heat, and from so long spent in that landscape, driving, staring out at the horizon.

This, then, was what I had been journeying towards: the ragged bush; a silent river-channel; the explorer's trail of emptiness. I closed my eyes; the light was pulsing against my eyelids. A pleasant, hazy faintness was stealing over me – it strengthened. After a while I became conscious of a sound, like the dry breeze inside the paper-barks. It came from a great distance, and it was close beside me, a soft voice, murmuring the same words over and over: 'Your life is spread before you,' it was saying – and as I heard this, and made out the words, I felt a wave of sadness overwhelm me. 'All you ever wanted,' it was saying. 'Your life itself.'

Judgement being passed on me. But whose – and why? Why now, so deep in the stream of life; why here, out in the backblocks? How ridiculous the whole thing was, how arbitrary.

In a calm, dismissive way, out loud I said: 'With one thought, I could do away with this' – and even as I spoke, and heard my voice, and heard the fear inside it, I understood the danger.

Then, very clearly, came the kite-hawk's whistling call: that first call – it seemed full of every warm and tender feeling I had ever felt, hope, care, forgiveness – and, in quick succession, the short, descending cries, one, two, three of them – only three – then nothing. Three calls, for nothingness. 'Three calls, and he would cast himself down.'

I listened, in the sudden silence, full of regret. And so, I whispered, this, now, is the end of my journey. I closed my eyes, I leaned into the bright abyss, and then above me, a fourth time – there had been, in fact, only the briefest of intervals – the kite-hawk cried.

# Two     Promised Land

# I

Shortly after the revolutions that dethroned communism in Central Europe, I made a journey to southern Bohemia, a region I had long dreamed of visiting, for its little towns, their cobbled streets and spacious squares, had been familiar to me since early childhood, when much of my sense of the outside world came from the old picture books I discovered on my parents' shelves. There had been a pair of large volumes, printed in Prague in the years between the two world wars, filled with pictures of medieval and baroque Czech buildings. There must have been an architectural theme to these publications, for there were never any people in their photographs: every palace and ballroom was deserted, the light was always faint, the sky dark and heavy. I knew the names of each of these castles, each church and hunting lodge; I would pronounce them, over and over, to myself: Jaroměřice nad Rokytnou, Český Krumlov, Hluboká nad Vltavou. I had clear ideas about their scale, the colours of the stone, the silence in the ornamental grounds, so that when I eventually reached Krumlov and saw its castle tower, when I walked through a sun-drenched Vranov nad Dyjí, which had been shrouded in my imagination by deep romantic shadows, or when I wandered in a crowd of German tourists through my medieval Hluboka and found it to be a nineteenth-century replica of Windsor Castle, each of these discoveries was like a little earthquake for me.

On occasion, though, things unfolded differently. One trip I made, almost an act of pilgrimage, was to the Moravian town of Kroměříž, where a late Titian painting, today celebrated and much sought-after for international exhibitions, hangs in the bishop's palace. In those days of early 1990 this painting, which depicts the flaying at Apollo's command of the satyr Marsyas, was little-known in the wider world: I had never seen it reproduced.

When I arrived in the town, after driving past Slavkov and the battlefield of Austerlitz, I was full of anticipation. I parked, and bought a ticket at the palace museum's entrance. In the early galleries, which were full of medieval altar-pieces, I had almost to restrain myself from breaking into a run, though there was no one else in the museum, and no sign of guards or attendants.

After several further halls and state-rooms I came to the Titian gallery. I looked round. At first, I could not see it. A kindly figure standing behind a desk on which a handful of postcards was displayed made a gesture with his arm, pointing not to the walls, but to an easel upon which a turbid splash of paint had recently been poured. Only after a few seconds did I make out the image. At once I averted my eyes and began walking quickly round the room, looking upwards at the frescoed ceiling, or out, through the high windows, at the eaves and attics and the sky – anywhere but at what I had just seen, the body of the satyr, suspended upside down, a knife against his skin, a look of languor in his eyes, the god, close by, intent, all in a blur of brushstrokes. Breathing slowly, moving slowly, taking care not to look back towards the painting on the easel – though sometimes I think I have never stopped seeing it – I went over to the postcard counter, and bought one, for a single crown. The man behind the table surveyed me, slipped the card into a grey envelope which he handed to me, made a little bow and escorted me half-way down the flight of steps leading to the museum's main entrance.

It was only after I had left Kroměříž behind that I began turning over this experience. How much had been coming into being and dying around me there! The bishop's palace would soon be full of visitors, the town choked with western stores and hotels. The Titian would be a brief stop on the grand tour. The Central Europe of my childhood, of black and white photographs and fabled sufferings, was almost gone, its last traces were vanishing around me.

I drove on for several days tracing a zig-zag route through provincial Moravia, and Slovakia, glimpsing everywhere the signs of empire in disintegration, whole worlds of custom, order and priv-ilege collapsing, falling into oblivion. At times during that journey I felt almost like some colonial explorer who carries in his blood-stream a fatal bacillus, an infection so virulent it will destroy all that he sees, and all he yearns to see – and it is slowly destroying his own life as well, for who will heed the explorer in a settled land when the joy of discovery is gone, and nothing beyond the frontier remains?

These thoughts resurfaced in my mind years afterwards, on my return to Australia, when I began making my way once more through the country, and seeking some strands of connection with the previous stages of my life.

One field that seemed particularly to speak to me was Aboriginal rock art, which was just then passing through a phase of great dis-coveries, with each new month bringing fresh claims of wondrous ancient finds. The carved monoliths and rock shelter paintings I first came across, depicted in coffee-table books, or wrenched from their place and enshrined in museums and art galleries, brought back to me something of the frescoed vaults and chapels in Central Europe.

I was struck, too, by the names and faces of the rock art researchers I glimpsed from time to time in television news reports. They had a European feel to them – one of them above all, the bearded, deep-accented George Chaloupka, a Czech émigré who headed the rock art project at the Museum of the Northern Territory, and who was chiefly responsible for revealing to western eyes the painting tradition of Arnhem Land.

On a visit to Darwin, a place where it is hard to avoid chance meetings, I came into contact with him, and so, across backgrounds and across generations, began a friendship that has taken on increasing significance for me – in part, at least, because of the eventful story of George's European life, a story which he outlined to me with the most painful reluctance in the course of our first meetings, a story I have since tried to piece together from snatches of his conversation and his anecdotes.

George was born in the small Bohemian town of Týniště nad Orlicí, in 1932, into an artistic family with strong patriotic and religious convictions. His grandfather was an amateur painter, and he retained, as he told me, a very strong memory of him.

'My grandfather died literally of shame and sorrow, soon after the start of the German occupation, when soldiers came into our house and confiscated his gun collection. He was a real Czech nationalist, a very proud man: the hurt was too much for him. After he died – I was only seven years old – I used to go up to his room and smell the oil paints in his chest of drawers, and the snuff and pipe tobacco. I can still smell them now. I wanted to be like him, really: undoubtedly, if I had remained in Czechoslovakia I would have become an artist.

'My father had been sent away to forced labour camp, in Germany; he was there all through the war. My mother and grandmother tried to bring us up with a sense of responsibility, of right and wrong. My mother's surname was Izak: you can imagine what effect that had. She had to prove to the authorities that there were no Jews in our family for the previous three generations. In fact our forefathers had been members of the Czech brethren (perhaps you have heard of them?), a religious group whose members adopted biblical names, many of whom had fled from Bohemia to Poland in the seventeenth century. I became very conscious, in this war-time childhood, of the sufferings of the Jews. My mother had a close friendship with a Jewish couple who were taken away.

'And so we lived, and waited, and endured. The great event of those years that stands out for me now is something history has forgotten: the Prague uprising, when the city rebelled against the occupiers. My elder brother went to fight. It was only three or four days later, when everything was over, that the Russians came through. That was the first indication of what would happen. Gradually, word spread among us of the details of the Yalta agreement. There was still, you see, a degree of freedom – two, three wondrous years.

'I considered myself a great cosmopolitan in those days: I was learning English, and reading English and American literature. I was interested in modern art, and the changing waves of intellectual fashion. My grandmother, Emilie Izáková, who influenced me in these directions, was a most unusual figure: she used to urge us to learn Esperanto.

'But as I tell you the story of those days now, from this side of time, I see the light was already fading: it was that Indian Summer known so well in all the countries of Middle Europe. When the coup d'état by the communists came, in February 1948, I had a sense of history slowing down, coming to an end.

'During that summer it happened that I was very much involved in the scouting movement: walking, hiking, wandering. I remember going on a two-week course to a castle, close to Prague. In the library there was a beautiful two-volume study of prehistoric art, and in its pages was a section devoted to Australia. I leafed through its pages, and saw a desert shield, a boomerang, a Wandjina.

'The leader of our course turned up on that first weekend in a uniform with a hammer and sickle pin prominently displayed on his chest. He told us all that we had entered a new era, and to start with we would need to select a more progressive name for our scout-troop. I was only seventeen years old and I could see the shape my life would have. It was during that weekend that I took the decision to leave.

'I told my parents I was going off on a cycling trip. My mother knew I wouldn't be back. I went by bicycle as far as Suchice. I found the newspaper kiosk, and bought the last detailed map of the border region they had, then went across the road to the park, to plan my route. I had gone half the distance to the frontier when a border guard stopped me, and asked me where I thought I was going.

'"To see the black lake Karel Hynek Mácha wrote about," I replied.

'"You'll get six months in jail for your black lake," he warned me – and I cycled on, as far as Železná Ruda.

'It was a very Bohemian scene: mountains on the left, peasants in the field on the right, harvesting. I put aside my bicycle, and began running up the hills, into the mountains, with the people in the fields behind me cheering me on. It was much further than it looked, up to the forests, but you have so much energy in that state. I ran straight into the barbed wire – I had cuts all over my legs, but I kept going. I really didn't believe that was the frontier. I'd heard stories about dummy fences, and rows of frontier troops in machine-gun posts behind them. After a while I heard voices. They belonged to foresters, speaking German – and when I heard that language, the sound of which I had hated for so much of my life, I was happy.

'They gave me directions to the nearest town. I reported to a US military camp, and I was brought before a Czech-American. He interrogated me, then handed me a ticket to Munich, and a coupon for a hotel.

'For several months, I waited in displaced persons camps, in Murnau, where the Blaue Reiter group had been formed, and then in Bad Aibling in the Alps. Originally, it had been a German air-force base: it was very well-equipped. It had a skating-rink, and I used to go out alone to that rink at night-time, when it was completely deserted, and skate there, round and round, and there, one night about nine months after I had reached Germany, and just before I was to leave on the boat for Australia, I had a vision: my brother, clear before my eyes, my brother Milo, and that was the day that he too succeeded in crossing the border.

'Once they saw that both of us had escaped, the authorities threw my parents and younger brother out of the little town that we had lived in. My father was an accountant; he suffered badly from asthma. They sent him to work in a stone quarry – you can imagine what that did to his health. For a long time we were unable to communicate at all with them. When I arrived at Fremantle, with my promised land before me, I knew that I had begun another life, and that I had also broken the lives of everyone I loved.'

George sighed, and rested his forehead on one hand. We had moved, during the course of this conversation, from his cluttered office in the Museum, for a stroll round East Arm Reserve to the Darwin Sailing Club, a huddle of low shacks and awnings close by Fannie Bay, where we whiled away the afternoon, watching the sun's glow on the pale green water, the boats bobbing and the smoke-plumes on the far side of the harbour.

It became apparent as the days progressed that the Australian chapters of George's life were harder, indeed, were almost impossible for him to describe, and yet their consequences surrounded him at every turn. I already knew them, at least in outline: how he had come from Western Australia to the Northern Territory in 1956, together with his brother, hoping to reach Melbourne in time for the Olympic Games; how he had found Darwin, and stayed on, exploring, wandering all through the ranges of the Top End, the Arnhem Land plateau, the Victoria River, the Stone Country, discovering the painted galleries and the rock shelters which lay there in their hundreds, unknown to European eyes. Yam figures, rainbow serpents, mimis, lightning men – such were the characters in the frozen scenes he came upon, then recorded, and placed in their sequence, step by step, through years of study, until the masterwork of his Australian incarnation was complete.

*Journey in Time* was a tall, unwieldy volume, full of George's photographs, accompanied by an understated text. During my evenings on that stay in Darwin, I would leaf through its pages, with their images of carved galleries and cloud-darkened landscapes, and feel the days of my childhood come back to me – those long, solitary afternoons, when I would sit cross-legged in the District of Columbia sunshine, poring over the photographs of southern Bohemia, wondering what adventures might lie waiting in those halls and shadowed gardens, if I were ever to explore them myself.

Dutifully, I made my way right through the book, emerging much better informed about the life-cycle of the barramundi, the colour scale of haematite and the distinctive properties of ironwood. As a source for George's own experiences, though, it offered little, or so I thought, until, just as I was about to close the book for the last time, I stumbled upon a modest 'author's note' recounting the origins of the manuscript.

*'Its beginning goes back,'* George had written, *'to 1958, when, in the heartland of the region's rock art at the East Alligator River, I*

*entered a rock shelter whose wall and ceiling were ablaze with multicoloured layers of painted images. Some were identifiable as representing the natural species that inhabited the riverine environment, others were of human figures, and some, as I was to learn later, were beings from the Dreaming. In the stillness of the day, I stood spellbound by their magic, captivated by their unique form and the brilliance of their execution.*

*'To discover what it meant, who the artists were, and how this tradition fitted in the cultural sphere of the local populations, I sought out the traditional owners of each area where I was to search for rock art sites. I was privileged to meet many people of generous spirit and great strength of character, who accepted me as a friend. A number of these men and women possessed a deep knowledge of their traditions. These people were my closest companions for more than two decades. They taught me all that I know of this land, their society and its traditions: 'they grew me up' in knowledge, I was taught to see the landscape, the shelters and the paintings through their eyes.*

*'Many of the people who took me through their land, and who during the long evenings spent round the camp fire taught me the traditions of their Dreaming, have since passed away. But it is really only their bodily self that is gone; their spirit lives on. I see them often in the bush, for they now approach me in their other manifestations. I know that the dingo which followed me for several days, and at night came to where I slept, is one of my friends. So, too, is the white-breasted sea eagle which flies to sit in a paperbark tree where I camp when visiting his land.'*

When George came back from a spell in Kakadu National Park, where he had been escorting a German documentary film crew through the galleries around Nourlangie Rock, I went to see him once again. His manner, and his bearing, even the light in his eyes had changed.

'I feel happier when I go bush,' he murmured. 'All our conversations, about the past, and Europe, were weighing on me, even though they made me happy at the same time. You look, you see, very like my father, or my father as I remember him. You have his build, his height. Somehow, it made those days very present for me. Nothing we have lived through ever leaves us, you know. Time abolishes nothing – that's the deepest lesson that life holds.'

It was mid-afternoon, his favourite time for talking. Often during those long exchanges I would plunge into a pit of memory, only to be rescued and returned to something more like external consciousness by the sound of George's low, quickly-dying laugh at the end of some story, and I would find myself once more, sitting opposite him, settled into one of the soft chairs in the main room of the Chaloupkas' garden cabin, with the day already shading into twilight.

Hunched towards me, close enough to reach out and touch my sleeve, George was ranging across years and subjects, quietly, almost whispering, because his wife, Pina, had fallen asleep in the room next door.

'For you,' he said, 'maybe my past holds some distant, exotic flavour. For me, it has a pattern. It is my evidence about life. When I came with my brother to Darwin, in 1956, in our minds we were poetic refugees. We never expected to stay abroad forever. It was then that we heard the news of the Hungarian uprising, and its suppression, and only then did we truly realise we would not be going back. And it was then that I gave up my European past, or so I told myself, and I became part of this country.

'I remember the day we arrived in Darwin. It was like reaching a new dimension. No one cared where you came from. Everything was ramshackle. There was nowhere to stay, so we camped in a rainforest, where the Casino is now. And that first evening, some crocodile shooters came in, and they brought with them a group of Aboriginal men, from Oenpelli, just across the river-crossing in Arnhem Land. For decades I have spent my life with these people, in their world.'

'Until it has become yours?'

'I don't think, of course, that can ever be. I know I brought Europe with me into my Australia, but the more we talk, and look back, the more I come to feel that the two halves of my life no longer make any sense if you take one without the other. I remember so much of those early days in Darwin, working for the Water Resources Division, discovering the land, opening up areas that were quite unknown to westerners. We had to make our own tracks. We used helicopters. We built gauging stations on the crest of the escarpment. And everywhere I got near to the rocks, I found rock paintings, not just in Arnhem Land, but throughout the Territory.

'This all reached very deep into me. When I tried to move on, after a decade, I started writing a long poem, a farewell, you could say, to the country.'

'Do you remember any of it?'

George leaned towards me once again and began reciting, smoothly, in a deep, slow murmur:

*'The blue moist coastline, bays,*
*Islets and lakes,*
*Snakes of rivers uncoiling,*
*Towards the sea of Arnhem,*
*In the Bonaparte Gulf or*
*The Gulf of Carpentaria.*
*Dry rivers dying shallow,*
*Accentuated by the river red gums*
*Down in the dry seared Centre*
*Below the Tropic of Capricorn . . .'*

He broke off, and buried his face, an instant, in the uplifted palms of his hands.

'I had reached as far in my imaginary journey as Yirrkala when I realised I couldn't leave. Not just because it was becoming my own country, not even because of the paintings, though I was astonished by the importance of the art as I began to come across it. I knew, of course, that as a European you only see the outward meaning you yourself give it – but I sought out the traditional owners, and went back with them to their old lands. I wanted to know what the paintings meant, otherwise they would have been in my eyes just dead art, archaeology. I collected all the information I could find on the sacred sites, the paintings, on who made them. I became particularly close, over the years, to certain Aboriginal people.'

'The people you mention in the foreword to your book?'

'Of course, to them,' said George, heavily.

He looked across towards me through the gathering dark.

'Perhaps, in a way, I had been hoping not to speak about this. Now, however, I realise how much my old companions summon up for me the past – the past in my country, as well as here. All the things I have seen, and lost, and hope to find again some day.'

I was surprised by this faint note of belief.

'But I was born a Catholic,' George said. 'When I came to Darwin, I helped to quarry stone for the Cathedral. And now, there are two layers of belief in me. I still believe you are your brother's keeper, that choice is within us. We choose good or evil. When I was younger I would not have believed that there was an afterlife. But today' – he moved his hands, in imitation of the scales in a balance – 'today, I am hoping. We are torn between reason and mythical beliefs. But really, what survives is not some physical part of us. The spirit survives: our spirit that looks on, the echo, I imagine, of our self. Perhaps we all leave something behind us: our achievements, our actions in life, our effects on other people. But even as I say this

I wonder if the Aboriginal influence upon me is coming out? Have I become part of their world, without fully knowing it?'

He laughed, then, after some moments, at last began to tell me the story of his two great friends from the Badmardi clan, the brothers Kapirigi and Namingum: each in turn, their lives, and character, what they believed, and loved, their knowledge, too, of trees, and food, and flowers, all this in the most gentle yet most detailed fashion, with the skill and tact of an eighteenth-century biographer, conveying the flavour, the essence of an absent subject, rather than the gross events of that subject's life.

After some minutes he paused, then reached for his copy, lying between us, of *Journey in Time*, opened the book and passed it to me.

'This,' he said simply, 'is Kapirigi, as I remember him.'

The dedication, in Gundjeihmi and English, was printed beside a photograph that filled both pages.

It showed an Aboriginal man, almost in profile, seated, spear in hand, legs drawn up to his chest. He was looking out from the edge of the escarpment, with the green plain in the distance. Above him was a pale blue sky, the colour almost bleached out by wisps of feathered cloud. Kapirigi's face, or what could be seen of it, was stern and grave. He wore a white band about his forehead. A pair of grevillea stems were thrust through it like heraldic plumes. Silver light played on the stone platform round him, as if at that second a beam of filtered sunshine had been illuminating him alone.

'Ah, Nipper,' said George. 'Nipper – that was my name for him, you see,' then, calmly, he continued, sighing. 'It was a very beautiful day, such a beautiful day, the day that he died. His wish was that he should pass away in his own country, and be buried in the traditional manner. We took him there together: myself, Pina, and his brother Namingum.

'Back we went, to this landscape we had explored so happily, and which we knew so well – Balawurru, Deaf Adder Creek, where the most wonderful rock art galleries surround you on every side. We stayed with him there for two weeks – the last two weeks. We cared for him, and we built the platform on which his body would be placed. I had never thought, until then, that I would be able to watch someone die. We had camped on a most beautiful lagoon, their favourite spot. Throughout those days, we had visits, from nurses, rangers, from the Aboriginal people.

'It was a calm day, when he was close to the end, and I went away from the camp for a few minutes to catch a fish, and to be alone with myself. All through that morning there had been a sea eagle above us, a white-breasted sea eagle, and Namingum was shooing it away, and telling us it was after Nipper's soul. I was upstream, and again I saw the sea eagle, flying low over the creek, and when it passed over the camp I heard the people start to wail – and I knew that was the end of Nipper. I ran back, and leaned over him, and I closed his eyes.'

There was a silence in the cabin: indeed, several minutes passed. The darkness thickened; tears were flowing down George's cheeks. He smiled at me, and wiped them away.

'It was very intense. Dramatic – a beautiful time as well, to look after him, to share his last days. He was dying of lung cancer. What we didn't know then was that the same thing would happen four months later to his brother. Namingum had come to stay with us, and lived with us in Darwin. Our doctor diagnosed him. When the time came, we took him to another place, and went through the same process of sorrow and caring. He was placed, in his turn, on a different platform. The final ceremony was held two years later, when the people came to collect their skeletons. They were ceremonially treated with red ochre, and placed in hollow logs, and we flew them to the escarpment, to lay them in a shelter where they would not ever be disturbed.'

'And they still look down on you? And one day, you might see them again?'

'In this way' – he tapped the book – 'I'm sure that I'll see them: I already do. I mentioned the dingo that followed my tracks. When I visited their country, last year, I heard the dingoes calling. It was the longest continuing call I've ever heard. There was a reply from the other side of the valley, and when I heard it, I thought of my friends.'

It was only several days later, at a farewell dinner in the Chaloupkas' apartment near the bay, that I heard from George's lips something of the sequel to these events.

We had been talking, in an almost joking way, around his ideas of Bohemian identity: how language shapes one's feelings and one's thoughts, how the hills and forests of his childhood were still present and vivid in his mind.

'And it never occurred to you,' I asked him, 'in 1989, when you heard the news coming out of Czechoslovakia, and all Central Europe, to try to return, to recapture what you were? Undo your poetic exile?'

'But of course,' said he, as if shocked that I could even ask the question. 'The moment it became possible, I made a journey to Prague, and to Moravia, and it was everything I had ever dreamed such a homecoming could be: the streets, the squares, the churches, the sound of Czech, the way it sounds like bird-calls, being spoken by young voices. We went through Hradcany, and we saw President Havel walk out in the courtyard of the Castle – it was something almost unimaginable for us, to have a writer once more as the president of the country, someone we had admired so much, for his stand against the regime.

'Together with my brother, I made a journey to our little provincial town, to visit the graves of our family. It was a Sunday. My brother stopped in the central square and went to buy a pack of cigarettes from a kiosk, and bumped into one of my old schoolfriends. The following weekend, it turned out, was our fortieth-year class reunion. I attended it. It was very touching, and very sad, to hear the stories of their lives. Many of them had suffered persecution under the system. At the time, just a month or two after the revolution, there was little anger at what had happened, little thought of revenge. One of my oldest friends had become an accountant, and worked for an insurance company. There were teachers, and a doctor, and two or three fleshy men – they were the communists.

'All through those weeks, though, however dear to me the medieval castles and the churches were, however beautiful the landscape seemed, however strongly I felt at home, there was always, if I can say it this way, always another part of me walking beside myself. I had not shared what my countrymen had experienced, and they had not been with me. They had not seen the rain falling in great sheets from the storm-clouds in Arnhem Land. They had no picture of the smoky, hazy sunsets above the Arafura Sea. They had never looked into a rock shelter and glimpsed the art of forty thousand years stretched out on the sedimented stone before them.

'There was a day when I was walking through Prague, near the Vysehrad, alone, and I realised that I had brought all the things I loved there, all the things I had missed all those years, I had brought them with me, and passed them into Aboriginal Australia, and found them there, disguised, waiting for me – so that I came to feel that every exile has in it a homecoming. Perhaps it seems ridiculous to you, but I always believed, in some secret corner of my heart, there was a natural connection, between Bohemia and the world here, the world of Kakadu, and Arnhem Land. Not just because there were so many scientists and researchers from the Czech lands who came here, like Brandl, who was from the Sudetenland, or Jelinek, whom I met here, just after the Prague Spring, in 1969, but in some deeper fashion, it is as if the two worlds run in parallel, and sometimes they come together. We had a very specific instance not so long ago last year.'

He drew himself back, and gave the barest outline of the story: early in the morning of a hot December day, the Museum received a call from the Protocol Office of the Department of Foreign Affairs. The President of the Czech Republic was paying a State visit to Australia, and had expressed a wish to stop in Darwin, so as to visit the rock art sites of Kakadu, which he had learned of from *Journey in Time*.

'Of course, there was a great excitement at the thought of this exotic foreign leader coming to the Territory. Everyone turned out. We met Havel at Darwin airport, and flew together by light plane to Jabiru. There was not so much time for us to talk together, although I had looked forward to the encounter so much: but, in the end, the talking was not the point of the visit.

'He was very keen to have a cigarette during the flight, because, as you know, he was at that time a committed smoker, and they told him: No smoking, absolutely, even for presidents.

'When we landed, all the Aboriginal people were waiting for us. It was a day when Kakadu was filled with its softest, most gentle light. Full wet season, but the Magela Creek had fallen, so we could cross it; a weekend, and there were families on the banks fishing together.

'We were welcomed by Big Bill Neidjie at Ubirr, in front of the paintings, and when we arrived, and I found myself standing in the rock galleries with the dramatist of Bohemia and the philosopher of Kakadu before me, I felt, for a moment, as if my life was in balance, that its two halves agreed and corresponded. Of course I knew this feeling would leave me, but it was something, even once, to have had it present in one's mind.'

Some months afterwards, George went on, in an even, careful voice, there was a development that changed the course of his life. At one of the regular check-ups he submitted himself to, he learned that he in his turn was suffering from cancer, which was already well advanced, and spread through several organs of his body. An operation followed. It had been, apparently, successful. In its wake, though, it was as if the patterns of his thought had shifted: life seemed swifter, emotions stronger, the past more full of shadow, until the present day had become for him almost exclusively a time of looking back, and reassessment.

'And perhaps,' he concluded abruptly, glancing at me with a disquieting directness, 'that is the light in which to view our conversations, which have given me such a nostalgic pleasure. Perhaps, too, that is the frame for the whole story that I have found myself telling you.'

'A very Bohemian story,' I said. 'One rich in change, and trials, and melancholy.'

'Melancholy? Perhaps,' he countered. 'But I sense a sadness in you as well – a restraint. You listen, and hold yourself back. Are you still, I wonder, somehow in exile, throwing yourself so deep in Australia the way you do – losing yourself in it?'

But I absorbed this blow in silence, for my thoughts were already far away. At his words, they had travelled back to Central Europe. I was once more in Budapest, in the last days of the falling empire.

It was a time when I had just finished a protracted journey to Romania. I was wrung out by what I had seen, and the Hungarian capital, by contrast, appeared like some near-perfect heaven. On one of the first mornings of my stay there, I made a visit to the Fine Arts Museum, and it was there that I came across the figure who, for much of George's story, had been hovering on the edges of my imagination.

In the main galleries of the museum, I noticed, there was a special exhibition, newly hung, devoted to a nineteenth-century collector I had never heard of – Karoly Pulszky, a scholar of the renaissance, although the details of his career, which were given only in Hungarian, escaped me. It was the eclectic choice of paintings, sculptures and drawings, their combined effect, like some sweet, synthetic potion, that caught me.

I walked around, and found my eyes returning to one work in particular: a quattrocento portrait of a young man, elegantly clothed, wearing a dark cap. There was a manuscript desk, of pale wood or stone, before him; he held a rolled-up parchment in one hand. Behind his shoulder, through an open window, a Campanian landscape could be made out, receding towards a horizon as deep-blue as the sea. I stared at this portrait for several minutes, until I became conscious of a tall man, with long, black, thinning hair, who was standing to one side, with an uncertain expression on his face, watching me.

'Eisler Janos,' he murmured, stepping forward, and shook my hand, with the air of anxious bravado that still in those days mantled chance meetings between Hungarians and western strangers. 'And might it interest you to know more about Pulszky?'

Dr Eisler's English, like that of many eastern intellectuals, was almost flawless, though heavily accented. His skin was pale, as if he passed his life solely in the ill-lit wood-panelled museum office where he first told me something of Pulszky's life.

'I myself,' he said, 'have always seen him in the portrait you were looking at. It is the painting he loved most, and the painting, we may say, that brought him down.'

'Brought him down?'

Eisler smiled, and sighed, and began: 'Pulszky came from a great political family. He was born in London, where his father, who had been Kossuth's envoy, was living in exile, after the death sentence passed on him by the counter-revolutionary government. The younger Pulszky was brought up first there, and then in Florence. In his father's salon he could meet the leading European writers and philosophers of the day: Herzen and Bakunin; Mommsen and Henry James.

'He pursued his higher studies in Leipzig, and in Vienna, and wrote his dissertation on the links between Raphael and antiquity. In his tastes, and his enthusiasms, he was international – and this flavour was evident to all around him. He was elegant and full of charm and style: after his family's return to Budapest, he used to ride his white steed from the hills where he had his house, down into the paved streets of the city.

'All these elements had made him into a brilliant figure, and of course he was hated for it, and envied by his rivals. Nor was this resentment lessened by his personal circumstances, for while he was still building his career in politics, he married the actress Emilia Markus, the "blonde marvel", who was said to be the most beautiful woman of her age. One of their children, Romola, you have surely heard of: she became the wife of the dancer Nijinsky.

'At this particular point in the development of the Hungarian nation it had been decided to create a state collection of paintings, and Pulszky, as the natural candidate, was entrusted with this task. For three years, he travelled, at frantic pace, here and there through northern Italy, sometimes changing towns daily, searching, hunting down his painted quarry. It was a sustained frenzy of collecting and connoisseurship. He was, you might say, the Berenson of Budapest. But his enemies were watching. One of the paintings he bought was the Sebastiano del Piombo portrait you were studying, which was sold to him as a Raphael, but which he bought knowing very well the correct attribution – because it was a masterpiece, because it was beautiful, because, perhaps, as well, he saw himself in it. He was accused of buying junk, and wasting the public's money – although, of course, the affair was much more personal, and complex, since it was unfolding in late nineteenth-century Hungary.

'There was a scandal in Parliament. He was forced, in his turn, into flight. It is only today that the political climate at last allows us once more to honour his memory, and to appreciate his life's work.'

'And what became of him?'

Dr Eisler looked away, as if into the middle distance, though he could see, through his window, only the grey brickwork of a neighbouring building.

'Pulszky went into exile, in Australia, a country where he believed he could escape from rumours. But he was a knight of the renaissance, unable to live among sheep-shearers. He found employment there as an insurance agent, but fell prey to depression, and loneliness – and, on the sixth of July, 1899, in a place called Myrtletown, in the state of Queensland, I believe, he took his own life.'

## II

A few weeks later, I found myself once more on the rock art trail, that ill-drawn road that always leads to unexpected places – although, on this particular occasion, as I was deep in central Queensland, and many kilometres down a well-marked track, with a skilled map-reader close beside me, I was feeling more confident than usual about my progress.

'So – tell me about this dude we're going to see,' said Cameron, folding his long legs into a new position, stretching, and in the same movement reaching out to switch off the music, a Glenn Gould recording of the English Suites which, as I was well aware, had been driving him to distraction ever since our fuel-stop at Injune.

I turned onto a dirt road. In the distance, our destination loomed at last.

'Is that it?' he said. 'It looks like hell' – and, in truth, Carnarvon Gorge was not wearing its kindest aspect.

Before us, across a plain of parched scrub and Mitchell grass, the pale cliffs reared up, their crests lost in swift-moving trails of cloud, layered, ragged, like some compacted atmospheric sediment, through which, from time to time, the play of lightning could be seen flooding the valley's entrance with spasmodic blades of light.

'He's a rock art expert,' I said, contriving my description carefully. 'One of the best-known in the country.'

'Another academic!'

'Not at all – I shouldn't think he's ever been near a university in his life. You might be quite intrigued by him, I think. He's very keen on cars – old American cars – and drugs.'

'Well,' said Cameron, 'there's certainly a basis for negotiation.'

We drove on, great wind-gusts smashing into the Landcruiser, rain-squalls scudding past on either side, as I scrounged up every odd detail I could remember about the life of Grahame Walsh, the grey wolf of the Carnarvons, whose redoubt we were approaching: his childhood misadventures; his underworld connections; his adolescent loves – design, photography and illegal weapons; his present mania for collecting, which had first showed itself in the purchase of the Saracen tank he used to drive round south-east Queensland; his many life-threatening accidents, all of them in their varied ways extreme, like episodes from some 1960s television series. There had been, as I recalled, a shooting incident in Toowoomba, a head-on collision that left him paraplegic for several months, and, of course, the sea-plane crash just off the north Kimberley coastline.

'But that's miles from here.'

'This was where he began: up the Gorge, ahead of us, in the tablelands, and beyond, to Salvator Rosa, and Mount Moffatt. If you're lucky he might tell you about the string of food and ammunition dumps he's secreted all through the central Queensland sandstone belt.'

'And this person is a friend of yours?'

'In a sense. I heard about him from a rock art scholar I know in Darwin, but I only met him for the first time quite recently, at the Bar Roma, in Sydney, right by the Capitol Theatre – maybe you know it, run by a family from Lecce, but covered in posters showing the Palazzo Schifanoia in Ferrara?'

'Listen, I come from Melbourne. I know all about Italian coffee bars – I'm not a savage.'

'No, of course not, just a photographer – so you'll have lots in common with Grahame. I can still see him that day: he was like an apparition. It was a cold winter morning and he turned up in white shorts, white shirt, white shoes and long white socks, carrying a mass of papers – and that was it, he was off. He had the most extraordinary speaking style, and every story on the very edge of the believable. But the oddest thing was, they were all, in every detail, true.'

'And he lives here – all the year round?'

Cameron was peering through the windscreen at the banks of cloud, which rose above us in banded tiers. Shafts of light came pouring down, and shone with a fierce glare upon the rock faces, while thunder could be heard rolling and echoing.

'All the year round – but this is almost a farewell visit. He's selling up. He bought this property twenty years ago, and set up his research centre here. But since then, more and more, he's shifted his work to the Kimberley. His great love is the Bradshaw figures now. You've heard about them?'

Cameron shook his head, as we plunged into a creek crossing, and submerged the front half of the vehicle in rushing water.

'They're not so well known yet,' I called out, over the roar of the engine, as we struggled up the steep far bank, and the sign we were looking for came into view.

'Takarakka Rock Art Research Centre,' it read in crude stencils upon a wooden board and underneath, in much larger letters: 'Private Property – Keep Out.'

'Very graceful, ancient figures,' I continued. 'He'll tell you all about them. They're in rock shelters, just beneath the ridge-lines, looking out across the river-valleys, all through the remotest parts of

the Kimberley. He thinks they're more than 17,000 years old –
because of the evidence from wasps' nests.'

Another sign appeared – the road, by this stage, had dwindled to
a scree of jagged stones: 'Private,' it said. 'Trespassers Will Be Shot.'

'Are you sure we had an appointment?' Cameron asked. 'And
what do you mean – wasps' nests?'

'Absolutely I'm sure – and the nests are fossilised, they can be
dated, so the paintings underneath them can be too. The Bradshaws
are worth your attention. Everyone who studies them goes slightly
mad, but then that's probably true of all rock art, anyhow.'

I braked sharply, and pulled off the track, for a cavalcade of vehicles was headed at speed towards us, bumping over the rocks and
wash-aways. In front was a police Toyota, then came two park
ranger trucks. They were the first signs of humanity we had
encountered for several hours.

'Dangerous Dog On Patrol,' said the next sign, and a few hundred metres on, after passing some tumbledown cabins, we came to
a halt in front of a low house which was almost wholly concealed
behind a screen of ferns, zamia palms and thick shrubs, their weep-
ing branches weighed down by purple flowers.

'Do Not Leave Car,' announced the last sign, hanging beside the
padlocked entrance. 'Sound Horn – You Will Be Met At Gate.'

I followed this instruction, several times, until there was movement amidst the shrubs and ferns, the gate opened, and, smiling,
stark-eyed, sallow, Grahame Walsh emerged. He was wearing a
khaki uniform topped by a deep brown Akubra which was in the
last stages of disintegration.

'You made it, Uncle,' he said, in tones of rapture. 'The
Carnarvons – escape from reality.'

From out of the shadows behind him came a Doberman, which
was walking with a pronounced limp.

'Is it safe?' asked Cameron, eyeing man and beast cautiously.

'Safe?'

'Safe for us to get out?'

'Of course – don't worry about him,' said Grahame, reaching through the window towards me, taking my hand in his, which was bathed in a clammy film of sweat, and shaking it repeatedly. 'He'll just lick you to death – won't you, Max?'

The dog, at this sign of attention, retreated nervously.

How relaxed he seems up here, I thought, as we moved indoors, pausing for a few minutes in his workroom for an exposition of his latest theories. Perhaps in this world the bleak part of his nature simply fades away. It was an unusually impractical environment, even for a bush scholar's cell. From floor to ceiling, bookshelves lined the walls. The desks were piled with manuscripts, loose-leafed binders and stapled sheaves of photocopies. The floorboards were concealed by drifts of paper, so that navigation or free movement was impossible. We stood, trapped, listening, trying not to over-balance in this swirling sea of print.

'Don't you ever get cold working in here?' Cameron broke in after a while, shivering, rubbing his arms, for the air-conditioning was arctic.

'Best temperature for document conservation,' said Grahame, indignantly. 'And for staying awake and alert as well.'

We edged our way into the main room of the house, which had a cave-like air. It had been built from dark bricks, and scarcely any daylight penetrated the screens of vegetation beyond the windows. There were no decorations or signs of domestic life. Above the fire-place an elaborate array of samurai swords could be distinguished, gleaming in the dark.

'They're beautiful,' murmured Cameron, walking across to inspect them.

'Aren't they? The love of my life,' said Grahame. 'Every cent I get I spend on them. I've loved them since I first saw one.'

I leaned back into a low armchair. The Doberman came hobbling over, and began affectionately licking my hand.

'What happened to the dog?' I asked.

'That dumb bastard.' Grahame waved in its direction. 'It's given me nothing but trouble since the day I took it, it's always been on edge.'

'But what happened to it?'

'It jumped into the way of a bullet.'

'It did what?'

'It was acting up, so I fired a shot just past its head, to calm it down, but the damn creature jumped the wrong way.'

'Poor thing,' I murmured, trying not to look too shocked, and stroking the dog's head, while it gazed up into my eyes.

'Poor thing? It's bad news! The owner just had to come up to file another report on it.'

'It's not yours?'

'No – it belongs to the cop at Injune. He was just here. It attacked a young boy at the gorge yesterday – tore half the child's face off.'

Very carefully, I withdrew my hand from the dog's slavering muzzle, got up from the armchair and went across the room towards the sword display.

'Get out of here,' Grahame growled at the dog, which struggled to its feet, and, radiating grace and sadness, limped away.

'Now – these swords' – he took one down, and ran his fingers along the blade – 'Isn't that beautiful? I get Japanese businessmen coming here wanting to buy them. They'd give two hundred and fifty for this one any day – but I'd never sell it.'

'Two hundred and fifty dollars?'

'Two hundred and fifty thousand.'

'Are they all worth that?'

'Near enough. This one's the star of the collection. See how beautifully balanced it is? It's a priceless work of art. I'd buy another like it tomorrow if I could ever find one, although it might be hard, on my income.'

'But it doesn't look as if you're on the breadline.'

'Looks can be deceiving. I made two thousand two hundred dollars last year, and it was a good year. That's what I eat – over there.'

He gestured towards the refrigerator; then, as if to prove his case, went over, tugged the door open, and produced a large slab of brownish material with a glazed sheen on its surface.

'The usual fare. Christmas cake from twelve months ago. You just keep cutting the mould off as it stratifies. And those as well.'

There was a stack of yellow cans beside the sink.

'Taiwanese tuna. No-name brand. You can live on that for seventy-three cents a day. Most people seem to use them for pet-food.'

'I suppose,' I said, feeling the conversation was getting a little out of hand, 'that with your intake of pharmaceuticals, a conventional diet doesn't really matter all that much.'

'You're not wrong, Uncle,' Grahame was saying, when Cameron, his voice strained, broke in.

He was standing at the door leading to the verandah, which was overhung by thick vines and shade-canopies.

'I think you better come out here, Grahame – there seems to be a large python on your garden table.'

'That's right,' said Grahame. 'The park rangers found him on the road the other day. Some tourist had run him over, so they brought him here to recuperate. I don't know how well he's doing.'

He strolled over to the python and bent over its head, which moved from side to side while its forked tongue flicked in and out.

'Is there any life-form on this property that hasn't sustained some dreadful injury?' I asked, appalled by this unfolding catalogue of horrors.

'No,' said Grahame, 'me included!' – and he picked up the python and cradled it in his arms.

Cameron pulled me aside.

'Listen,' he whispered, 'this man's a sky-pilot. We've got to get out of here before he shoots us both!'

'Calm down,' I said, although I too was beginning to feel a certain alarm, mixed in with the drowsy midday numbness that wet-season storms so often provoke. 'It's just that he's just a touch eccentric. You won't meet too many people like him in your life. And, besides, he said he had something to show us – something important.'

'What – a bullet in the head?'

'Just trust me – he said it would be a nice surprise.'

'Come out here,' called Grahame, his voice full of enthusiasm, the python by now coiled around his neck. 'The storm's gone past – it's headed over Deepdale – no danger any more of lightning strikes. I'll take you to the look-out.'

We clambered up through thick undergrowth, along the steep ridge that reared up behind the house, tripping, losing our footing, slashed by branches and stung by tree-ants, until we reached a bare rock-ledge. Before us the white cliffs of the gorge entrance, framed by clouds and plumes of moisture, loomed like a stage-set.

'There she is,' said Grahame. 'That's the sight that always sets me free. Silent country. On a day like this, you can't hide from the truth about this landscape!'

'And what's that?'

'It destroys the mind,' he said cheerfully. 'It undoes consciousness. That's what it's been doing ever since Europeans came here.'

'And you love it for that reason?'

'Love? Of course I came here because I thought it was beautiful. I searched all over Australia for somewhere I could live, and it was a toss-up between here and Mount Barnett in the Kimberley. This is

a very sombre spot: a hidden world's inviting you in. Absolute solitude – there's something about being surrounded by rock. But love?
It's much more than that.'

He turned his bloodshot eyes towards me for a moment.

'At first the Gorge taught me humility. When you get deep into
these valley systems, and it's sunset, and you hear a rumbling in the
distance, and you see vast land-falls, then you begin to realise that
you're in a greater world: solid, inhuman. The gum-trees up there
on the ridge-line with the tableland, they're primeval creatures,
eight metres round the girth. And look at that rockface, and the
stratigraphy of all the floods: a million years in a single metre. Look
at the ferns on the slope beneath. Look at the play of the light and
shadow. The first time I saw the Gorge I realised I was escaping into
a different domain, very close to us, and very alien.'

'When was that?'

'One Easter. It was hot, and it was raining. There were broken,
heavy cloud-fronts: it looked like today. I was a teenager, and I came
up with the Shell rep from Roma. There was nothing here, that far
back. No lodge, no ranger station. We walked in up the river from
our campsite. It took all day, and as we went through the Gorge
seemed to me like Camelot: all mist-shrouded hills and far-off thunder. It was the kind of weather when the Aborigines thought spirits
were walking, and the black trees came alive. And then I saw the
rock art: an old cattle duffer called Little Billy Dingo took me in the
first time, to see the stencils down near Moolayember Pass, and from
then on I realised I was going to give my life up to it.

'That stirred things up at home. My old man didn't like the
Gorge, or care much about the past. It was my mother who hypno-
tised me into archaeology. Knowledge was no burden to carry, she
used to say. And she thought you had to collect to understand. She
was happy when I began to bring back my own rock samples, and
to win prizes for them at the Roma show. And now, the longer I've

been living here in the shadow of the Gorge, the more I've found. The more I've seen, and the more I've needed to see: the engraving sites, the stencil hands, the galleries up beyond Cathedral Cave. Death was big business here, you know. It's alive with death – this whole landscape was a mortuary site for the Aborigines. For them, these ranges were all sources of energy. The rock was a living, powerful thing, created by the ancestor spirits. Every inch varies. Every inch has its secret. See the top of that cliff face over there, that looks so smooth and untouched by human hand? It's full of burials. They were all covered over by a rock-fall thirty years ago. And that little crack in the trees, over there? That turns into a false gorge that leads up to a cave burial of seven bodies. When you move through here, you're moving through a universe that's utterly dominant, and every part has got its story.'

'So how come you want to leave?'

Grahame turned and gazed at Cameron, who had asked him this question. His manner was by now altered: a weight and grandeur had possessed him.

'The Gorge is changing,' he said at last. 'You don't discover a place like this. It waits for you, and it discovers you. It points your way through life, and tells you when to move on. When I came here I could feel its strength pouring into me. But now – there's too many people coming and going, passing through, being here but not see-ing, and over time the effect's like discharging a battery, draining away all the energy the place used to have. It's becoming like any-where in the world, covered over with human meanings. That's what remains for us now, almost everywhere, and we're all feeding off that barren fruit. For me, what we're looking down on now is already like a memory. To come up here and have it in my eyes is physically painful.'

'And once you're gone, will you ever come back? Didn't you ever think you might want to be buried here yourself?'

'Think? Of course. I've already picked out the burial chamber. Over in the ranges, far away.'

He waved towards the banks of cloud, which were just beginning to block out the few remaining patches of pale-blue sky.

'High up the face of Mount Moffatt, in a cave that's aligned with the first rays of the sun at the winter solstice, just like the tomb-shafts at Abu Simbel. And I've designed the coffin, and had it made: it's polyhedral, stainless steel, with symbols on the faces representing the themes of my life.'

'And what are they?' I asked, sensing, by now, the flurry of disclosures that marked the climax of every conversation that I'd ever had with him.

'That would be telling,' he said. 'A man has to keep some secrets, Uncle: secrets are the motive force of life.'

'Why Mount Moffatt, then?'

'Do you need to ask? It has an energy you can feel from far away. It's lovely, and solitary, untouched and unravaged by the hand of man. When you get there, it's quiet and pure – it's a lonely, lonely place . . .'

'And you're a lonely, lonely man?'

'Absolutely: how did you know I was going to say that?'

'A wild stab in the dark of your imagination.'

'Well, you hit the jackpot.'

'But what if we don't altogether vanish, and there's an eternal cycle? What would you choose to come back as?'

He hesitated.

'I don't suppose I could be an initiated Aboriginal man, in the Kimberley, pre-contact – or maybe even Thomas Mitchell, coming through the Carnarvons for the first time?'

'No – it has to be the present day. And you have to be an animal. It's an identity game. President Mitterand used to play it with his ministers, during Cabinet meetings.'

'Honestly? Maybe I should pay more attention to politics. But if it's an animal, there's only one choice for me.'

He stared out, his profile sharp beside me in the moist blue light, and I followed his gaze, out over the gorge and the darkened valleys, over the ranges and the precipices.

'And what's that?'

'You can't guess?'

He looked at me with an air of surprise.

'I have no idea.'

'The whistling kite, of course – *Haliastur sphenurus*. Don't look so startled. They're the most amazing birds – the ultimate survivors. They just float, and soar, and every rubbish-dump and slaughter-house has got them. They exist on what everybody leaves. They never kill. They make the best of whatever's around them. They've got taste: they're an ugly, drab-looking bird that nests in the most spectacular of places. You might catch sight of one, and your eyes could just glide over it, but they're beautiful to me – and out of all the birds of prey, they have the most heart-rending call.'

As I listened to these words of his, which brought back to me my own experiences in Cape York, at the junction of the Lynd and the Mitchell, an idea I have never wholly broken free from came over me: suddenly, the Outback seemed a place of echoes and repetitions, where one lives over things experienced before; where, like lines of sand-dunes, they come to meet one; where time is not at all the smooth, unbroken, forward flow we sense around us, but something yawning, full of rifts and voids, amidst which we navigate, almost unknowing, so that our advance from second to second is little short of miraculous. These thoughts, and their implications, sank in on me as we stood together at that look-out. I fell silent, lost in them, for several minutes – and not until we were safely back at Takarakka, and Cameron had begun making discreet, urgent signs to me that we should leave, did I find myself once more conscious of the conversation.

'But wait,' I heard Grahame say, in tones of alarm, for he had intercepted some of these departure signals. 'You can't go yet. You haven't seen the surprise I promised you.'

He left us, only to reappear with a look of triumph on his face, brandishing a rusty, battered sabre.

'What's that?' said Cameron, in a nervous voice, and he darted an accusing look in my direction.

'A real piece of history. It's Leichhardt's lost sword! There's no doubt about it.'

Grahame held it up, then placed it delicately before us on a low coffee table.

I stared at this weapon sceptically, and ran my fingers down its pitted blade. It looked, on first glance, like the kind of thing one sees in theatrical supply shops.

'It was found in an Aboriginal burial, in the Valley of the Ruined Castles, close by Reedy Creek,' he went on, softly. 'An old stockman came upon it while out mustering. It was deep inside a cave, with skeletons. He took it back to the station and stuck it between the slabs in the wall of the old homestead. I saw it there, once, when I was visiting in 1977, then a couple of years later I was recording local histories in Cloncurry, and I ran into an old-timer who'd been out working on Reedy Creek, and he told me all about it.'

'And what makes you think it's genuine?'

I gazed at it even as I asked this question, and it began changing before my eyes into a lovely relic, wondrously preserved by fate.

'The whole look of it – its feel, its condition. It's obvious it's been carried by someone who didn't oil it, someone who had no idea how to use it. The blade's been bashed and slashed against the rocks, but for a long time now it's been out of the weather. Just what you'd expect if an Aboriginal warrior had taken it a century and a half ago, and kept it with him – in life, and then in death. It's true you find unusual things in burials round here. I've heard of an old fighting-knife, a notebook, a felt hat – but this sword is in a class of its own.'

'But there's nothing to connect it to Leichhardt.'

'What do you mean? I thought you knew all about him. He tells the story himself, in the record of his first expedition. He was passing through the Eastern Carnarvons and looking for rope to repair his harnesses. You don't remember? Here.'

He handed me a tattered, ill-bound copy of the *Journal*, open at an early page. I looked, and read out loud:

*'As I passed a native camp, which had only lately been vacated, I found, under a few sheets of bark, four fine kangaroo nets, made of the bark of Sterculia; also several bundles of sticks, which are used to stretch them. As I was in the greatest want of cordage, I took two of these nets; and left, in return, a fine brass-hilted sword, the hilt of which was well-polished, four fishing-hooks, and a silk handkerchief; with which, I felt convinced, they would be as well-pleased, as I was with the cordage of their nets.'*

'And what could be more reasonable?' I rounded off.

'I think he was romanticising about the brass hilt,' said Grahame. 'The hand-guard's just ordinary metal. But this is the kind of weapon he would have had with him, exactly: a nineteenth-century Prussian military sword. See? There's the blood-runner. He would have brought this with him when he sailed from Europe, late in 1841. It's a very distinctive style, meant to cut and slash. There's just not much in the way of German stuff from that period in Australia. And anyway, how would it have got into Robinson's Gorge? That's a really remote location – it's tiger country out there.'

'So how did you get it?' Cameron asked.

'It came up,' said Grahame, cryptically. 'And I wanted to have a piece of Leichhardt's past. It wasn't that I thought he was a particularly interesting guy. In fact, I think he was a bit of a nutcase, treating his men the way he did. He had no conception of how far he was pushing them. I've read that *Journal* through and through. It shows you very clearly what he was like – exceptionally weird – and it also shows him just tumbling from one disaster to another, and in Australia if you carry on like that you always come unstuck in the end. Just look at his diet. Steamed roo and flying fox. A shingle-backed lizard. Cockatoos. Greenhide. Tree-gum. Listen to this.'

He picked up the book, and flicked through: '"A crow was shot and roasted – and found to be exceptionally tender". Just imagine being with the bastard. The unions would have really reared up over the way this guy carried on! He was obviously an incredible bushman, and very lucky that he even got through, the first time, when he went up by the Gulf. All the explorers were mad, but some of them were more successfully mad than others.

'No. The reason I wanted the sword is because he was lost without trace, because he belongs to the kingdom of the unknown, the broken, the disappointed. He's out somewhere in the desert, with no one looking over him, his bones are scattered, all the creatures that he once ate have fed off his carcass, and he's passed onto another level. He's become a dream that's out there, haunting the interior, and haunting us as well. Here. You try it.'

He passed the sword to me. It was cold to the touch, and heavy.

'Isn't that a perfect balance? Real German workmanship! That's a tradition I admire. They turn up everywhere in the discovery of Australia.'

'They do?'

'Of course – there was Leichhardt, Strehlow and the missionaries, von Mueller. And in the Kimberley, above all. Every bastard that chased anything up there was either a lay preacher or a German: look at Ernest Worms, the Pallotine priest at Broome, who won an Iron Cross in the Great War and became a learned elder of the Kimberley tribes. He used to go on long journeys through the rock art valleys of the north, and strip off his clothing, and give it as payment to his Aboriginal guides. And there was the Frobenius Institute Expedition, under Petri, with Schultz, and Kleist, and Lommel . . .'

'I hadn't realised this was such an enthusiasm of yours. All that European gloom, and sadness, and complexity, reaching out this far into the bush – sinking into your heart?'

'But this place is sad, and complex,' said Grahame, an air of sudden, joyful animation possessing him. 'This is where the darkness is. These are our temples, and our medieval churches: our frescoes of the damned and the saved. Here, all around us in this tropical Inferno.'

'And it took Germany to show you that?'

'I was making it up myself, until I hit this vein. It just knocked me over – strong, commanding, full of poise and depth. I've soaked myself in the records of the Frobenius Expedition. I'm even republishing them in English.'

'You are?' By this stage I was sure he had toppled over into the realms of fantasy.

'Absolutely – I'll show you.' And off he darted into his study.

'Aren't you convinced yet?' said Cameron from the corner armchair, where he was trying out the Leichhardt sword. 'Your expert's completely off the planet.'

Even as he said this, Grahame rushed back in, clutching a large paperback which he thrust into my hands. In red letters on the cover, printed above a blurry photo of Aboriginal men holding warspears, were the words: *The Unambal*.

'That's the real thing, that book,' he said, his voice trembling. 'Full of heavy science: circumcisions and creation dances; magic chants, and songs, and painted Wandjinas.'

'I thought your bag was the Bradshaws,' said Cameron.

'My bag?'

'Your speciality.'

'They are. But the Wandjinas, they're out on the edge. The things you see, deep in the north Kimberley: they would blow your head apart.'

'What kind of things?'

'Stone arrangements. Great avenues and circles, as high as a human being. Hewn altars on the high plateaus. Crystal rocks. There's rain magic, devil myths. Serpent carvings, megafauna, sexual cults.'

'And are you going to write about them?'

'Maybe, towards the end, perhaps, after I've finished my autobiography.'

'And what's it going to be called?'

'*A Wasted Life*.'

'Well,' I said, 'at least you've got a publisher.'

And I glanced down at *The Unambal*, and flicked to its title page: 'Takarakka Nowan Kas Publications', the colophon declared, in bold letters, 'Carnarvon Gorge'. Just above those words was an emblematic figure, male, legs splayed, with hanging phallus, and plumed head-dress, clasping a maze-like set of circles in its outstretched hands.

'I like to keep control of that side of things myself,' said Grahame.

'So what do you do when you want to put a new book out? Just sell another samurai sword?'

'Something like that. You're not interested in the Leichhardt sabre, are you, by any chance? I could give you an explorer's discount.'

'That's very kind of you to offer, but I think it would be just a touch beyond our price range.'

'Truly?' He shook his head. 'Well, I'll give you this copy of *The Unambal* anyway, no charge.'

I leafed through the book. The story that emerged was one of great pathos. The author, Andreas Lommel, an orientalist, had, as Grahame told us, been a member of the Frobenius Institute mission to the Kimberley, which arrived in north-west Australia from Frankfurt a year before the outbreak of World War II, and began work copying engravings round Port Hedland, before its members were transported by mission lugger to Walcott Inlet.

Here, they found themselves deep in the territory of the Wandjina. These ghost-like, wide-eyed figures seemed to be everywhere in the caves and rock-shelters of that wild and precipice-filled region. The researchers made repeated visits to the painting-sites, guided by old men of the Unambal, often taking circuitous routes, obeying the rule that one must follow the exact path, including all the detours, taken by the ancestor-beings whose images are painted on the rocks.

While Helmut Petri made his famous overland trip from Sale River to Kalumburu, Lommel stayed behind at Mary's Spring homestead, and it was here that he was introduced to the poet Allan Balbunga, and to the secret Kurangara cult. In silence I read through the passage where he describes this friendship, together with the things he learned – and I have found myself drawn back to these few pages ever since:

> 'A poet is no ordinary person. He must be a medicine man. He
> must know how to send his soul in a dream over great distances
> into far-off lands, there to have strange and remarkable
> experiences. Above all he must have access to the underworld,
> the home of the dead.'

His art consists in giving shape to dream images – a task that often requires desperate work for days on end, and a literal recreation of his language as well.

> 'With grand sublimity, he does violence to this language as he sees
> fit. He tears the words apart, puts new vowels in them or he drops
> syllables and moulds the words until they seem to him to have the

*sound that they must necessarily have for the portrayal of his experiences.'*

Lommel goes on to describe the great corroboree he witnessed, a sad and serious ceremony, in which he saw a sign *'that this life of the Aborigines, so beautiful and so unique, will only last a short time longer, to then disappear forever and pass away.'*

Although he had been given such deep insights into the Unambal, Lommel was not able to publish his book in Germany for many years. As a result, his invocations of a dying world no longer have the warning force of prophecy, and the entire work is suffused by an air of dream-like retrospect.

In 1954, together with his wife, Katharina, an experienced rock art copyist, he at last returned to the Kimberley and visited important sites round Gibb River station. Here he worked intensively with local Aboriginal informants, recording their mythologies, spending lengthy periods in caves and rock shelters, beneath the gaze of the Wandjinas, most of which, as subsequent photos show, have undergone a dramatic decay, almost to invisibility, in recent years.

# III

Some months after this encounter, I woke one morning in my swag, well-rested, with the strong conviction that I had been back in my dreams to Carnarvon Gorge. For a few moments, I had no clear recollection of where I was. Without stirring, I looked round. Scrub, spinifex. Small, gnarled trees. A spent fire. A homestead with out-buildings close by, abandoned, its corrugated iron walls rusting and half torn away. Further off, a hill, or pile of monumental boulders, deep red, glowing in the light of dawn. After a minute's gazing out across the landscape, a slight movement caught my eye. Gradually, in the shadows alongside me, I made out a figure, bearded, clothed in khaki, perched in something very like a lotus position. Grahame Walsh? No – in fact, I realised as I swam up to full consciousness, it was his human opposite. I was in the Pilbara, on the most implausible of missions, together with the monarch of the rupestrian world, Robert Bednarik, convener of the International Federation of Rock Art Organisations, author of some four hundred scientific papers, a man who, contrary to life's usual pattern, became more, rather than less, a figure of the imagination, the longer one knew him. I stumbled out, and went across.

'Breakfast,' I asked, optimistically. 'Coffee, maybe?'

'I don't eat much in the bush,' said Bednarik, in his precise manner. 'I only seem to need about five hundred grams a day. I proved it to myself some years ago, on a walk across South America, when I ate very little and experienced hardly any weight loss.'

'Don't you even drink anything hot in the morning?'

'Very rarely. It's a waste of energy, keeping a fire going, and besides, I must have an unusual metabolism, I require very little liquid to survive.'

What about the rest of us, I almost said, and wandered off to collect some firewood. I made my way towards the homestead. It had the painful poetry of Outback ruins: strewn on the stone floor were discarded toys and keepsakes, a tennis racquet, a child's dress bleached by wind and rain, still on its hanger, a wooden hairbrush with long blonde hairs tangled in it, an iron bedstead, an inlaid rosewood box, the lid missing.

I looked back to the campsite, and wondered if I should call Bednarik over, and if such things would speak to him at all. I could still picture my first meeting with him some years before, when, on a rain-soaked day, I had gone, at George Chaloupka's suggestion, to see him at his office in Caulfield.

'You might find him a rather driven kind of individual,' George had warned me, sighing, as if the very thought of Bednarik was enough to fill him with weariness.

'Driven – but I thought he was Czech?'

'The name may be Bohemian, but the man is Austrian. Surely you can tell from his accent? I'm sure Bednarik regards attributes like national identity as irrational and meaningless. But every time I see him I can't stop myself from thinking of an Austrian ski-instructor or mountain-guide, giving orders as if the whole world depended on him.'

Made more curious by the whiff of cultural antagonism lurking in George's words, I pressed on into deepest south-east Melbourne.

The International Federation's rather busy letterhead gave a list of more than twenty member organisations, among which my favourite was the *Association pour le Rayonnement de l'Art Pariètal Européen*, although the number of affiliated bodies keeps expanding, so that one day soon, perhaps, there will be no room for any correspondence, and Bednarik's stationery will serve purely as an index of the constant spread of rock art studies, to ever newer and more appealing frontiers of enlightenment: Macedonia, Uruguay, the Canaries, the Ariège.

From this imposing note-paper, I had been expecting some large, glass-fronted headquarters, full of secretaries and conference rooms. But at the street address I found instead a little terrace house, at the door of which Bednarik greeted me with great formality, before ushering me down a darkened corridor to a cramped study. I sat on a flimsy wooden chair, almost without speaking, all day long, while he unfolded, in rigorously sequential fashion, his evolutionary arguments, his contrarian theories, the blueprints of his scientific world-view: the spread of early man across the globe; the cognitive capacities of *Homo erectus*; the origins of art and body decoration; the importance of drilled and perforated ostrich eggs.

From time to time, as the hours passed, I would find my attention wandering. There was a large, peculiar plaster-cast on one wall: maroon in colour, with scored, ungainly lines across its surface. They depicted, in schematic manner, a pair of animals joined by their tails. I could not keep myself, at one of the rare pauses in Bednarik's exposition, from breaking in, and asking what this object was.

'My Tasmanian tigers,' he answered, with a dreamy sigh. 'It is a petroglyph, from the Pilbara. I discovered it in 1966. Don't you see the stripes on their bodies? At the time when I found them, it was the only such depiction known on the entire Australian mainland.'

'The Pilbara,' I echoed, somewhat hazily, for at that stage far north-west Australia was as remote as the moon to me.

'Yes. I started out on my Australian journey there. I worked as an electrical engineer for several years. Undoubtedly it is one of the world's greatest rock art provinces.'

'And an impressive landscape, apparently.'

'A landscape that poses many questions.' And he gave a little laugh, the first I had heard him give, a sign perhaps of the sense of humour I would later come upon, well-buried in the convoluted paragraphs of his research papers, or even in their titles. How charming they came to seem to me: 'Palaeolithic Love Goddesses of Feminism', 'Mariners of the Pleistocene', or my favourite of recent years, 'To be or not to be Palaeolithic'.

'Many questions,' Bednarik repeated. 'It is almost a conceptual echo-chamber.'

'That sounds wild.'

'Wild?'

'Maybe one day we'll be up there together, and you can show me what you mean.'

'Maybe,' replied Bednarik, with a sceptical expression.

And here we were. I reminded him of the conversation in his study.

'But it's true,' he said. 'An echo chamber – exactly. Can you imagine the impact of this landscape on a twenty-two-year-old immigrant, coming to the Pilbara for the first time? It exploded on me. Geology rules here. It makes the statement. I had never seen anything like this. I had never even seen the sea before I came to Australia. I had never seen mountains like this – these eroding boulders, these ancient basalt ridges. I had only been a rock-climber in Austria and north Italy. All I knew was picture postcard limestone peaks. So when I got here it took me a long while to feel at ease with this topography. Then, one New Year's Day, when I was working at Tom Price, I climbed Mount Nameless, alone, up the hard side, the steep side, without rope.'

'And you felt at home when you got to the top?'

'That would have been very sentimental,' Bednarik said, in his sternest fashion. 'No. I simply felt my understanding grow. You see, I had already been to Port Hedland, and then I worked on the Burrup Peninsula, and found the rock art there. And I realised then that my dream – the dream that made me leave the country of my birth, and brought me as far away as Australia – the dream of making valuable discoveries, would be fulfilled, so the Pilbara became my new territory. You see, when I was a teenager, growing up in Europe, in those difficult years, it was the great French archaeologists who were my gods. I used to read them all the time, and copy out their drawings, and imagine myself in their footsteps, but I never thought I would be able to contribute to their field.'

He shook his head, as if he had just made some extraordinary confession, and this was in fact by far the most detailed account I had heard Bednarik give of his world, and origins – origins I was suddenly intrigued by, and eager to discuss, a story we had never touched on, though I had spoken to Bednarik so regularly by telephone in the months preceding our foray that I was immersed in his ideas. What was he, I wondered; from what point on the blurred palette of Central Europe?

But at that moment, just as I felt myself about to make inroads into this mystery, there was a shifting and a stirring from the swag stretched out on the far side of the Landcruiser, and Megan, the photographer deputed to record Bednarik's great discovery, emerged, rubbing her eyes.

'Any breakfast?'

'Robert doesn't believe in breakfast.'

'Oh – right. So: what do you think, now you can see it in daylight?'

And she pointed to her swag, for swag design had been the subject of deep controversy between us the previous evening, though Bednarik, who slept on a tiny square of thin foam-rubber, played no part in this exchange. I had to admit, as I surveyed the symmetrical trapezoid in which she had been cocooned, that it was a thing of simplicity and beauty, far more suited to the Pilbara than the elaborate device I had struggled with throughout my trips in the interior, a swag that felt it was a tent, that hung from hooks and poles and guy-ropes, that leaked, and seemed designed for the efficient transfer of sand from the environment into the folds and stitching of its mattress – so much so that I had often worried, if I were to go with it into the Simpson, that whole dune-fields would vanish and I might face prosecution under various clauses of the national parks act.

Preferring to steer clear of the swag comparison, I asked 'Aren't you at all curious about why we're here? Don't you want to know? After all, today's the day.'

'It's your secret,' she said, with overwhelming indifference. 'I figured you'd get around to telling me in your own time.'

'Well,' I began, 'we have a splendid story. Robert's made a find that changes the whole picture of Australia's European settlement.'

'That's not strictly true,' interrupted Bednarik.

'Isn't it?' – and I had an unpleasant vision of our journey, speeded up, planes flying, hotel doors swirling open, the

Landcruiser lurching through creeks and washaways, all this super-imposed on piles of fifty-dollar notes blowing in the wind.

'No: it's a detail of history, maybe. Scientifically, of course, it's quite irrelevant. What's really important in my present work is the replicative archaeology. The sea journeys I've been making in rafts built to prehistoric design from Timor to the north Australian coast.'

'But perhaps,' I said, 'just for a moment, we could keep to the detail of history, folkloric and trite and journalistic though it may be. Robert' – I turned again to Megan – 'was up here, in July . . .'

'Just after the Alice Springs rock art congress,' he interrupted.

'. . . Yes, with a group of experts and enthusiasts, looking at sites all through the Pilbara – and, close to here, he came upon a stone platform, with western signs carved on it, and a date.' I paused, for drama. '1771.'

Megan said nothing.

'It turns upside down all the standard assumptions about European penetration of the inland!'

'I guessed it must be something like that,' she said, still with dev-astating calmness.

'But that's not exactly right, either,' said Bednarik.

'Perhaps, then, you should tell her. I'll drive, and you can give us a precise, objective account – to the extent, of course, that objectivity is ever possible, given our dependence on the information we receive through our senses, and on our conceptual frame.'

'I'm glad you made that qualification,' said Bednarik, with the air of a sceptic whose immediate worries at least have been allayed.

We packed up and drove on through the Pilbara landscape, that so resembles false-colour film, with its purple rock-platforms pro-truding from the spinifex, and ranges on the horizon dancing red and mauve inside the heat-haze. We passed by Hillside Station, and by Woodstock; we drove through Bonney Downs junction, and the crossing of the Shaw River, as Bednarik told his story: how, on a low ridge of broken, weathered stones, close by a well-known Aboriginal engraving site, he had stumbled on a rose-coloured panel facing upwards to the sky. On it were four faint, weathered emblems, aligned with each other, that immediately caught his eye. Their edges were sharp. They had the look of marks made not by pounding-stone but metal, by a knife-edged blade. There was a familiar Aboriginal anthropomorph, with hanging phallus – but the rest were something else. One was a spoked wheel, polygonal, with a pair of hands clutching it. Alongside was the puzzling date, a year long before the colonisation of the north-west coast, and a neat capital 'H'.

'H for help,' put in Megan.

'H for Holland – H for Hans,' retorted Bednarik. 'Why speculate? Who can tell?'

And on he swept: the physics of dust accretion and rock erosion; the eighteenth-century marine exploration record; the remarkable formula he had discovered some years ago that allowed him to estimate the ages of rock carvings viewed through a microscope.

'But how do you get the carvings to the microscope?'

'I take the microscope to them, of course. I have my field instrument. Didn't you notice the silver case I have with me? In fact, I am the only rock art researcher who regularly carries a microscope to sites.'

'Aren't they rather bulky things to be scrambling about with, up rockfaces and mountainsides?'

'Not at all. Mine only weighs eight kilos. There are times when I carry it with me all through the day. I built it for lightness.'

'You built it yourself?'

'Naturally. From Russian, Chinese, German and Japanese parts. And I have a pocket microscope as well. See?' He produced a delicate, flute-like object, black, with chrome wheels and levers, which he held out between my eyes and the windscreen.

'You have to turn here.'

'But this is the Mount Newman railway line,' I protested – and indeed we were about to cross the embankment.

In front of us, one of the stately, blue-liveried locomotive-teams was just then coming into view, the train of ore-cars behind them screeching as they negotiated a bend in the line. We watched them flick slowly, grandly by.

'That's right – you take the Newman access track. The carvings are almost directly on it.'

'How handy.'

'Handy?'

'For tourism.'

'I hope there won't be anything like that!' said Bednarik fervently.

He lapsed for several minutes into an injured silence at the thought of strangers traipsing across his beloved Pilbara rock-piles, until at last, just as we were passing a scatter of low hills, he raised his right hand in the most imperious style.

'We have arrived,' he said in a low voice, as though there was a danger he might be overheard.

From the back of the Landcruiser he fished out a small silver briefcase, and a purple sunhat with the words 'Australian Rock Art Association' emblazoned in gold letters on its brim. Solemnly he put it on, checked his reflection in the window, straightened it, and headed off at a brisk pace, across the railway, through the mulga and the spinifex, then climbed, in big strides, up a steep pile of shattered tawny rocks.

We both gave pursuit, but by the time we reached him he was standing, one foot resting proprietorially upon the summit, gazing out, his jaw clenched tight, rather in the pose of Sir Edmund Hillary on top of Everest, although the view was hardly Himalayan: dry grass; dry riverbeds; twisted gum-trees; low ranges smudged along the horizon's line.

'One should always keep one's imagination in check, on first coming to a site like this,' he said. 'When you first see rock art it looks so confusing, and you wonder: how ever am I going to fit all this into my scientific picture? At some places I have spent a whole day just sitting still, in silence, trying to make sense of everything. It is almost like a form of meditation.'

'Yes, but where are they: the carvings?'

'You're standing on them.'

I looked down at the rock-slab beneath my feet. I moved to one side.

'Where?'

Bednarik leaned down, and pointed. At last I began to make out a faint set of marks, much smaller in size than I had expected them to be, and more discreet, and private – almost hidden by the angle of the sunshine on the rock. They were as he had described them: four signs, a paler shade of rust, as if stamped into the texture of the stone. I gazed down, wondering if I could sense the presence of the man who had been there so long before us, commanding myself to feel exalted, touched by history.

'Well, what is your reaction?' asked Bednarik, almost shyly. 'I must tell you, even for me, now I am here again, out in the field, this is an event, to find something so unexpected – no matter that it is from a chronologically recent period.'

He bent above the carvings, stroked them, blew upon the surface of the rock, peering at it from one side, then another, giving a running commentary all the while on what he saw, becoming more enthused and animated with each inspection.

'Of course,' he said, 'it's quite a fantasy – but one can invent a story of how these carvings came about. It seems to me the most probable theory is this: that we are looking at the emblem of an isolated man, that a shipwrecked sailor, a European, cast away, or marooned, on the Indian Ocean coastline was somehow able to survive, and he fell in with an Aboriginal group.

'Together with them, he would have travelled along the river-course, deep inland, perhaps over several years, to where we are standing now, two hundred kilometres from the sea – and then, close by one of the ceremonial centres of his adopted tribe, he carved his own message into the rock, never expecting it would be seen by men or women of his own civilisation. He was naming himself, recording himself. It is an act of preservation; adaptation; survival. Psychologically, I can't help feeling there is a statement here before us: with the ship's wheel, and its spokes, carved so carefully, and the hands on it, and there – do you see? – the masts and the rigging above? To me it says, as if in words: I am a sailor, from far away.'

'That's a very intuitive, non-rational thing for you to come up with!'

'Maybe it is,' he shrugged. 'But we are in the middle of the Pilbara – there's no one to hear us.'

He reached over, and flicked open his silver case.

Slowly, both hands outstretched, balancing, almost slipping once or twice on loose boulders, I edged my way along the jagged sum-mit-line to the end of the ridge. I looked back to where Bednarik was kneeling, poised above his microscope, with the bare plains behind him stretching away – and, for a secret instant, I saw there, gazing down at that stone memorial, not the president of the International Federation of Rock Art Organisations, not the scholar, not the scientist, but a lone explorer, reaching his hands down into time's boundless murk.

It was late that afternoon, close to the edge of nightfall, after a hot day of inspecting bare red rock-piles, each one of which seemed to me indistinguishable from the other though Bednarik treated them all like long-lost friends. We drove at last out of the back country, down the Roy Hill road towards Munjina. We were within a few kilometres of the highway, the lights of the roadhouse just becoming visible, tucked into the folds of the Hamersleys, when a procession of vehicles, bunched tight together, approached, and began to pass us: bush trucks, a group of three of them, their windscreens missing, their bumpers trailing in the dirt, then came battered traybacks, and ancient Commodores and Kingswoods, with rusted panels, or great dents and gouges in their bodies, and these vehicles, hardly any of them roadworthy, were interspersed with brand-new Toyotas and Patrols. All of them were heavily laden with Aboriginal passengers. All of them were moving very slowly, without lights. We waved as we passed each one, but no one gave us any sign of recognition, and, like some heraldic hunting-party, they swept by and dwindled in the rear-view mirror, their dust-trails dissipating, stained pale pink by the last rays of the sun.

Shaken by this encounter, as if we had passed a train of ghosts on their way to some supernatural ceremony, I pulled up some minutes later by the diesel pump, jumped out, and went with Megan and Bednarik to collect our room keys.

'If you're looking for the funeral, you've missed them,' called out the manager as I slid the glass door open. 'Love, turn the television down. The reception!' He shrugged apologetically. 'It's awful at the moment – we seem to do best this time of day with Channel Seven.'

'A funeral – at a roadhouse?'

'Big Aboriginal funeral down at Woodstock. They were here all day, the place was that full you couldn't move. They've only been gone a few minutes, down that back road to Marble Bar. You're not with them – or the drillers, or the road repair crews?'

'I can't say we are.'

'So what are you blokes doing out there?' He inclined his head towards the window, and the darkness beyond the road-trains, and the illuminated signs, as if towards a storm-tossed ocean.

'Just discovering a historic site.'

'True? One that's going to rewrite the books about north-west Australia?'

'Very likely.'

'So you'll be wanting a feed, then?'

I glanced around: plastic chairs and tables; the smell of fried food from the kitchen; display shelves full of motor parts and fan-belts; cakes, and camping gear, and long-life milk. Could it be, I wondered, that I had actually come, through long habituation, to be fond of roadhouses, their staleness and their anonymity, the air they always have of onwardness and transience and lukewarm excitement? I was still turning this idea over some while later when our meals, vast piles of gravied meat and boiled potatoes, appeared.

Bednarik and I were talking through his current fraught relations with the rock art establishment when the manager came over to us.

'The newspaper,' he said in joyful tones. 'I knew I'd seen you before. You work for that newspaper, don't you?'

'From time to time,' I answered, unheroically.

He sat down with us.

'And you too?'

'Robert is the country's most famous independent rock art researcher.'

'Oh, well, we won't hold that against him. Listen.' He turned to me with an air of great candour. 'That investment section you put out the other month – I really rated that!'

'I didn't know you were a regular reader.'

'No, of course not – we only got it by accident. A truckie brought it in from Hedland. He had a governor wrapped up in it.'

'A governor?'

'From an engine – and a fuel filter as well. So: when's the next one coming out?'

'The next what?'

'Investment special, of course.'

'I'd have to check into that, and let you know.'

'That's the shot. You've got to look after the pennies up here, with all the floods, and all the bushfires in the park. And what about the girl with you? She's not eating anything?'

'She's a vegetarian.'

'Is that right?' He burst out laughing. 'She won't get far up this way, then, will she?'

He retreated to the service counter, and the evening went on, the food congealing on the table, the television newsreader's voice just audible, and the conversations of the truck-drivers and the Telstra technicians drifting round us, until hours had passed, and Bednarik and I had made our way along an imaginary rock-art trail, across the Pilbara, and the desert, to the coastal dunes at Sandfire, to the Kimberley, to the Bradshaw regions, and to their connoisseur, Grahame Walsh.

'Have you ever by any chance been to Takarakka?' Bednarik asked me, pronouncing the name in a tone of voice one might reserve for some feature of the underworld.

'Yes – just the other day, in fact.'

Bednarik digested this information.

'And was there' – he hesitated – 'a dog there?'

'Max, you mean: the Doberman. Sure.'

'I went on a visit once to Takarakka. There was a group of us, rock art scholars, and my wife came as well. She had her knee in a cast just then. We all went off, as you would expect, to see the art sites in the caves and amphitheatres up the gorge. Obviously she had to stay behind' – he leaned towards me – 'and that dog attacked her. She was stuck for hours up a steel ladder on the side of Grahame Walsh's water-tank, with the Doberman barking and growling below.'

'Well,' I said, rather wishing there was a photographic record of this scene, 'I don't think there'll be any recurrence of that problem. Grahame just shot the dog in the back leg by accident, and maimed it. Anyhow, he's sold the property. He's moving to Brisbane – and then perhaps on to the Kimberley.'

'I had no idea.'

'Yes, it's all change – but then it always is with him. There's a new woman in the picture.'

'Really?' Bednarik was blushing. 'I'm quite shocked.'

'It's a dark world he lives in: sex, and guns, and gloom, and drugs.'

'Drugs,' echoed Bednarik, now sounding appalled.

'Yes – generally pharmaceutical ones, I think. I suppose you never take any?'

'Only for professional purposes.'

'And what might they be?'

'When I was walking across South America, for example, and I was in the upper reaches of the Amazon, I had a theory that the harmalines in the potions mixed by the local Indian tribes generate visions of jewelled, dragon-like creatures in everyone who ingests the drink – so I was careful to try some.'

'You surely don't mean ayahuasca – the drug of telepathy?'

'Yes, exactly. It was the polite thing to do – and it was an ideal opportunity.'

'And what happened?'

'I felt nothing.'

'Nothing – from the strongest hallucinogen known to man? No jewelled dragons?' I said, quite loudly. The road-train drivers at the next table looked at us with some surprise.

'Nothing, no.'

'Maybe,' I said, 'it's a question of temperament.'

'Of expectation, I would think,' responded Bednarik, with the utmost seriousness. 'And also of cultural formation.'

'Cultural formation?'

'Yes,' he said, with a trace of embarrassment, as though touching on something he had long forbidden himself. 'Europe – Vienna – the Austrian world. You know, that kind of thing.'

Only some time later, during the last day Bednarik spent with us on that Pilbara journey, did the subject come up again. We had been scrambling our way up the ravines and creek-beds of the Hamersley escarpment all morning, in a vain rock art quest.

After several hours we gave up, and drove in to Wittenoom, an asbestos-mining town, long since abandoned, and largely dismantled in recent years. Little remains of it today beyond a grid of streets, and sign-posts, and telephone poles, all covered over by a screen of scrub and spinifex, through which, occasionally, the eye is drawn by the outline of some caravan or ramshackle dwelling. We skirted the town-site, and took the winding road that leads up Wittenoom Gorge, past Cathedral Pool, the mine, the black tailings, and Lang Hancock's fast-decaying camp, until we reached the end of the line: a creek crossing where the road comes to an abrupt stop above a broken causeway. For some time we sat in silence there, beneath the paperbarks, listening to the running water and the bird calls and the faint noise of impact the sun seems to make in summer as it irradiates that landscape.

At last to my surprise Bednarik, who had said nothing all day, turned to me.

'It truly is untameable,' he said.

Since I had never heard him begin a conversation about a topic other than rock art, it took me a few moments to catch on.

'What is?'

'The mountains, I mean.'

He waved a hand up to the ramparts, which at that point in the canyon formed a near-complete circle high above us.

'These great mountains make a statement, it seems to me. They say: here I am, what are you going to do about it? This combination of grey-green leaves, and yellow spinifex, and deep-red ironstone – this is what makes the Pilbara for me. I see it all the time. It's the same everywhere across this region.'

'You see it in your mind?'

'Whenever I close my eyes I can see it,' replied Bednarik, as if this was the most natural state of affairs in the world. 'Do you know, I lived at Wittenoom, once, long ago, when I first came to Australia. It was a large, built-up place then, with hotels, and shops, and houses everywhere, and look at it now! I even remember buying a book by Sir Mortimer Wheeler in the bookshop: an introduction to archaeology, which I still have today. Wittenoom had something alpine about it, as a place, I always felt.'

'Alpine?'

'You look up, and you seem to lose balance, and this feeling of vertigo is somehow expressed in that view. This slope, up there before us, it invites me to scramble up and look at those rock shelters: I imagine it murmuring to me – "Robert, Robert, come." But of course, if I had to scramble up in this heat I would be half-dead by the time I got there.'

'It speaks to you?'

'It tells me the values that are dominant elsewhere really don't apply here. This is a very different kind of place. For me, coming here wasn't a culture shock alone, it was an environmental shock. I looked up, and I saw. Each mountain you come upon seems perfect, as if they had been designed by an architect. Most of them look like castles, like German or Spanish or Indian fortifications: don't you see?'

He gestured high above us, and for a moment I could almost see the flags and crenellations, and tiny silhouettes of guards and sentries standing their watch against the bleached-out sky.

'Ah yes,' breathed Bednarik. 'I was fascinated when I saw them.

How much solidity there was in these structures. This landscape can never be domesticated. You could never turn the Pilbara into some kind of theme park. No – they are the very reverse of the beautiful limestone mountains I knew in the northern Alps.'

And on he swept, carried beyond geology into murkier reminiscence, his eyes wide, his hands beginning to make soft, nostalgic, rather Central European motions as he spoke.

'You know the biggest climb I ever did, the last climb I made in Europe, was fifteen hundred metres vertical: a classical climb among alpinists. It was the Hochtor, on the Ems River, and when I went up it, the icicles on the overhangs were two metres long. How far away it is, and yet, walking along that ridge of the Hamersleys today, with the rocks above me and the plain below, I was feeling the most wonderful sensation, just walking, almost as if I was back on the Dachstein or the Hochtor.'

'You're returning to your past,' I said.

'Of course not. But I do find myself thinking more and more about aspects of human development, it's true: about the way children grow into their grandparents, or the way familial traits emerge and assert themselves in time.'

'You're thinking of your own family?'

'My grandfather was a keen palaeontologist. On one of his explorations, in a high mountain cave, he discovered the skeleton of a cave-bear, and he assembled the bones into the correct skeletal order. Eventually he had it displayed in an alpine hut in Upper Austria. Much later, when I was about forty or so, I began asking my mother in Austria about all this, and tracing the parallels, and becoming intrigued by them.'

'So the love for rock art is hereditary!'

'Oh, I would still be sceptical. Maybe there is some predisposition to think about the past, to go out into nature analytically, to seek to understand it.'

'And were you very close to your grandfather,' I asked, 'when you were growing up, and going on all those walks, and climbs?'

Bednarik's eyes remained fixed on the red peaks high above.

'Both my grandparents were killed by a Russian soldier in the occupation army, who wanted to take my grandfather's bicycle. My grandfather protested, and was shot. His wife cried out, and she was shot too. The soldier got three months in jail. My grandfather – irony of ironies – had welcomed the downfall of the regime and the arrival of the allied soldiers, even the Russians, for he had been, at great personal risk all through the war, a strong anti-Nazi.

'During my life in this country, I have thought about him, and his example, often – as you can imagine. On a visit to Austria, which I have returned to only very rarely, in 1981 I think it was, I went by myself – you could almost say it was a pilgrimage – to see the original cave where he had found the bear's skeleton so long ago.'

For several minutes I said nothing. The sadness of his answer swept through me and it filled my mind with memories.

Abruptly Bednarik turned to look straight into my eyes.

'I wonder about the first travellers to pass this way. The first explorers. What was their reaction, when they saw this landscape, so strong, so unfamiliar? I wonder if they were as overcome as I was, when I came here as a young man and found a new world. Were they fearful, awestruck, excited? It would be interesting to me to know how they described their experiences.'

And on this point at least I was able to enlighten him, for I had read the journals of the first European to chart those ranges, the sublimely literal-minded Augustus Gregory, who passed through the valley of the Fortescue, the iron gorges of the Hamersleys, and the foothills and fringing deserts, without betraying in his daily record even the faintest flicker of interest or enthusiasm.

More than a decade passed before the poet of the Outback, Ernest Giles, approached the massif of the Pilbara in 1876, on the return leg of his final expedition; but Giles was a man of the desert, and the mountains were veiled from him, literally, by the onslaught of the ophthalmia he endured all through that stage of his journey. It was left to his companions to guide their leader through country wilder and more implacable than any he would ever see. It was they who told him of the vistas stretching out before them, the colours and the outline of the far-off peaks, two of which he christened: the Governor, and Mount Robinson. Both have kept their names to our day, and guard the road that goes winding from Mount Newman to Munjina and Karajini, between the vast iron-ore mines of the Ophthalmia Range.

Though deprived of sight, Giles caught somehow the pitiless and pulverising tone of this country. His narrative of inland travel, *Australia Twice Traversed*, is often thought of as a love song to the landscape, but in the pages he devoted to the Pilbara fear and horror steal into his words. He describes not just his surrounds, but their bleakness. He sees a field of battle, claimed by decay and vengeful death: death advancing, reduplicated, a death that mirrors the dimming and the failing of his own imagination:

*'The flies kept eating into our eyes, which were already bad enough. This seemed to be the only object for which these wretches were invented and lived, and they also seemed to be quite ready and willing to die, rather than desist a moment from their occupation. Every little sore or wound on the hands or face was covered by them in swarms; they scorned to use their wings, they preferred walking to flying; we might kill them in millions, yet other, and hungrier millions would still come on, rejoicing in the death of their predecessors – as they now had not only men's eyes and wounds to eat, but could batten upon the bodies of their slaughtered friends.'*

## IV

A year went by. The rock art trail went cold. Then, one morning, very early, a call came in. There was a bleak, half-familiar voice on the line.

'You're there!' it said, sounding disappointed.

'Is that Grahame Walsh?'

'I just rang to invite you to my party, in the new house, in Brisbane – the Eccentrics' Party.'

'Why, that's very kind of you, Grahame.'

'Yes, I've been trying to get through to you for ages. It was last month, in fact. You've missed it.'

'Oh – that's a shame.'

Silence.

'And how did it go?'

'Not too badly, I guess: no fatalities. Everyone who came had to dress up as an eccentric of some kind. You wouldn't have had any trouble. We even had the pool thematically decorated.'

'As in swimming pool?'

'That's right: you could have gone for a dip. There was a boat moored in the middle, with an articulated Indian skeleton on board, shrouded in nuns' black broadcloth, and holding up a Coca-Cola tin.'

'Heavy symbolism.'

'You're not wrong, Uncle. And there was a heap of little mines in the water, all around, made out of Japanese fishing floats, with upside down golf-tees stuck on top of them, very lifelike.'

'And that was Charon's ferry on the River Styx?'

'Yes – the dark, fatal river that waits for us all.'

'So the mines were a bit superfluous, really?'

'You can never be too careful.'

'And what were you wearing?'

'Well, I came in a bloody Samurai robe with a dragon on it that I got in Japan, and I had a Samurai sword in my belt at the start of the evening, but pretty early in the proceedings I thought I better hide it, in case I dropped someone. The guests all had their own approaches. Pauline, my publisher, came as me, in desert boots and long socks. There were absent-minded professors, and real professors who didn't need fancy-dress. George Chaloupka turned up, and he was in a pith helmet and safari jacket, looking just like Gunga Din. By the way, I've just been on a quick trip to Kununurra: we drove back through Darwin. I saw George there. He's pretty sick again. In fact, I don't think he's got too much further to run.'

'Really?' I said, horrified. 'Are you sure? I spoke to him just the other week. He said he was doing fine.'

'No,' came back the voice, with grim precision. 'Death's wings are close above him. I could tell, without him saying. If you want to see him again, you'd better fly up now.'

A few days later, in sad and solemn frame of mind, I got off a plane at Darwin airport. There, waiting for me in the arrivals hall, beaming, was George, with Pina close beside him. He stood straight, his eyes were clear, his face was tanned a walnut-brown.

'You look magnificent,' I said, a touch surprised, and it was true. He seemed to my eyes then like some luxuriant native plant, putting forth rich new wet-season shoots. We went outside. All round the terminal the air was thick with smoke. Kites wheeled over the runway. On the horizon, across the harbour, one could see a ribbon-line of bushfire flames, advancing, dissolving, spreading through the sky.

The Chaloupkas, as they told me, had just moved back into their large house near Fannie Bay. Their various rock art projects, catalogues and monographs were all in train, but Grahame Walsh was not entirely wrong: death had drawn close to them once more. Mick Alderson, the last of George's old Aboriginal friends from

Kakadu, had recently passed away. His daughter, whom I knew from previous visits, was staying in the Chaloupkas' cabin, and could be seen flitting through the garden from time to time.

I spent some days in Darwin, talking to George and Pina, and making brief journeys into the surrounding country, or going through my half-finished projects and piles of notes. One evening, when we were sitting side by side on the upstairs verandah, George began to tell me about his most recent journey back to the Czech Republic and the impressions he had been left with.

'Although I never really believed this would be possible,' he said, 'there is only a very slight part of me that still belongs there now. I shall keep making visits there, of course, but in the way one some-times walks down a street where a young girl one knew, long years ago, once lived. I went back, this time, as before, to Týniště, and to Brno. I visited old friends, and graves, but it's all different now. The airport at Ruzyně is completely changed – shops everywhere. And even though the tourist industry in Prague is busy exploiting Kafka to the hilt, I don't think Kafka himself would have been able to stand it for a second.

'One particular morning, I was reading the newspapers in a little coffee-house in the back streets between Hradčany and Strahov. I sat there alone, looking over the heads of all the tourists as they went hurrying by, and I thought of how it used to be: shadows, and silence, all that haunting, life-giving sense of melancholy. I felt then much as I suspect the Aboriginal people across Australia must often feel, as though everything that had been mine, and mine alone, was being eroded away by time, and by the presence of strangers – and all the sights and sounds and tastes of childhood that I can still remember were doomed to van-ish. I had the idea that I should make a driving trip through the towns of Moravia, of the kind you once described to me: I was even planning to visit the bishop's palace at Kroměříž, but the

Titian was away on loan somewhere, as it always is, it seems, these days.

'Once, you know, I even dreamed that I might buy a little apartment in Prague, in the Mala Strana perhaps, and I would go back every summer and spend time there, but now!' – he shook his head – 'When we were in Kakadu the other day I looked out across the grass plains, those wide plains, burned, or dry and yellowing, the way they are all round old Mudginberri station: dusty grass, smoky grass. You can see such colours nowhere else. And I realised that in my mind now I have come to find European forests dark, and monotonous, and threatening. Here you can lie safely under the casuarina trees, you can walk through the stringybark forests and find them filled with sunshine.'

He paused. I looked across at him, for I had been struck by something he had said. How clear it was! When I first met him, I used to think he was the image of some prophet from the Old Testament, frescoed on a high cathedral vault. But now, as he himself perhaps imagined that evening, he had come to resemble the sad-eyed, white-bearded elders one sees in records of the Centre from a hundred years ago: old men, full of ritual knowledge, of kindness, of understanding that was not passed down. One stares into those faces, caught in the grain of photographic prints, and feels half-sick with sorrow. They kneel there calmly, their hands clasped, but the wisdom in their eyes is long since gone; the landscape has gathered all their words.

Next morning, just before the dawn, George and I set off for a brisk walk along the beach at Fannie Bay. For a long while, our silence was broken only by his breezy greetings to the various strollers, joggers and dog-walkers we passed.

'Good morning,' he would cry out in his distinctive accent

through the murk, and, with differing degrees of embarrassment or reluctance, these kings and queens of Darwin's social set would grunt some response as they drifted by.

Only when we had reached the halfway mark of our journey, and were retracing our steps home, did we begin talking, and George quickly raised the subject that was uppermost in his mind.

'I feel, I must say, quite worried just now, about my own state,' he said.

'Your health, you mean?' I asked quickly.

'No – but I find I have such a weight of sadness pressing down upon me. I don't know any more, in truth, if I'm depressed or not, or if I have been all my life. I was always quite emotional, but now I find myself constantly being moved almost to tears. I have to keep away from emotional scenes on the television – and as for the real world, and all the dreadful things in it . . .'

It was daybreak. The first rays of sunlight were flooding through the sky and onto his face, where I could now read a look of the deepest anguish.

'But is that such an awful failing?' I said. 'To be consumed by sorrow, when one of your oldest, dearest friends has passed away, when that death resonates so strongly with those of your companions in Kakadu, all those years ago? When everything seems to be vanishing and dying, and magic Prague is slipping through your hands, and all the dreams of Central Europe that sustained you through your life have come true, and died, also, in their own way? I don't know I'd call that excess of sadness: if you didn't feel sad, I'd think you had a heart of stone.'

He nodded, and stroked his beard. We walked on.

'No, I don't have a heart like that. But I am too susceptible. That is my failing. That is the imprint I have absorbed from life. I find now there are days when I can barely concentrate, and still I have my swan-song to write.'

'What's that?'

'My book on the Dynamic Figures of Kakadu and Arnhem Land. It is the task I have been preparing for all my life: childhood in Bohemia; years of trudging through the art sites, learning them, and taking all their grace and beauty into my eyes. And now everything weighs down on me. I feel as if I have not one more word to say, and all that has gone before seems meaningless. But look at us!' He laughed. 'Look at where we are!'

He turned to me. I stared back in some puzzlement, for the darkness of his words had plunged me into a melancholia of my own. I turned away, and took the measure of myself, as though in secret: I had reached one of those still points in life when our dreams and illusions break, and we watch them go, and lament the moment of their passing, even though its glamour lifts us up.

'And where are we?' I asked, thinking we must have reached some place of historical significance: some explorer's landfall, perhaps, or a sacred site.

'Here,' he said. 'Just here – at this moment, on the beach at Darwin. The green water, hazy sky. Mangrove arms and inlets, boats at anchor, a light plane coming in to land. What could be sweeter than the casual moments of our life? How blessed we are, after all the things we both have seen, and lived through, and fled from, to be here, together, walking in the early daylight, on a silent, gentle shore. And look! . . .'

The sun had climbed above the smoke-plumes and the flecks of cloud. Its heat began to warm us.

'. . . Look at the gleam on the cliffs, there. Don't you think they're almost like the pink bluffs one sees round Kununurra?'

'The promised land.'

'What do you mean?'

'Don't you know the story? Early in the twentieth century, the leaders of the Zionist Movement were looking for a Jewish homeland.

They fanned out across the world on great exploratory missions. They came to Australia, and searched through its empty spaces. They were very keen, at one point, to buy up all the country round Argyle and the Ord and Lissadell – that whole stretch of the East Kimberley. There were talks with the Emmanuels and the Duracks, and the other station-owners. They even approached the West Australian Government, but maybe Palestine began to look more promising: it all fell through. History would have been very different, don't you think, if Tel Aviv had been built where Wyndham is today. Think of the native title problems.'

'Go on – you're joking!'

'Why would I joke about such a thing? It would have been a strange kind of haven, at the end of exile, to find salvation eighty kilometres up the Cambridge Gulf.'

George, perhaps wisely, let this topic go.

'How I should love to visit the Kimberley once again,' he sighed. 'Travel up the Drysdale River Road, to Kalumburu, see the art sites, the Wandjinas, the Bradshaws, but I suppose I never shall. I spoke to Grahame Walsh the other day. Have you been in touch with him recently?'

'In a sense,' I replied, with some caution.

'He sounded dreadful,' George went on. 'Alone, despairing, afraid of shadows. He is the proof, if ever I needed it, that love unchecked turns into obsession.'

'Love? Love of what?'

'Rock art, of course. But not rock art itself, as much as what it holds out to us: the image of the past, cultures that are gone, men and women we can never bring back to life. And yet there is the hope, always, that we can know them, almost touch them, feel what they felt, and dream their dreams more intensely even than they would have themselves, because the veil of the millennia hangs between us and them, and makes their world more beautiful, full of richer, deeper magic to our eyes. So' – he glanced at me – 'your inquisition's over. You know our secret now, our heart's desire, and isn't that what you want too? Isn't that what everyone who's drawn into the Outback wants? To lose themselves – to escape – into the arms of time?'

# Three     Sturt

# I

At the height of a burning inland summer, on January the 27th, 1845, Captain Charles Sturt and his exploring party, bound northwards towards bleak plains and sand-ridge desert, were compelled to halt and seek shelter at a large water-hole which lay beneath a line of reddish-coloured hills. Sturt, who was nearing his fiftieth birthday when he first encamped at this spot, west of the Darling, and far beyond the settled districts of New South Wales, had been charged with unusual guidelines for his expedition. The official instructions from Lord Stanley, the Secretary of State for the Colonies, advised him to seek out a mountain chain or watershed, believed to lie towards the centre of the continent, around a latitude of twenty-eight degrees. His true goal, that tormented and spurred him on increasingly during his advance into Central Australia, was the unknown sea geographic opinion then placed at the heart of the inland. So confident was Sturt of the reality of this feature, and of his destiny as its discoverer, that he had hauled with him, over the

133

five months of his journey out from Adelaide, a neat little boat, hewn from red cedar wood, in which he hoped to 'plough the waters' of the central sea.

The subsequent fortunes of this vessel were mixed. It was carried northwards with his party towards the desert. It shared in Sturt's retreat, until he was forced to abandon it: in a mournful gesture, he launched the boat, unmanned, upon the waters of the rockhole. At some point in the future it was caught by the rushing waters of a flash flood and smashed in pieces. A later explorer, William Tietkens, found some of its fragments, and sent a specimen to the Melbourne Museum. Years afterwards, a traveller noticed one side of the boat, lodged in the fork of a tall gum-tree some distance to the south, at Evelyn Creek. A piece was given to Sturt's descendants, who offered it to the Adelaide Gallery, while another piece was once to be seen in the mining city of Broken Hill.

All this, though, was still to come when the Captain arrived at the little rocky glen and found himself 'on the brink of a fine pool shaded by trees and cliffs.' An engraving in Sturt's two-volume *Narrative of an Expedition into Central Australia*, which only at this point begins to shed its wooden, perfunctory quality, shows 'Preservation Creek' as Sturt and his men encountered it. The sketch is Sturt's own: it depicts a broad, curving reach of water, its soft lines punctuated by outcrops and bars of stone. On one side is a flat, sandy bank; on the other, boulders, and a forbidding precipice. Relief filled the Captain's mind when he first saw this well-concealed oasis, for he and his men had been in the most desperate need of water. But as the days of his stay there turned into weeks, and his search teams failed to find more native wells or enduring river channels in the vicinity along their forward route, and the sun licked up those few water-holes and pools they had encountered in the ranges behind them, the truth stole across his mind: '*It became evident to me, that we were locked up in the desolate*

*and heated region, into which we had penetrated, as effectually as if we
had wintered at the Pole.'*

Sturt made repeated, futile sorties and survey probes, eastwards,
westwards, through the gibber plains that lay around them, returning to the 'Depot', as he soon came to call the encampment, ever
more anguished, frustrated and stupefied. Here, in his tent, set apart
from the members of the exploration team, he pondered, and
devoted much of his time to writing. In addition to the published
account of his journey, a private record survives, together with a
lengthy memoir-letter he composed each Sunday for the benefit of
his wife, Charlotte Christiana, who had been strongly opposed to his
departure on the expedition.

On the face of it her objections were well-founded. Sturt's fame
as an explorer and a hero was already established, for more than a
decade-and-a-half earlier he had succeeded in tracing the River
Murray from its higher waters down to the ambiguous point where
it flows out through Lake Alexandrina to the Southern Ocean. But
now he was in imperfect health, his eyesight was failing, and he was
abandoning four young children to launch himself on a voyage he
regarded as a form of perpetual quest, a quest as much dream-like
and imaginative in nature as it was strictly geographic.

Sturt's temperament, despite his military background and his
Olympian manner, was reflective, self-questioning, melancholic. A
wall of glass hung between him and society; he was a man born for
loneliness, for absence from the things he loved; he had the horizon
always in his eyes. Signs of this element in his nature emerge even in
the most conventional accounts of his life.

He was born in India, the eldest of eight sons. His father, an
impecunious Bengal judge for the East India Company, came from
a well-known Dorset family. At the age of five Sturt was shipped off
to the mother country and brought up there by relatives. He
attended Harrow school together with Lord Byron, that institution's

most celebrated inmate, and the sole recorded incident from these years concerns his stint as fag to the same Duke of Dorset lampooned in some of Byron's youthful verses. One day Dorset sent Sturt up a tall tree to retrieve a nest full of crows' eggs. Sturt, climbing down, broke one of the eggs in his mouth; Dorset thrashed him. Sturt, outraged at this injustice, threw a bat at Dorset; for this crime he was forced to run the gauntlet of the whole school. Despite experiencing such humiliations, Sturt professed to have loved his schooldays; but there was no money to send him on to Cambridge.

He was commissioned as an ensign in the Thirty-Ninth Regiment, and embarked on a military career which took him, even before he came to Sydney, as far afield as the Pyrenees, Canada, France and Ireland, and which made possible the taste for international comparison that surfaces from time to time in his Australian narratives.

After his first journeys of inland exploration, and a brief spell in England, where he met and married Charlotte, he returned to New South Wales and fell swiftly into the financial difficulties that were his family's best-established tradition. Sturt decided to overland a herd of cattle to South Australia, an enterprise for which he proved ludicrously ill-suited. He ran short of supplies along the way, but was rescued by his friend, that most glamorous of the early explorers, the wild, extreme and solitary Edward Eyre.

Not only was Eyre the pioneer of desert voyaging, and the first proponent of the theory of the inland sea: he was Sturt's ideal, and inspiration, and, in some measure, the secret companion of his imaginings, the 'excellent friend' Sturt wished both to live up to and to go beyond. Eyre, in fact, rode with the Captain some distance on the first stage of his desert journey, talking with him, encouraging him, before the party struck out towards unknown terrain.

With Sturt on this venture travelled a full complement of livestock, eleven horses, and fifteen men. Several of these individuals, who had been hand-picked from hundreds of applicants, the Captain knew already from survey work or from his overlanding fiasco. His deputy, James Poole, was a red-haired Irishman of persistent ill-temper. The head stockman, Robert Flood, 'this man with the instinct of a Native in the Bush', had a well-known tendency when in town to drink, a trait shared by John McDouall Stuart, the draughtsman of the party, a dour figure who would eventually far surpass Sturt in achievements and become the first explorer to cross the continent from south to north and back.

But these men, the Captain's companions during months of isolation, drift through his story like half-remembered ghosts. They are scarcely there in more than name. Sturt had a romantic yearning for intensity of friendship, and the focus of his thoughts all through the journey – the Patroclus to his bush Achilles – was the expedition's charming doctor, the twenty-eight-year-old gentleman, John Harris Browne. Not only does Browne serve as Sturt's conversation-partner and sounding-board, and as his fellow-traveller through the most blasted, molten wastes and deserts, he is a man of fine feelings, and noble soul, and self-restraint, a younger, sweeter version, as it sometimes seems, of the Captain himself. There are grounds for believing that Browne passed, in some fashion, into the very fabric of Sturt's emotions and his ideas. The doctor had been keeping his own journal of the expedition's progress until they were well beyond the Darling, at which point Sturt ordered him to stop writing. But from then on, Browne and he spent long hours together, sitting opposite each other, talking through their experiences, Browne acting almost as the Captain's eyes, picturing for him in words the landscape and the distant features Sturt himself could hardly see.

There was another man on the exploring party with whom Sturt's relationship was closer yet, and odder still: George Davenport, a former convict, whose unusual history I first came across by chance in an obscure volume published by the Barrier

Field Naturalists' Club to mark the expedition's centenary. *Sturt 1844–1944*, a slender book of the utmost elegance, has a cover illustration of the Captain, implausibly idealised as an Australian bushman. He is seen from behind, poised on the crest of a tall sand-dune, staring out, one hand shading his eyes. He wears long trousers, a short-sleeved shirt and a stylish slouch hat. Inside the Mitchell Library's copy, beneath the colophon, with its details of the Sturt Memorial Committee of Broken Hill, is a message in a neat cursive hand: 'With the compliments of Claudia Underwood, Secretary'.

Davenport, as the Club's researchers relate over the following pages, in a breathless present tense, was a soldier at Waterloo, entrusted with carrying the colours of his regiment. Sadly, he was an epileptic, and his emotions at the onset of the battle were rather different from those of Stendhal's Fabrizio: feeling a seizure coming on, he scrunched up the colours, stuffed them in his pocket, and knew 'no more'. After the fighting, he was found wandering the battlefield uninjured, was court-martialled, and judged guilty of desertion.

It was many years later, during Sturt's brief spell as commandant of the garrison on Norfolk Island, that he encountered Davenport, whom he befriended, and whose protestations of innocence he believed. It happened that a ship was driven on the rocks of the harbour during Sturt's time on the Island. Both he and Davenport took part in the rescue of its passengers, and this became the pretext for the Captain to ask for, and to gain, the pardon of his convict friend. After Sturt's marriage and return to Australia, Davenport made contact with the household, greatly to Charlotte Sturt's initial horror, for he was a Caliban, unbearably ugly to look at, while Sturt himself, like all in his family, was a man of the most striking grace. Davenport eventually became the Sturts' cook and servant. He was present at the birth of the Captain's eldest son, Napier, whom he at once clasped fervently to his breast, and for whom, ever afterwards, he preserved an almost paternal affection.

When Sturt, in the teeth of the most despairing protests by his wife, at last set off on the first stage of the Central Australian expedition, Davenport, who was far from a natural candidate for such a journey, gave pursuit, overhauled the Captain on the banks of the River Murray, and demanded to come. It is hard to believe that he was not sent on this mission by Charlotte Sturt, and though we almost never hear his name in the expedition journal, we may picture him there, at the Depot, alongside the Captain, tending, fussing, caring – the hideous intimate, the all-knowing imbecile – much like the slave beside the Roman emperor, deputed to whisper constantly in his master's ear: 'Be mindful of what you are'.

Davenport's path through colonial life after the return of the expedition was worthy of some Dickensian sub-plot. He invested his seventeen months' pay in Adelaide sections, had a lucky hit in the goldfields, and opened an inn which attracted a roaring trade. He never married, but in later years became obsessed by the desire to make Napier Sturt his heir. He died in the same year as the Captain, a man he resembled in the purity and intensity of his longings, shortly after dispatching to Napier Sturt a letter in which he had enclosed a golden chain.

Such were the faces Sturt saw at the Depot, as he paced the sandy margins of the waterhole, or strolled in the shade of the overhanging gum-trees, and day passed into day. Sometimes one or other of the expedition's officers would ride out with him on the vain, repeated transects he made during the first weeks at the Glen, as much to escape the 'gloomy silence' as to uncover a safe route ahead.

From one of these journeys, on which he was accompanied by Browne, Flood and the young servant Joseph, Sturt records, in terms of near-religious exaltation, an encounter that would have seemed to his readers' ears remarkable, though bushmen in remote areas still talk of such experiences today: '*We were in the centre of the plain, when Mr Browne drew my attention to a number of black specks in the upper air. These spots increasing momentarily in size, were evidently approaching us rapidly. In an incredibly short time we were surrounded by several hundreds of the common kite, stooping down to within a few feet of us, and then turning away, after having eyed us steadily. Several approached us so closely, that they threw themselves back to avoid contact, opening their beaks and spreading out their talons. The long flight of these birds, reaching from the ground into the heavens, put me strongly in mind of one of Martin's beautiful designs, in which he produces the effect of distance by a multitude of objects gradually vanishing from the view.*'

Whatever others might imagine, Sturt insists these kites, patrolling their lonely deserts, had held power of life and death over him and his party in those few moments before they wheeled away and returned 'to the lofty region from whence they had descended'. So struck was he by this visitation that in his published narrative he included at this point an illustration of the fork-tailed kite, *Milvus affinis*, in Gould's limp lithographic likeness.

For the Captain had become by this time as responsive to the signs of nature as to the ideas of man. When a dove or parrot overflew the Depot, he saw the shining waters of the inland sea as its certain destination. When the crows and shrikes and hawks at last deserted him, it was a portent of the expedition's end. A favourite kangaroo-dog was always at his feet, nudging, nuzzling, panting. His relationship with the horses, who have characters, and figure by name in his narrative, was almost Iliadic. He christened features of the landscape after them; they plead with him when he runs short of water, circling him, pulling off his hat to gain his attention, and he relates in heartbroken words the sufferings of each of the animals in turn as they fall on the plains of the stony desert.

They were purer, truer than the camp and the world of men, from which Sturt turned his eyes increasingly as the ordeal wore on, preferring to deal alone with Browne and cloister himself in his writing tent, there to ponder his dreams of life, his intense states of feeling, his remembered joys and sadnesses, the truths about his nature he was struggling to confront.

In his memoir to Charlotte, a memoir that reads much like an internal monologue, or confession to his conscience – though he addresses her as 'Dearest' repeatedly, pleadingly – Sturt returns often to the sense of dread and foreboding that so afflicted him.

On his departure, as he tells her, he had stood with Eyre upon the banks of the Murray and spoken of his 'doubtful enterprise', then, alone above the river, he had a vision of his wife upon its waters 'almost as distinctly as if you had really been there' – and his mind flew back to the time when their peace and happiness were unbroken, 'and when I could look on the clear blue sky without a feeling of regret.'

Sturt had come to believe that his departure on the expedition, which on one level he justified to his wife as an essential step to secure the family's finances, was somehow a betrayal, an act of transgression for which he would have to pay a price. He was troubled by the fear that she had already died during his absence; or perhaps one of their children: Napier, or the fickle Charles, or Evelyn, the 'wild Australian boy', who did in fact die young in India, from cholera, or his daughter 'Missey', Charlotte Eyre Sturt, a woman of unsurpassed loveliness, who never married, and remained in her parents' house, sewing, working through the odd piece of music, displaying in advanced form the signs of her father's high-strung, nervous temperament.

Just before his march into the Barrier Range, and towards the Depot, Sturt's suspicions deepened. *'I turn my thoughts towards home with the most gloomy apprehensions. I have taken it into my head that both you and Napier have been snatched from me, and if such should be the case I am sure I do not know what I should do.'*

There had been words between them at his leaving; but how much he loved her! He goes on to set down a statement that tells much about the expedition's course and outcome: *'I have ever seen reason to be grateful to you for your care and anxiety – and you must lay to the account of a distempered mind any of those feelings which I evince either of petulance or unkindness. I am sure I was too unhappy myself to consider the unhappiness I was inflicting on others, and a very little more would I sincerely believe have made me put an end to it all.'*

Unsurprisingly, the men and the officers noticed that their Captain was sometimes overwrought; they commented on it among themselves, and put it down to the strength of his ambition and his burning lust for fame.

The journey, then, was not what it had first seemed to be – a smooth, well-planned advance towards the Centre. Sturt conceived it more and more as time went by in private terms; he described it to himself as if it were a work of the imagination, a literary epic that he was composing even as he advanced.

What was he seeking at the continent's veiled heart? A space as abstract as the grief that lurked inside him. What was he fleeing, and leaving behind? Not only all he cared for, and held dear, but need, and pain, and love itself. Where was he bound? Like every noble or beautiful thing, to the kingdom of death – that kingdom he longed to see with his own eyes, to endure, and to return from, with golden words upon his lips.

At first, at least, theirs was a kind imprisonment. The Depot gave the party water, ease, and rest. The horses were knocked up, the men exhausted, while Browne and Poole were both suffering from scurvy, a disease then little understood, which produced disquieting symptoms: blackened flesh on the limbs, nosebleeds, a taste like copper in the mouth. But as this seclusion dragged into its third month, and there was not the faintest variation in the weather, Sturt found himself watching the sky 'with extreme anxiety' for signs of cloud – only to see how *'week after week the sun rose and set in inexhausted splendour, and every cloud that rose upon the horizon was beat back by a moon as bright and I had almost said as hot as the sun itself.'*

The heat and the confinement wore upon the Captain's nerves, until he came to regard himself as subject to some mocking sentence, some plague imposed upon him by the heavens. *'It appeared as if we were the last of creation amid the desolation and destruction of the world. There was a solemn stillness around, not a living thing to be seen, not an ant, not a cricket or a grasshopper.'*

Nature and its patterns had been turned upside down. Seeds planted in the creek-bed were burned to cinders by the sun's rays as soon as their shoots cleared the soil. The horses sweated even when they walked. The upper leather of the men's shoes was burned as if by fire. There were strange meteors in the sky. The ground was warm as far as four feet down. Sturt charted the mean recordings of his thermometer with painful care, and described the heat's effects: *'Every screw in our boxes had been drawn, and the horn handles of our instruments, as well as our combs, were split into fine laminae. Our tyres fell off the wheels, and the drays rattled all over. The lead dropped out of our pencils, our signal rockets were entirely spoiled; our hair, as well as the wool on the sheep, ceased to grow, and our nails had become as brittle as glass. We were obliged to bury our wax candles; a bottle of citric acid in Mr Browne's box became fluid, and seeping, burnt a quantity of his linen; we found it difficult to write or draw, so rapidly did the fluid dry in our pens and brushes.'*

———

With agonised excitement, Sturt went on, all through the journey, recording these extremes. The hot wind from the interior so over-whelmed him *'that I shall never forget its withering effect. I sought shelter behind a large gum-tree, but the blasts of heat were so terrific, that I wondered the very grass did not take fire. This really was nothing ideal: every thing, both animate and inanimate, gave way before it; the horses stood with their backs to the wind, and their noses to the ground, without the muscular strength to raise their heads; the birds were mute, and the leaves of the trees, under which we were sitting, fell like a snow shower around us.'*

Sturt took a reading, on this occasion, with the thermometer in the sun, then moved it into the shaded fork of a nearby tree: *'In this position I went to examine it about an hour afterwards, when I found that the mercury had risen to the top of the instrument, and that its fur-ther expansion had burst the bulb, a circumstance that I believe no traveller has ever before had to record.'*

In fact, as those who frequent the Corner Country and its lonely cattle stations in our time well know, Sturt experienced nothing unusual in the way of weather. There are even grounds for believ-ing that he passed through this region, and the stony desert that bears his name, and the eastmost sandhills of the Simpson, during an exceptionally gentle season, so frequent were the supplies of food and water he stumbled on, so abundant the wildlife, so well-settled the Aboriginal tribes.

Yet the Captain converted that landscape into a wilderness quite charged with hidden meanings: *'Providence had, in its allwise pur-poses, guided us to the only spot, in that widespread desert, where our wants could have been permanently supplied, but had there stayed our further progress into a region that almost appears to be forbidden ground.'*

For a while Sturt's spirits were cheered by an Aboriginal man who stayed with them at the Depot, sleeping close beside the

Captain's tent, and fanning old enthusiasms, for this visitor described an inland water where the waves broke higher than his head. With his departure depression set in, and boredom: 'a gloomy silence pervaded the camp'. Browne and Sturt, 'almost heart-broken', scarcely left their tents except to visit the stricken Poole, who was lying helpless on his bed, his mind wandering, his dreams becoming fanciful, while the scurvy that had seized him 'like a tiger' intensified its grip.

Sturt was not much troubled by the psychological condition of his men – he had his hands full in his own universe. Poole, though, made the strange suggestion that two navigation cairns should be built upon the tops of nearby hills to guide the party onwards, an idea the Captain quickly took up 'to keep the men in health', even though he knew the peaks soon became invisible in the country they were travelling towards. And so a pyramid, rather like a memorial in its appearance, was built to precise specifications upon an isolated summit, where Sturt hoped it would stand for ages 'as a record of all we suffered in the dreary region to which we were so long confined' – and he has his wish; it can still be seen there to this day, at the end of a twisting access track, its stone blocks being slowly prised out of true by the elements.

Above the Depot, the morning of the twelfth of July dawned overcast and calm. Throughout the previous week the air had been charged with moisture. Clouds would gather, thicken, then, in sudden, mystifying fashion, disperse. All through the camp there was action, preparation. Sturt decided to send back his ailing deputy, together with a small team of men, as soon as rain made movement possible, to the Darling, and thence to Adelaide.

But Poole was restless, ill at ease inside his tent. He demanded to be moved into an underground room the men had dug beside the creek-bed when they had first encamped there six months before. In those days Sturt, who had come to dislike Poole, and now saw him as a 'mischief-maker', treated the ailing man with exemplary kindness and compassion; he spoke to him softly, and bore his tempers. For the first time in the journey, Poole had become an object of vague interest to the Captain, whose thoughts went naturally to ideas of death and sacrifice, for he knew his deputy was 'in danger', though it was not felt to be immediate.

One day, while waiting tensely for the rains to fall, and scanning the sky, and the shapes and progress of the clouds, Sturt, 'to give a change to the currents of my thoughts', walked along the creek with Browne, and the two men continued their 'ramble' a few miles further, for all the world as if they were a pair of Lake poets.

*'I know not why it was, that, on this occasion more than any other, we should have contemplated the scene around us, unless it was that the peculiar tranquillity of the moment made a greater impression on our minds. Perhaps the death-like silence of the scene at that moment led us to reflect, whilst gazing on the ravages made by the floods, how fearfully that silence must sometimes be broken by the roar of waters and the winds. Here, as in other places, we observed the trunks of trees swept down from the hills, lodged high in the branches of the trees in the neighbourhood of the creek, and large accumulations of rubbish lying at their butts, whilst the line of inundation extended so far into the plains that the country must on such occasions have the appearance of an inland sea'.*

At this point one can almost hear the sigh in the Captain's voice.

At last, around the middle of that day, the arrangements were complete. Poole's chamber, where at night-time the temperatures fell very low, had been equipped with a fireplace and a chimney. The patient was carried from his tent. The Captain supervised, walking by his deputy with an air of benign interest, and was much struck by a particular coincidence, which chimed with his way of seeing things. For as Poole was being brought across the camp *'towards the room he was destined to occupy for so short a time, I pointed out the pyramid to him'* – the new-built navigation cairn upon the peak that bears Poole's name, and serves as his monument – *'and it is somewhat singular, that the first drops of rain, on the continuance of which our deliverance depended, fell as the men were bearing him along'*.

The following night the Captain went to bed in turmoil. Rain, a gentle, mist-like rain, had come and gone. Now it began once more, and he could hear the echo of the imagined waters of the inland, those waters with their rushing, splendid roar.

Sturt prayed *'that the Almighty would still farther extend his mercy to us'*, and laid his head upon his pillow, underneath which he had placed, as always, a Bible belonging to his father-in-law. In this state, with both forms of love so neatly bound together, and faint thoughts of the dying Poole on the edges of his consciousness, he drifted off – and all night long the rain poured down *'without any intermission, and as morning dawned the ripple of waters in a little gully close to our tents, was a sweeter and more soothing sound than any melody I ever heard. On going down to the creek in the morning I found that it had risen five inches, and the ground was now so completely saturated that I no longer doubted the moment of our liberation had arrived.'*

The return party mustered. Its departure neared. Sturt went to Poole, and told him the dray in which he would be borne off was ready, and 'he felt much'. But he did not at first show it, to the Captain's great relief, for what he really loathed in Poole was not so much his sickness, the discoloured legs, the paralysis, the chunks of flesh that hung down so repellently from the roof of the man's mouth, but his vehemence, his 'violent bursts of passion', his lack of self-control. Sturt watched as Poole was lifted from the stretcher into the carriage – but when at last the moment came to say goodbye, to his vexation and embarrassment Poole broke down and wept bitterly.

With a 'beating and a bursting heart' – for separations in the desert are always poignant affairs – the Captain saw the little cavalcade move off, and turned to thoughts of his own advance, but the going was so wet he was delayed. He had made no more than four miles progress from the Depot when young Joseph from the return party overhauled them, and gave them the news of Poole's death.

Together with Browne, Sturt rode back to 'examine the remains of our unfortunate companion'. They were startled to find not some tortured corpse but a body possessed of a 'singular fairness of countenance.' He had died without a struggle, in the act, as the Captain rather oddly mentioned to his wife, of taking some of Mrs Sturt's favourite medicine. Both the Captain and the doctor expressed surprise at Poole's passing. 'God knows,' wrote Sturt, as though to avert his own suspicions from himself, 'it was an event I had not foreseen' – but he could see how death, and rain, and freedom had come together, and he admits to experiencing a sense of guilt at having sent Poole away to die like some scapegoat in the desert. There was no wood for a coffin, so the dead man was rolled up in a blanket and laid upon his mattress instead. They buried him underneath a grevillea tree that stood close by the underground room: his initials, J.P., and the year, 1845, were cut into a blaze on the bark, where, over time, their outlines would blur, and spread, and be transformed almost into abstract shapes.

## II

Drawn by this story, and above all by the dream-like quality of Sturt's descriptions, I resolved, almost as soon as I began reading the expedition *Journal*, to make a voyage of my own into his landscape, and through the desert that still bears his name. I was able to bring off several brief forays in this direction, to Innamincka, to the

Corner Country, even to the plains that lie round Preservation Creek. For some while his northmost point, amidst the sandhills of the Simpson, from which he returned defeated after eighteen months of fruitless struggle, eluded me. So I felt relief almost as much as joy when at last, in mid-December, I received a commission to travel, together with the photographer Johnson Venn, from western New South Wales to Birdsville, a route which would allow us to trace, in a few days of driving, almost the whole of the Captain's year-long progress, as he picked his way through creek-beds, across dune-fields and bare flood-plains.

All seemed to have fallen into place. I had a gifted, if irritable, companion for the road; the Outback in the heat of summer as dramatic stage-set; and a long-imagined destination, rich in myth and history, towards which our white Landcruiser could head.

At mid-morning on the day the red-soil plains were at last spread out on the horizon before us, and this joint odyssey should truly have begun, I found myself not on the open road but standing close by Johnson, speaking in a low voice, arguing. We were on the crest of a low red bluff, just beyond the street-grid of Broken Hill, a city that has always had a certain charm for me, in part because of its lavish, baroque-flavoured civic architecture, its spires and balconies and steep-pitched rooves, so reminiscent of some Central European provincial town.

But on this occasion the charm had vanished. All round us, gathered in one of those tight knots that mark out a waiting media crowd, were reporters, photographers and television crews, and off to one side, surrounded by federal police, was the object of collective attention, tall, flame-haired, square-faced, with green eyes set close together: the independent member for Oxley, Pauline Hanson, who was at that time close to the peak of her short-lived celebrity, and by far the most recognisable human being on the Australian continent.

'This wasn't what you said we'd be doing,' hissed Johnson, staring at her and speaking into my ear. 'Don't you remember? Open spaces. The explorer's trail. Creative self-expression. A journey into the heart of the Outback? And now you've arranged this. It's so thoughtful of you: a photo opportunity with the Far Right. Is there some connection I'm missing?'

'We were in the area,' I whispered back, wondering how the two of us were going to endure an extended spell together. 'And I didn't arrange it. What did you want me to do? Refuse? Why don't you just go and take your picture?'

'Well, you're not putting yourself out, I notice. I'm doing all the work. Have you actually ever met her? No! So here's your chance. You ask her. Go on! Everybody's packing up to leave. It's now or never.'

'I'm not that on-key this morning, Johnson,' I said. 'In fact,' I went on, looking across at him, 'I'm quite off-key, to be absolutely frank with you.'

'Is that right?' said Johnson to this, vindictively. 'Tell me something I hadn't worked out already. Inland blues! The Captain's shadow! It doesn't make any difference, anyway. It's your turn!'

Thus prodded, with great reluctance, reassembling the journalistic instincts I had been discarding in preparation for our journey, I strolled across to the political group, and towards its diva: 'Ms Hanson,' I began somewhat tentatively, for throughout the months of her rise to fame, the newspaper I wrote for had subjected her to the most relentless hostile coverage. I introduced myself.

'I know who you are,' she said in frigid tones, and I was on the verge of making some reply, when, without warning, a wave of faintness swept through me: the blood drummed in my temples, the light drained from my eyes. I swayed on my feet, I half expected to collapse before her on the ground. Perhaps, I felt myself thinking, in a distanced fashion, it was just as Johnson said, and I was in the midst of some Sturt-like reverie – or one of those moments of self-intoxication the great correspondents of the past describe, moments that came upon them like a blow, once, twice in a life-time, at the brink of combat, or under fire. But was this really quite such an occasion? I gazed at her, and at her slanted eyes.

'And I know who you work for, as well,' added Hanson, with the same cold indignation, into which a certain puzzlement had now crept.

'You're very well informed,' I managed to say, almost gasping as I spoke.

'That's my job,' she snapped. 'So – what is it?'

'A picture,' I went on, still barely able to pronounce the words, staring through the sheen of light that was pulsing in my eyes.

A picture. But how to capture her, as she was in life, that instant? Half fear, half anger; half grace, half ugliness. That broad face; the wide nose; the hair, which was familiar, in some distant way, the ochre hair – like an Aboriginal tribesman's, painted for the dance; like Odette's, when Charles Swann first saw her.

'A suggestion,' I managed to bring out, 'for a picture – something different.'

'What?' she said cautiously. 'I think by now I've seen it all.'

'It occurred to us,' I went on, with a sense of relief, for Johnson had drifted inconspicuously over – but at that point I realised I had forgotten what I was about to say.

'Yes?' she prompted.

'It occurred to us – that – that your hair has the same colour as the sandhills and the landscape all around us.'

'And so?'

'And so – we thought it would make a striking image if we took a picture of you, lying on the ground, with your hair spread out around your face, and its red mingling with the earth's redness.'

Hanson raised her eyebrows, and gave a little smile: 'Is he always like this?'

Johnson darted a sharp look at me, and jumped in: 'You could almost say that it would symbolise your message, reaching into the Outback.'

'Really,' she said. 'And what did it symbolise when you were trying to break into the lounge-room of my farm with that other photographer last year?'

'Johnson?' I said, by now recovering some sense of my own presence. But what exactly had just happened? A political reaction? A nervous seizure? Some crevasse, maybe, in the smooth, untroubling gradient of life?

'Yes, look, I'm sorry about that,' Johnson countered. 'You know how things are. It's a demanding business, and that was a long time ago now.' He gave her his most winning smile. 'So: how about it?'

'I think, in spite of everything, it's a good idea,' she answered. 'I know that might surprise you, but I get so bored of the same old things: being asked all the time to hold a gun or pose in a fish and chip shop or hug baby kangaroos. I'll just get rid of this old top-coat.'

She passed the garment, which was a spent shade of pea-green, to her political adviser, David Oldfield, an individual whose face and bouffant hairstyle were just then becoming familiar, for he was reputed at that time to be the manipulative hand behind Hanson, the creator of her policies, the partner of her thoughts and dreams.

'David,' said Hanson coldly. 'Here.'

'And what's going on?'

She told him.

'It's a dreadful idea. It doesn't project the right image. We want you to seem more normal.'

'Normal?' said Hanson, her voice rising, and looking at me, her face a mask of horror, as though she herself was a student of all that was extreme and elevated from the daily course of life. 'Normal?'

'Yes, normal,' said Oldfield, with an air of annoyance. 'We want everyone to be more normal – don't you remember? Normal houses, normal families – the world would be a great deal happier if there was more normality in it. You know what we're trying to do with One Nation,' he went on, turning to me accusingly. 'You know what we stand for, in the bush. Journalists!' He made a gesture, as though to express a depth of horror beyond words.

'Well done!' said Johnson in my ear. 'Brilliant!'

We retreated. Our day of reporting pursued its course – political rally in the local hall; press conference; street walk. I strolled along at a safe distance from the scrum ahead, looking up to the facades of Argent Street, and pondering the viability of my mental state: lack of concentration; a proneness to daydream; extreme suggestibility. Were such things at all compatible with the requirements of my professional life? I was lost in these reflections, and in the disturbing realisation that Hanson and Odette Swann had, if only momentarily, occupied the same space in my mind, when a tall, ingratiating man with a walrus moustache fell into step beside me.

I recognised Hanson's second confidant, David Ettridge.

'How do you think it's going?' he inquired in the pleasantest of manners, and, when I looked at him uncomprehendingly, he smiled and waved his hands as though to express the elusive subtleties of political life. 'The day, I mean, the whole One Nation campaign – the rally – how did it seem to you?'

'Just between the two of us?' I said.

'Of course.'

'I thought it was completely surreal.'

There was a silence as he allowed this unhelpful judgement to sink in.

'So!' he tried. 'Where are you two going from here?'

I told him.

'You see, that's wonderful – you're staying with our theme,' he said triumphantly. 'You can't get away: from the political frontier to the geographic frontier. And what are you actually looking for out there?'

I shrugged, and gave a distant non-committal smile.

'Well, we're all looking for something, in the end, aren't we?' said Ettridge, with great enthusiasm. 'We're all poor lost souls looking for light, and freedom, and salvation.'

He nodded and tilted his head, as though appraising his own sentiments.

'In fact, you could say that's what we're doing on this trip: looking for enlightenment, and trying to bring it as well.'

'Is that right?' I said. 'That wasn't really the impression I was getting.'

At which point he leaned towards me.

'You do understand,' he whispered, rather abruptly, 'that Pauline Hanson wouldn't pay attention to people like you.'

I glanced at him.

'Of course she wouldn't,' he went on. 'She listens to us. She's interested in what we have to say.'

'And why are you telling me this?'

'Just because it's important you know it.'

'Know about your role in things, you mean? To give an accurate record, one day. For posterity's sake?'

'If you like.'

'And she pays attention to you two. You're the great shaping influences in her ear.'

'Yes – she's pure gold, of course, to market. Look out' – a conspiratorial lightness flowed into his voice – 'she's coming back this way. Listen: for the moment, just like you said, that stays between the two of us. I think she wants me . . .'

Hanson was, indeed, beckoning towards him. Ettridge's manner shifted, almost imperceptibly, into a more pliant, servile gear. He went forward.

'No, David,' said Hanson, with an air of great satisfaction, as if wrong-footing her staff was one of the sweetest pleasures of her life. 'No, not you – I want to talk to your friend. We were having such a strange discussion.'

'Him?'

'That's right – alone.'

She gave a flick of her fingers in the direction of her security detail, who retreated some way from her. They hovered just within earshot as Hanson paused outside Schinella's Fruit Villa for a chat about immigration. I stood to one side, waiting, leaning on the door frame, hoping there would be no repeat of my previous reaction to her presence, until she drifted on, gazing into the passing windows.

'What was all that about before?' she said, after half a block, as I kept pace, wondering vaguely what to do in the event of an assassination attempt. 'About the photo – in the morning?'

'I'm sorry it didn't work out,' I said. 'It would have been a good picture.'

'You don't really have any idea what's going on here, do you? None of you media people ever get the point.'

This was said in a calm, even manner, with great assurance, as the shop windows, and our reflections in them, ghosted by.

'Well, I'll tell you – there's a revolution going on. We're taking this country by storm. Nothing's going to stay the same. Everyday people are rising up, and the politicians don't know what to do. They're defenceless, just like the Aborigines when the white man came.'

I said nothing, and let this image with all its sadness sweep through me.

'Sometimes, in fact,' she went on, 'I actually feel like those first explorers, those pioneers, going through the Outback.'

'It's a comparison that hadn't occurred to me, I have to say,' I answered, startled by this join between two separate worlds. 'We're quite interested in the explorers as well. In fact, we're about to begin travelling in the footsteps of one of them, right through until New Year.'

'And what made you decide they were so fascinating?' she asked, almost indignantly.

'They were pioneers, of course,' I said. 'Only the frontiers they were looking for were in themselves as much as in the outside world.'

'Well, I don't know I feel like them in that way, exactly,' said Hanson, pursing her lips, as though it had been a close call.

'But you do see points of comparison?'

'What did they travel with?'

'I'm sorry?'

'What did they have with them? Burke and Wills, and Oxley, and all the others – what kind of animals?'

'Pack-horses, and bullocks, the first ones – and then, later, when they realised what the far Outback was like, how waterless it was, they started using camels.'

'Camels?' She gave a backward nod towards her retinue. 'They do look like camels, don't they: with little humps.'

'Almost invisible humps.'

'But they're still there – only, in fact,' she concluded, rather sadly, 'I'm the one who's the beast of burden, and they're all riding me. Let's have a look in here.'

She plunged into a run-down shoe-shop, where she picked up and began examining a pair of white high heels.

'I don't know this is really your kind of place, Ms Hanson,' I ventured.

'Isn't it?' said Hanson, her mood now changed, as though her brief statement of credo had lifted a weight from her back. 'You'd be surprised. It's extraordinary the kind of things you find some-times in towns like this. I bet you only ever shop in David Jones or

Grace Brothers. And anyway, you can never have too many pairs of shoes. As a woman, you have to highlight your best features.'

'Your legs, you mean?'

She stretched them out, first one, then the other, and stared down at them, rather in the way young horses, with an air of quiet amazement, sometimes inspect their front hooves.

'You don't like them?'

'No, no,' I said hurriedly. 'They're magnificent – astonishing.'

And, this point cleared up to her satisfaction, we walked on, in silence, towards the police compound and the courthouse, and back, meeting not a single member of the voting public, though a small group of tracksuited Aboriginal children did record our progress from afar, and as we came within earshot they smiled, and swore, and giggled, and ran away. Eventually, we reached the haven of the Theatre Royal Hotel. The security team, her inner circle, and the few remaining diehards from the media followed her in. A mood of indolence was hanging in the air. The betting channel had monopolised the attention of the men in overalls and work-boots at the bar.

'David,' called out Hanson to Oldfield. 'The juke-box!'

Oldfield made a selection; the machine began to play 'Suicide Blonde'.

She turned to the little table where Johnson and I and the other journalists had just sat down.

'Up-to-the-minute choice of music,' said Johnson, in his most scathing manner.

'Oh well, we like to move with the times in One Nation,' she answered, looking round. 'It's a genuine Outback scene, this, isn't it? Warm and soft, and nothing ever changing. The real Australia!'

'If this is the real Australia,' muttered Johnson, in a stage whisper, 'then we're all dead.'

'But maybe we are,' I ventured, with a sudden expansive conviction that no theory so far-reaching should be left unexplored.

'Maybe we're all just drifting through an after-life, and this world is dead – and that explains the sense of emptiness the Outback gives.'

'It's not dead in an interesting way,' said Johnson. 'It's just dead. Devoid of culture – inactive.'

'If it's not cultural enough for you down here,' chirped Hanson, 'why don't you come up with the TV crews, both of you, and have a cup of tea with Pro?'

'You mean the artist?'

Johnson, who had raised his camera, for he had the disconcerting habit of taking pictures at the same time as conducting a conversation, looked quite appalled.

'Yes. Pro Hart – he's an Australian icon. He helped out with our rally here today and I've always wanted to meet him – after all, we've got the same initials.'

'How convenient,' I said.

'Convenient?'

'Yes. When you want to give him presents, you could give him a monogrammed suitcase, for example, without actually having to buy one.'

'Well, I don't know the friendship's going to go that far,' said Hanson, looking sceptical. 'But if you want to come up, you'd be very welcome.'


Pro Hart lived on the high side of town, in one of the most unusual compounds I had ever seen. The main house was a well-defended Queenslander, and alongside it rose a gantry-like structure of corrugated iron, which contained Pro's collection of Bush and International paintings. We tagged along as he gave the party a special guided tour.

Johnson whispered as we went: 'What were you doing, on that

street-walk, swanning about with her? Little policy consultations? Private confidences? It's the oldest trick in the book.'

'What was I supposed to do? Tell her to get lost?'

'At least that would have been consistent with our editorial line.'

Hanson descended on us.

'Are you two planning your next savage attack on me?' she asked airily.

'No, of course not,' I said.

'Absolutely,' said Johnson.

'Don't you ever agree on anything?'

'We have rather a volcanic professional relationship,' I explained.

'Well! I'm not sure who to believe! But Pro's going to show us his personal favourites, in the living area. You might want to come and take a picture of me, Johnson, with my permission, just for a change.'

We trooped along the corridor. Ahead of us, beyond the television cameras and the federal police, the artist was in full flight, giving quick descriptions of each canvas he came to in turn.

A few minutes later, when the tour was done, we retreated to the verandah for urgent consultations.

'In trouble again!' said Hanson to neither of us in particular, shaking her head in mingled reprimand and commiseration, as she glided by. 'See you next time. Don't get too lost in the desert!' And she gave a quick wave as she was ushered into the back seat of her Commonwealth car.

'Thank God that's over,' said Johnson.

'Just tell yourself that was the aperitif,' I tried, feeling he was on the verge of mutiny. 'And now the open road. No politicians. Only emptiness, and silence, and the spirit of the inland, for weeks ahead. White Cliffs – Wanaaring – Innamincka – Birdsville – what could be a greater privilege?'

'The frightening thing,' he replied, slowly, 'is that you're inviting me into a nightmare, and you sound as if you're looking forward to it.'


Within a few days, though, to my relief, I felt our journey beginning to take on an easier, more collaborative rhythm: sunrise, motel coffee, quick departure, morning drive. For hours in the passenger seat as we passed through bare red landscape I would close my eyes and wait for the bush's revivifying powers to take effect, or hunch over and lose myself in the pages of the Captain's *Journal*, resurfacing only briefly at roadhouse stops to check our much-annotated maps of the Corner Country and south-east Queensland.

Beside me Johnson passed great pools of time in his own brand of silence, singing softly, drumming his fingers, gazing through the windows of the Landcruiser, only giving in occasionally to his creative impulses. Then he would hit the brakes and stop the car beside some unprepossessing subject: a piece of burnt and twisted metal; a fence-line receding to the horizon; a shredded truck-tyre; a freshly-decapitated kangaroo, from which he would chase off the outraged crows. Sometimes half an hour passed before we were ready to drive on, and I endured these episodes of photographic inspiration as calmly as I could, but when we had our third pause in one morning for ground portraits of a blue-tongued lizard, I felt the time had come to make a stand.

'Johnson,' I said, 'if we don't push on we're never going to get there.'

'What's the matter,' he called out from behind his lens, his voice muffled. 'The heat getting to you?'

'It is at least forty degrees.'

'Here,' he said, holding up his pocket camera. 'Take a picture of me.'

'Take a picture of you stretched out on the road taking a picture of a lizard in its threat display?'

'Art lurks in strange places,' he said as I complied.

Towards the middle of the day we reached our first navigation point, and turned off the White Cliffs road onto the Silver City Highway, a corrugated dirt track that winds northwards from the Barrier to the Grey ranges, closely following Sturt's route, beneath quartz hills, across bare plains, until it strikes the shallow watershed of Evelyn Creek, and descends at last towards a plateau strewn with piles of weathered, deep-red stones.

'Well, I still think a book of photographs of road-kill would be a valid project,' said Johnson. 'You could even write the text: "... While travelling with this gifted photographic artist, in the furthest reaches of the Outback . . ." – something like that, maybe.'

'Thanks!'

'So what's the attraction of this place you're in such a hurry to get to?'

'Tibooburra?'

I reached behind the seat and pulled out the centennial guide-book to the Corner Country, and gave it to him.

'It's a very high culture kind of destination. Just take a look at the last page – there's a story that might appeal even to you. And it's not that I'm in a hurry. I only want to get there in time to see the murals during daylight.'

'Murals?'

'At the Family Hotel: they're famous. There's a group of paint-ings round the bar, by Clifton Pugh, by Drysdale – and there's one above all, much more recent, that I wanted you to see.'

'Does every town in this part of Australia have some world-shattering art treasure in it?' said Johnson, flicking through the pages of the guide as I drove on. 'We're supposed to be in the bush. It's like driving through the Roman Campagna! And listen to this. Here's the story they choose to sum up a century of settlement.'

He began to read aloud: '"A few years ago at a local gymkhana a young policeman irresponsibly over-imbibed. When rebuked by his sergeant, he promptly thumped him under one ear, and kicked his fallen white helmet down the street. After being graciously permitted to resign, he walked over to the Family Hotel and there on the noticeboard he wrote these words: "*The song has ended but the melody lingers on*." For God's sake, it could come straight from a Slim Dusty chorus.'

'You see!'

'Well, okay, so maybe you're right, and it is my kind of place after all.'

He lapsed into a silence which lasted until Tibooburra's communication tower was visible ahead. We drove in, with the curiosity that comes after every long haul: trees, old houses, a general store, how tender and delicate they all looked after a spell in the emptiness.

'It's seen better days,' said Johnson impatiently, for human subjects stirred him less, I was beginning to realise, than emblems of the disarray in his own life.

I steered him towards the Family Hotel, where I abandoned him and went in search of food and water. When I came back I found him lying prone on the bar, his camera aimed straight into the centre of the best-known mural, the drunken, naked Bacchus surrounded by a host of Outback maenads. Beside him were Liz and Peter, the owners of the hotel, with whom I had spent many hours talking on my previous visit – with whom, in fact, I felt I had forged the first links of a warm friendship. They were sitting together, providing Johnson with a curatorial overview. I lingered in the doorway, listening.

'Clifton Pugh painted this in one night, or that's what his wife said, in '65 or '66. Then after it was painted, he, his wife, and her boyfriend bought the pub, and he was the silent partner. He used to come up and paint across the road in a little shack,' said Liz.

'The locals reckon he was an arrogant bastard,' said Peter, with a certain satisfaction. 'In fact no one's ever said to me they liked him. He used to paint in the nude, you know.'

'He was probably a bit eccentric,' said Liz. 'And good on him – someone of Clifton Pugh's calibre who can do what they want is just what places like this need. After all, what would this hotel be without the paintings? Let's be honest – just another dingy Outback pub. You'd have to find some other way of distinguishing the bar, like the signatures at the hotel at Tilpa, or the ones they used to have at Noccundra before they cleaned it up. You'd think they would have cracked and peeled by now, these murals, but no: the only damage comes from human interaction, and there's not much of that.'

At last, I went up to the bar, put my hand on Johnson's shoulder, and interrupted this exchange. Peter looked at me and smiled in the open-ended way bush people use for visitors they can't quite place.

'You don't remember me?'

He shrugged.

'But I was here only a few months ago.'

'We get twenty thousand tourists a year.'

'I remember you,' said Liz, 'kind of. But we were overwhelmed by your charismatic friend.'

'My what?'

'He's had us in stitches.'

'He has? But he's supposed to be depressed and unhappy.'

'Unhappiness is no bar to a sense of humour,' Johnson said to me. 'And how exactly do you want the photograph to frame the picture?'

'I've got bad news for you: this isn't the mural I had in mind.'

'You don't mean the caricatures?' said Liz. 'Those silhouettes of the Menindee stockmen, or the Flying Doctor over there?'

'I meant the one next door.'

'True? The Dream?'

'Ever since I first saw it, it's stayed with me. There have been times when I wanted to drive all the way to Tibooburra just to have it once more in front of my eyes.'

'Better go on through then,' she said, 'and see how it holds up.'

There, almost at eye-level, was a fresco of a sand-coloured landscape, rectangular, white-bordered, much smaller than I remembered it. At its centre was a pale, schematic human figure, while the red stones of the desert were rising from the ground as if to claim it.

'That's the painting?' asked Johnson. 'And that's the title? I should have known: "Sturt's Dream, Our Destination." My God! It may be beautiful, but I hope that's not where we'll end up going. And don't expect me to take a picture of it either.'

'Why not?'

'There's nothing there – it's an image of nothingness.'

'But that's the point of it. It's Sturt in the desert, and his hopes evaporating, disappearing, passing into the air.'

'Face it,' said Johnson, with an edge of exasperation in his voice, 'he was a loser in the end, wasn't he? He staked everything on an idea, a fantasy, and when it refused to materialise he wouldn't give up. They had to drag him back into civilisation. He would have happily stayed out there with his men and died in the middle of nowhere. Strange kind of hero to choose.'

'I never said he was a hero. I said he was open, and he had a softness to him that was quite unusual for a man in his position, in his time. He came from hierarchy, and order, and he found himself out in this – and he had to describe it and make sense of it.'

'Which you said he didn't do particularly well.'

'He tried. Towards the end he wrote his journal almost as if it was a poem. And slowly the landscape took him over: he became himself more truly. He felt all the love and all the yearning that had escaped him in the world.'

'And it never occurs to you,' said Johnson, 'when you talk about him that way, that you just might be talking about yourself.'

I let this sentence of his, which had been pronounced with a harsh laugh, resonate a while inside me, and I stared at the mural, and the human form dissolving into the dunes and the gibber plains.

'That's not the kindest remark you've come up with so far on the journey,' I said, at last.

'I'm not trying to be unkind. I'm just beginning to wonder if you haven't got it all wrong. The Outback. The inland. You think you know it, but you don't. You make your week-long visits in your hired Landcruisers; you drive through, you write about it, but you always bring your theories and your ideas. You're looking at it with the eyes of your explorers. For you, it's a world of suffering, and exhaustion, and danger, and death, but for me, whenever I've been out in it, it's been alive, and bursting with life. All of it, western and Aboriginal, human and animal. Haven't you ever gone out across the sand-dunes in the early morning and seen them covered with tracks and prints and markings? Or been in some crowded bush hotel at night, or listened to the old-timers in a place like this, the doggers, the boundary-riders, the fifth-generation families? What I see round here is life. Life, survival, victory – against the odds!'

'You're certainly having a very frank exchange,' said Liz, who was standing in the doorway, smiling, arms folded.

'Oh, we believe in complete professional openness,' I said.

'Don't you want to hear about the mural at all?'

And then, in a soft voice, as I allowed the shockwaves of this little dispute to ripple over me, and wondered to myself how much truth there was on Johnson's side, Liz began to tell us the story of 'Sturt's Dream'.

The artist, a Dutchman, a man of moderate reputation in his own country, a specialist in near-abstract landscapes, had pulled into Tibooburra one evening two years earlier, together with his wife.

'They'd been out for weeks,' she said, waving her hands expansively. 'Weeks alone, beyond Innamincka, off the Birdsville Track, in the sandhills and the gibbers, and this was the hot time of the year, remember, like now, all heat hazes and purple distance. Those colours, and the desolation of the stony desert, and the ruins of the Aboriginal missions, had put them on some kind of edge. I felt almost sorry for them when they pitched up here. They saw the murals, and – well, you know how it is, this place either chimes with you or leaves you cold – and they were overwhelmed. They came up to us and said they wanted to paint a mural of their own. Peter was in a good mood; he said: "Go for it," and we came back in the morning, and there it was, almost finished. They stayed on for a few days. I was glad to have met them. They were one of the gifts of living here – and so is the painting, too. Not many people notice it, the way you did,' she shrugged, and a note of regret came into her voice. 'It doesn't seem to draw too much comment at all. But I think the artist felt it was his masterpiece, and he minds that it's so far away. He minds it very much. In fact he says he hasn't felt at home anywhere since he came out to the desert. He stays in touch, and sends us catalogues from time to time of his exhibitions in Europe. There's nothing in them like the Dream, though, I'd have to say – nothing at all. Sometimes, when I come in here at night, alone, after all the guests are in their motel units, and the last of the locals have gone, I can almost feel him here, beside me in the room, as if he's come back to look at his painting once again.'

We fell silent, all three of us, and this far-off figure seemed for a second to hover, fully present, at our side.

'Is it the way you remembered it?' asked Liz.

'More beautiful,' I said, in a whisper.

'It's Sturt's vision of the future, I always like to think. Perhaps, if it means so much to you, you should both drive out to the Glen, and have another look around, before you keep going north.'


But by mid-morning of the next day, as we headed onwards, it was clear the detour had not been a success. Only after several hours spent in pointed silence, as we drove through an unending sequence of sandhills and claypans, did Johnson deign to make his comment.

'For me,' he said, 'I have to tell you, that was fairly underwhelming.'

'The Depot? You surprise me. There I was, for the last hundred kilometres, thinking you'd been stunned into quiet, reflective historical awareness.'

'You didn't say anything in your advance build-up about the brand new stainless steel shearing-shed, or the homestead across the creek, or all the black drinking-water pipes, and storage-tanks, and heritage signs. Or, I notice, about the tag-along tour group, not to mention the Lightning Ridge opal-miners having their breakfast barbecue at Poole's grave.'

'So the mood's a little different these days. You could try to use your imagination. Anyway, it still has a kind of splendid desolateness. We were just unlucky. When I first went there there was no one, and it had the strongest atmosphere about it.'

'Tell me about it. No, seriously,' he went on, when I laughed off this suggestion, 'I'd like to hear. Can't you tell yet when I mean things? I know you think I'm hating every second of this journey, and it all means nothing to me, but that's not true. It's not true at all, in fact.'

'Johnson,' I said. 'Who'd have thought it?'

'You see, you're still not taking me seriously.'

And so, very cautiously, I began to tell him about my journey to the Glen, and my first ideas and pictures of the Captain, my intimations of his presence, like some shadow lurking in the map-lines of the Centre: how I used to come across his exploration trails drawn on the nineteenth-century charts of Australia: Australia in the days before there was a Northern Territory, when the outlines of Lake Eyre and Lake Torrens were still unknown. I could make out a line, snaking across the blankness, through the country we were crossing at that moment: Sturt's route, annotated with cursive legends: 'sandhills without limit', maybe, or 'samphire plains'. And though I had always been left cold by stories of heroic exploration, when I began my own attempt to find a way into the continent there was something about these precursors that spoke to me.

'What?' asked Johnson.

'But don't you see, if there was a simple answer to that question, they wouldn't speak. It's not just what you think it is, that they were romantic, or tragic, or literary, or all three in equal measure; or that they've fallen out of fashion now; or that all their traces are vanishing and fading, and that there's the pleasure of ruins about them. There doesn't have to be a reason for everything. Sometimes places or people can just be attractive. Anyhow, when I first drove up to Tibooburra, along the same route we took, through Fowlers Gap, and past the Barrier Range, I was only just beginning to be interested by Sturt. I hadn't read him: all I knew was the standard line, that he was incompetent, and comical, and that he and his men were marooned, out in the Corner Country, for months on end. I was passing Milparinka – the road was much better in those days – and I saw the turn-off marked to Depot Glen. I drove in, very slowly, watching the heat-haze on the horizon, and by the time I reached the Depot it was almost the middle of the day, with not a soul around. Of course it would have been best if you'd seen it like that: the desert's always different when you're there alone. I left the car, and walked along the riverbed, beneath the gum-trees, until I found the Glen. I followed it up past where we went, to the rocky bar, and back. It made a strong impression on me: it had the kind of silence I associate with battlefields, the silence of places that have seen things. There was a pair of wedge-tailed eagles nesting in one of the old trees on the far bank, and one of them kept flying above me, circling so low I could hear the sound of its wings. At first, the things I noticed there were the small details: driftwood wedged in tree-forks; the smell of the white-gum bark; the patterns in the sand from kangaroo-tails. Everything seemed peaceful. I lay down on the sand, stretched out, and I watched the clouds moving through the canopy of the trees for a long time. After a while I felt the mood of the landscape beginning to change: suddenly, the branches above me seemed low, the rock-face on the far bank was confining.'

'A prison, instead of an oasis?'

'A prison, if you like. Or a place in which one could be remade. I stayed, lying there, maybe for half an hour, listening, in the silence, and I had the sense that I was, quite deliberately, conducting an experiment with myself.'

'Go on.'

'It's not easy to describe,' I said. 'I haven't tried to tell anyone this before.'

'Some revelation?'

'No, but it was so quiet there, so still, that I could hear distinctly something I had never heard before; something I imagine we aren't supposed to hear.'

'But what?'

'I can only tell you what I think it was. The sound of the self, the sound of my own consciousness. I could hear a low, soft noise, like a wave, whispered, constant, impossibly far away. And I stayed listening to it for a long while. It was only with great difficulty that I was able to break its spell. I lifted myself up from the sand, and I knew it would be dangerous to lie down there again.'

'Extreme! Metaphysical! Weird scenes in the backlands!'

'Johnson,' I said, reprovingly, but as I turned to look across at him, I noticed that his eyes had filled with tears.

'It's nothing,' he murmured as we swept round a sharp corner, down into a red plain, its edges picked out by stunted trees. 'And when do we reach the stony desert, anyway?' he demanded.

As if on cue, the landscape began to change. The dunes, which had been a pale, bleached-out pink, took on a deep red blush. Their angles sharpened. The claypans and the mulga thinned and fell away. Ahead of us, in a tree-lined valley, lay a homestead, an airstrip, a scatter of bungalows, stockyards, iron tanks.

'That must be Merty Merty station,' said Johnson, staring at the map. 'What a name! And from here, we go on to . . . to . . . Strzlecki Creek.'

'It's Strzelecki, actually,' I corrected him. 'He was an explorer too. It's one of the odd mysteries of Australia that everyone insists on mispronouncing the name.'

'And who was he?'

'He was Polish, in fact. A geologist. One of those half-fake noble-men who fetched up in Sydney in its early days: a charmer, and a gold-finder, and mountaineer. When Sturt hit a flowing creek, on his great push north beyond the Depot, for some reason he named it for Strzelecki. Maybe he had a soft spot for Polish officers, from his days in the Napoleonic wars. You see that high red sandridge? It's mentioned in the journal. It's going to run with us north-west from now on, past the gas-fields, past Innamincka, and Cordillo, all the way to Moonda Lake and Birdsville.'

'God – Birdsville,' sighed Johnson. 'Always Birdsville. The way you pronounce the name, you'd think it was some place of pilgrimage.'


And in this at least, my fellow-traveller was right: we were on a pil-grimage, one whose earliest moments I could still recall from the seamless days of childhood, when my eyes first fell on an impressive-looking hardback, slip-cased, guarded by glass panes in a tall cabinet. *The Dead Heart of Australia* seemed to me then like some magic adventure-book, though the concerns of its author, a Scots professor named John Walter Gregory, were, at least on the face of things, geological.

He set off, well-equipped for survey work, on a northward expedition in late December 1901, at the head of a string of camels, and led his team of students straight across the Lake Eyre Basin, the Diamantina Valley and the Tirari Desert. Gregory's account of their mission, originally composed as a series of letters to the Melbourne *Age*, has many peculiarities, but none were quite as immediately appealing to me, at least at that point in life, as his preface, in which he retells the Dieri creation story of the Kadimakara.

These 'strange monsters', as he explains, were the first inhabitants of Central Australia, which was once a fertile tableland, cloud-covered, well watered, while the heavens above it rested upon the trunks of tall gum-trees. The Kadimakara lived amidst the forest branches, but were tempted by the lush foods of the lower world. Here they were marooned by the progressive destruction of the tree-cover – and their large bones can still be found today across the bed of Cooper's Creek. This legend, which was much discussed at the time of the expedition, for the skeletons of giant marsupials and birds had only recently been found on the banks of Lake Callabonna, provoked alarming reflections in Gregory's mind: '*The assertions made to us as to the fatal fury of the heat, the delicacy of the fragile camel, and the appalling scarcity of water, as well as the warnings to beware the fate of some early explorers in the Lake Eyre basin, suggested a fresh explanation of the Kadimakara legend: might it not be an allegory on the experiences of Sturt*' – whose sufferings, as Gregory remembered, were so extreme that when the first word of them reached Adelaide, and

Charlotte Christiana read her husband's letter-journal, her long brown hair was instantly turned to white.

The geologists enjoyed a smoother passage, in part because of their reliance on the help of Aboriginal companions. Even the bleakest country caught their eye: still sand-dunes, with wind-waves carved into their sides, reminded Gregory of the fossil-ripples one might see on London paving-stones. Timbered landscape along the desert watercourses brought East Africa to mind. But the most striking section of his narrative is a brief intermezzo in which Gregory recalls his own boyish yearning for bare wilderness: '*The world never feels so wide and so unfettered as in the desert, with its low horizon, its long, open curves, and its unequalled expanse of sky.*'

This feeling is elusive, for the desert has a way of disguising itself as an enemy that must be fought: '*Its distances are vast, and they have to be wearily traversed; its heat is intense, and it has to be patiently endured; its secret water-holes have to be traced by the few faint clues, which even the subtle ingenuity of Nature has not been able to conceal.*'

It is only at night, when hidden from us, that the desert comes into its own, when the explorer no longer struggles with his difficulties, but rests in peace and feels at one with his surroundings: '*The air is cool and bracing; the low, brown hills that looked so near, but are so far, can no longer mock, or the mirage tantalise.*'

Silence descends, a silence so pure it brings higher understanding: '*At length, the camels grow quiet or wander out of hearing, the embers are cold, even the last prowling dingo has gone to its lair, and there is nothing to break the absolute quiet but the steady, audible thump of one's own heart. The camp is wrapped in a silence that appears to have crept down with the stars, and is more delicious than the sweetest music.*'

And at this point, almost in a whisper, Gregory introduces his elemental theme, the theme that runs through all the stories of the Centre, and that we have barely succeeded in hiding from ourselves today: '*Feeling so close to the stars and so intimate with them, enjoying the glory of the solitude and silence, even the idea of death in the desert loses its horrors. The passage from the strenuous struggle of the day, with the garish, glaring sunlight, to the full peace and soft beauty of the darkness seems emblematic of the passage from life to death. No other conditions present death in a more attractive guise. Nowhere else can the joy of rest be more truly appreciated and the beauty of darkness be more fully realised.'*

Gregory proceeds to quote the German romantic, Jean-Paul, who was half in love with extinction all his life, as a suitable authority, for Jean-Paul viewed death's darkness as a phenomenon rather like the twilight, making all objects seem more beautiful to those in its grip.

*'As we keep our watch in the desert-camp,'* Gregory resumes, by now wholly in the spirit of the first explorers; his world has become a photographic negative of life, and love, and movement, *'we seem to have half crossed the threshold of the star zone, and we feel an irresistible attraction towards the better rest and fuller silence of the long, desert journey, that lies before us all.'*

Five years elapsed between the end of the expedition and the appearance in London of Gregory's book, which received polite reviews before sinking into oblivion. Something in the text had plainly struck the publisher, John Murray: unusual effort was expended on the presentation of the volume. It was bound in ochre cloth; its pages were as white as ivory, its words were interspersed with haunting photographs. On the front cover was an image, inset, valentine-shaped, of desert sand-grains, edged by a line of gold, and though this book has been recreated since in facsimile, the copy lacks the feel of the original, which one may still encounter from time to time behind the panes of rare-book cabinets.

Gregory led to his precursor, Sturt. Sturt, though, to whom; or where? As I was making my first attempts to read my way into the desert, and build myself a route along the Captain's footsteps, the words and the emotions of twentieth-century travellers seemed far less present to me than Sturt's recollections, scratched out by night in the stillness of the Depot. This view of mine had almost hardened into a conviction when I came across the name of a young British ecologist, Francis Ratcliffe, who had been dispatched in the mid thirties to the arid, dust-blown terrain round Birdsville, a town he both loved and loathed.

From the back country he drove through, the dead triangle between the Simpson, the Channel Country and Lake Eyre, Ratcliffe wrote long letters home, letters so intense in their sweep and detail that they form, almost unedited, the text of his *Flying Fox and Drifting Sand*, an evocation of the Australian landscape, published in Britain in 1938, which became a guide and companion to me, though it has long since been forgotten by the wider world.

'*It is essentially a collection of observations, impressions, and reminiscences, on the whole more subjective and trivial than scientific and serious,*' Ratcliffe wrote in the preface to the Australian edition, which appeared only in 1947, when the passage of time and war had changed his portraits of the sand-dunes and the lonely, decaying homesteads into little cameos.

Ratcliffe formed a dark impression of the Centre. His first journey up the Track, from Marree through the channels of the Cooper, to Goyder's Lagoon and Clifton Hills, was enough to set him on edge: '*It was some time before the empty vastness of the land was brought home to me in full force. For several hours the flatness combined with the sandhills to limit the view. I remember the moment of realisation well, for something like a shiver ran down my spine as I took it in – the first real sweeping view, which opened up around us as we passed over the top of a scarcely perceptible rise. I shall not try to describe it, for I should certainly fail.*'

Indeed, for all his joy in recording nature, Ratcliffe never seeks to catch the desert landscape. Instead he gives that landscape's effect on him, which was unsettling in the extreme. At this first encounter with the desert, he felt he was looking 'round the bend of the earth', into shimmering emptiness: '*It was hard to grasp that the distance we could see, which looked so very distant, was but a mere step along the road we had to travel.*'

He tried to imagine the scene without its coat of grassy spinifex, when the film of green had given way to blinding, uninterrupted glare: '*Even with this green I thought it was just about the cruellest and most inhuman world that it was possible to conceive. Little did I guess that within the next day or two I was to be introduced to worlds still more desolate and terrifying. I was uncomfortable and nervous now: later I was to be really scared – scared that something in my mind would crack, that the last shreds of my self-control would snap and leave me raving mad.*'

As to the nature of this emotional crisis, Ratcliffe is less than clear, although it was bound up with his passage through the Cooper's and Diamantina's flood plains, and his experiences in the empty wastes and ranges south of Birdsville. In his narrative he provides at least a surface reason for the fear the Cooper inspired in him, when he and his fellow-travellers dropped down towards the river's main channel, at three-quarter light, with the western sky glowing a luminous green: '*The dry bed of that dead river, which rose in the plains of inland Queensland, and vanished in the salt-pans of Lake Eyre without knowing the sea, was the most eerie and haunted spot I have ever visited. Moreover, it was haunted by no friendly and comprehensible ghosts, but by the spirits of broken tribes which died misunderstood.*'

North of the river, matters only worsened, with the stony desert unfurling itself before him, until '*the world became little more than a rolling shingly plain, the lumpy red-brown sterility of which accentuated the empty blueness of the sky*'.

Ratcliffe eventually surrendered himself to the grip of nightmare.

This, he decided, was a region more awe-inspiring and desolate than any sand-dune desert could be, and as the car drove on, *'through great sweeping slopes quite terrible in their barrenness'*, he often had to shut his eyes against the *'unnatural'* landscape.

For a man of science, a product of the modern 'renascence in general biology', these were strong reactions. They conjure up the words Sturt chose to fix the image of the desert that now bears his name, and this itself gives a clue to the notions passing through Ratcliffe's mind. At the time of these forays into the Centre he was in his early thirties, he was about to marry and begin a settled life. The broader world was on the brink of conflagration, and the shadow of that future reached across him, like a dune of darkness.

For Ratcliffe, much like Sturt, had read himself into the landscape, and saw his own fears and longings reflected back to him. So much in fact did he read there that he seems at times almost to be absorbing the Captain's thoughts, as if they had been left like some mineral deposit upon the sandhills and the stones. It was not, then, or not only the vision of a cruel, inhuman world that brought him to the edge of breakdown. Ratcliffe saw, in the iron-shod plains, something darker still, which Sturt also glimpsed and shied away from, and which has left its ghost in the opening to the second section of *Flying Fox and Drifting Sand*.

Here Ratcliffe recounts the words of advice he was given when he headed for the inland, for that tortured landscape of broken hills, red and brown and yellow: *'It is terrible country you are going into. You will be glad to escape from it; but it will get you, and ever after you will find yourself longing to go back.'*

Longing to go back, because he was receptive to nature, and because the land had its grievous splendour, and he could trace the chains of biological cause and effect all through its constantly repeated terrain? Or for quite another kind of reason: because he had looked into that empire of formlessness, and death, and found it beautiful, and fallen half in love with it? Because oblivion, and stillness, and silence were calling out to him?

## III

With such a companion in the forefront of my mind, it was no surprise to me that, when at last we drove into Birdsville, in late afternoon, after a journey passed in near-complete silence, I was in a state of agitation and barely able to take in the buildings, the sand-hills on the far horizon, or the dust-laden sky in which storm-clouds could be made out, floating high above us, trailing rain-veils, pink-stained, their shapes and colours shifting, so that it seemed almost as if we were staring upwards from the ocean's floor at a parade of tentacled sea-monsters in constant, sinuous motion.

'Not much here, is there?' said Johnson, in his most annoying manner.

He made two full circuits of the township, gazing round, raising his camera for brief viewfinder examinations as he drove: a water-tower; a museum; a service station; a block or two of houses.

'You don't think so? It's got a kind of beauty. It's almost the way I imagined it. In fact, I feel like I've been travelling towards this place all my life.'

'But that's you,' he said, caustically. 'I have to deal with what actually exists in front of our eyes.'

He pulled up outside the hotel, and stared along its verandah appraisingly.

'This has been before everybody's eyes already,' I said. 'In fact, it's probably the most photographed building in all Outback Australia.'

'Yes, but the artist always tries for something new.'

We went indoors. The main bar, a side bar and dining room were all deserted. Each had the disquieting look of places recently abandoned: half-drunk glasses on the tables, a television blaring in the corner, cigarette smoke in the air. We searched the hotel's corridors and store-rooms for several minutes, glancing anxiously at each other, until Johnson raised a hand. I followed as he wound his way towards a row of motel units, from which we could now hear the sound of voices arguing. We rounded the corner. A man was sitting at a table, hunched over an aviation chart, the last rays of the sunset bathing his face. At his side, leaning over his shoulder, was a large woman, who glowered at us.

'Who are you?' said Johnson with a desperate urgency.

'Aha!' said the man. 'That depends.'

'Are you from the hotel?'

'I think you'll find they've all gone down to the Diamantina waterhole for the New Year three-legged race.'

'But not you?' continued Johnson, sounding relieved.

'No, I'm a publisher,' replied the man, as if this explained everything. 'I'm flying across the Simpson Desert. My co-pilot' – he gestured towards his companion, who shrugged, rolled her eyes, and stormed into the motel room behind them, slamming the door. 'We're having a little disagreement about the route.'

'What kind of books do you publish?' asked Johnson, sitting down. 'Anything photographic?'

'Well,' said the man. 'Where to begin? I run a healing meditation course, called "The Way of the New Millennium." And we put out the *Golden Age* magazine in Adelaide. Perhaps you've heard of it?'

'No, but I'd like to,' said Johnson, who seemed to be slipping into the rhythm of this exchange. 'In fact, I'm from near Adelaide myself.'

At which point a battered Hilux drove into the courtyard, and pulled up in front us. A woman, blonde, with striking features, leaned out of the cab window: 'You were looking for me?'

'We were?'

'Nikki'll help you out,' declared the publisher. 'She's looking after the hotel. And she's a healer too, like everyone round here.'

'A writer, and actor, and blues singer, primarily,' said the woman in the Hilux. 'But I do work with shamanic energies as well. Why? Problems? Jump in, anyway.'

I rode round with her to the front of the hotel, explaining our project and the progress we had made.

'And you stopped at Cordillo, and at Moomba?' she said, sounding incredulous. 'For the desert, and explorers, this is the only place to be.'

She waved a hand as she led the way indoors. The front saloon, as though by some magic of hers, had filled with a bush crowd: managers from the outlying stations, bar-hands and worn-faced ringers, Aboriginal women balancing their children in their arms. Over the next few hours, in the hotel's back dining-room, as the noise of celebrations echoed round us, Nikki told me something of her trajectory through life, and her connection to the town.

She was the sister of the hotel's owner, Kym. She had first come to Birdsville almost twenty years before, shortly after a syndicate of partners bought the building, which was at that point nothing but a burned-out shell, with wild dogs in the outhouses, and a western taipan nesting in the kitchen stove. Together with her sister, she ran the business during the early stages of its resurrection. Tales are still told across the Channel Country about those days, when Amazons were in charge at the Outback's wildest hotel. At last she took the decision to move back to Adelaide, and was torn at once by vivid dreams, in which she found herself retreating to the desert. Two months after her departure, there came a turning point. She was hospitalised with acute liver damage and told she had no more than five months to live. That sentence made her look closely at her life. At this point in her story Nikki raised her hands, as though they were the scales of a balance, and moved them slightly to indicate the decision she had faced. It was only at this moment that she had begun to edge towards the spiritual domain.

'I began the work, which I would find hard to explain to you, that allowed me to heal myself.'

Some days went by after this conversation. Johnson and I busied ourselves with our journalistic tasks. We found our way round Birdsville. The low-slung houses, and their occupants, began almost to seem familiar. Then, early one evening, just as we were planning the next stage of our mission, I was handed a note by one of the bar staff.

'Your trip to desert all arranged!' it said, in neat capitals. 'Departure tomorrow morning.'

After a brief search, I came on Nikki in the hotel's front room, gazing out at cloud patterns in the western sky.

'Of course,' she said to me with a cryptic smile, 'you have to go out into the Simpson. I couldn't let you just drive on to Bedourie or back down south. In fact, that's really where we should be talking now. On the crest of a high dune, maybe, with the light shifting on the gibbers, and the wind blowing sand-grains into the air. Then what I'm saying might seem to make at least a little sense. But there are some things you have to understand first.'

'That it's a magic place?'

'That it has a way of throwing back at you every effort you make, every single thing you do. I felt drawn out here from the very outset, and I thought it was because I could sense its splendour. But that's just the entrance ticket. The desert delights in levelling and stripping us down to the bone. If you have fears when you come out here, those fears will be reflected back to you. When I first felt the pull of the landscape, it was on the simplest level, without understanding what it was, and only long days and nights spent out here have helped me to some beginnings of intuition.'

She took my hand. 'I wish I could even begin to heal you.'

'Do you?'

'But don't you understand,' she replied, smiling, 'that that's why you're here?'

'Really?'

'Yes. You've been in the world, and now something's driving you out here. No one comes to Birdsville in these months without a reason.'

'But we came to trace the path of Sturt's journey.'

'Exactly. And what was he doing here? The desert's a mirror: this funny little town has a lot more going for it than just the race weekend and the pub. Why do you think the explorers were drawn along these particular dune-corridors? There are ley-lines out here. There are energy-grids. You go and talk to those gnarly old ringers. They'll tell you the same thing. You go up to the bar, and ask Frankie Booth, and Jimmy Evans. You can't live and work out here and not know. If you sit here, with the wind blowing and the sun beating down, and you close your eyes and listen, you can feel the desert's heart beat. And that,' she said, folding her arms, 'will bring you happiness – and transformation, too.'

She got up.

'I think you'll like your guides.'

'Who are they?'

'You'll find out soon enough. And you should listen to them. They're real desert people.'

'You mean they're Aboriginal?'

'Not exactly,' she said, and she retreated through the kitchen's double doorway, laughing as she went.

Desert people, I whispered to myself. The desert. I remained at that table for several minutes, staring out, conscious that every dream of mine had been absorbed into those words.

I waited, watching the sun's descent towards the dune-fields, and the clouds. Only when its beams were flooding through the windows did it occur to me to take a farewell walk through the town. I went outdoors, and made my way along the main street, pursuing my own shadow eastwards, and possessed by a desire to return, as soon as possible, and live there, amidst that emptiness, in a place I scarcely knew at all.

I had reached as far as the Diamantina crossing and the waters of the flood-channel by the time the twilight was done. After some minutes there, listening to the wind rising and falling, I began to retrace my steps, looking back towards the town, which seemed at that moment almost crushed by the overhanging bowl of stars and sky. At last I found a short-cut along the river, a rough track leading beside the caravan park and a block of new-built houses, then veering round towards the airstrip, and the low shape of the hotel, that home, for me, all through our stay, of dreams. And despite its reputation as a place of revelry, it seems to have played this role in the dreams of another of its inmates, the explorer Cecil Madigan, our last precursor, who was often on my mind during those days.

Madigan was an individual of great intellect and will. He was a Rhodes scholar at Magdalen College. He travelled, when only twenty-one, as meteorologist on Douglas Mawson's Australasian Antarctic Expedition. In the Great War he served as a Captain in the Royal Engineers, then worked in the Sudan for a decade as Assistant Government Geologist, before at last discovering the Centre. His fondness for this world was as much dictated by its beauty, and the depth of its past, as by its scientific promise.

*'The dominant characteristics of natural Australian scenery,'* he wrote at the outset of his career, *'are greyness, age, loneliness, stillness, and, above all, peace. Rome, Greece, Egypt, Babylon, are of yesterday compared with the age-long sameness of our great silent continent. The turmoil of history has passed this land by. Before ever*

*the mushroom growth of the human race had sprung up, countless millions of suns had arisen, shone upon the great desert disk of the interior, just as it is today, and sunk in a blaze of red.'*

His campaign to penetrate the desert began in 1929, when he carried out the first programme of aerial photographic survey undertaken in Australia. Flying west from Birdsville, he found a bleak monotony: *'There were no ranges hidden behind the sandridge ramparts, no water, nothing to record from the air but some slight changes in the relative sparseness of the vegetation. The whole expanse below was like a pink and gigantic circular gridiron, ribbed with close sandridges from horizon to horizon.'*

Knowledge, though, could not remove the desire in him for experience, and there was an urgency about this need in Madigan which communicated itself to others. A decade after his desert overflights, he secured support for a full-scale ground expedition from his friend Allen Simpson, a prominent industrialist and keen ornithologist, after whom, in a prudent stroke, Madigan had already named the desert. Setting out from Andado station at the head of a scientific party, he crossed from west to east, with nineteen camels, in the cool season of 1939, a year of unusual rains. The journey is described in his *Crossing the Dead Heart*, which, like most accounts of Central Australian voyaging, is as much self-portrait as record of travel and topography. Though the tale is genial and full of incidental wit and detail, a tone of stillness, of internal silence, comes strongly through. Cold weather swag management, the structure and the vegetation of sand-dunes, wild yams and their fibrous flavour: Madigan seeks to catch the everyday, but his mind drifts constantly elsewhere, to the vanished stories of his Aboriginal precursors, to the traces of abandoned pastoral ventures, to the expedition's sponsor, who was dying in a hospital in Adelaide, and to whom a cheerful private message was dispatched by radio: 'All going well. Natural history collections mounting. Beautiful

coloured desert wrens and finches, some probably new.' A good
selection of these rare creatures, fairy wrens, perhaps, or emu-wrens
or orange chats, had been shot by the expedition's field biologist two
days earlier when rainfall delayed their progress at a camp-site eastward of the Hale.

Throughout this mid-stage of the journey, up and down the sand-
dunes, Madigan was in his scientific element, but as the destination
neared his mood began to shift. He describes the scene he saw upon
the Mulligan, when the rabbit-proof fence, or its remains, like the
defence-wall of some ruined empire, came looming into view.

It is dusk, and traps and poison carts lie about. The word-portrait
he gives has an odd resemblance to photos from the early days of
Antarctic exploration, which show great, icebound ships bathed in
ghostly light: '*The country was bare and undulating, with broad
rounded sandridges and little live sand. We crossed several claypans, glaring white in the moonlight. This last two hours seemed very long. The
moonlight gave a rigidity and unreality to the scene, and seemed to inten-
sify the silence. The country became flatter, with dry swamps in which
stood scattered and dead box gums stretching upward their bleached and
ghostly limbs. Complete silence fell upon the party.*' It descended, too,
on Madigan, for the 'glamour' of his adventure was dying, the task
was done.

'*Perhaps,*' he mused, '*this was the last of the hard journeys I had
started out upon so hopefully twenty-eight years before, to end them
in this desert place. For some of the young men in the party it was
the first real living they had known, but they had all before them.
Would I ever be out on the trail again?*'

The camel team marched on. Rain poured down. The expedition
was briefly stranded on the edge of salt-bush country, close by the
deserted homestead of Annandale. What else to do but play cards,
and read aloud from a handy text of Shakespeare's *Henry IV*, and
discuss the malign effect of brolgas and frogs upon the climate?

In the last pull, Madigan's thoughts were scattered. He devoured an emu-egg omelette, and felt uncomfortable on seeing signs of young bird amidst the golden puree in his bowl, '*though why these signs of change should so put one off does not bear analysis, as it is all in the egg anyway.*'

Beyond Listore Creek, the sand-dunes changed their colour, turning a washed yellow, depriving his eyes of the flame-like desert red, the same iron oxide glow, he noted, that lends the blush of rouge to women's cheeks. Only when their goal appeared in view did his spirits lift: '*There before us lay the gibber plains of Birdsville, with the few scattered tin houses shining white not half a mile away. This bare and wretched little town, the most remote in Australia, was a beautiful sight. It looked better to me than a city with dreaming spires.*'

Town and expedition, after the briefest greeting ceremonies, headed for the bar of the hotel, and drank toasts: to Mr Simpson, to themselves, and to the desert, until it became uncertain precisely what toast was being drunk. Madigan, after a short presence, withdrew, his thoughts, as he recollects, filled with memories of Antarctic and Sudanese journeys, for '*unlike my friends in the bar, I have never been able, often to my regret, to throw off dull care and become thoroughly hilarious and hearty on a joyful occasion.*'

He turned his mind to this problem and I have often pictured him as he must have been, all through that night's empty hours, pacing in some back room of the hotel. There he is, the last explorer, his windswept, hawk-like face frowning as he looks within and sees the desert: past time, in its bleak array, and the future close ahead, for World War II was looming, the time for science and exploration was fading. Madigan himself would soon be dead of heart disease, a tradition died with him, and it is a curiosity that, for all his searching and surveying, not a single feature of the Simpson bears his name.

———

The next morning, at the appointed hour, Johnson and I were packed and ready and eager to set off with our unknown guides. No one came. In part to break this spell, I went into the back dining-room and started to inspect the paintings hung along the walls. Each depicted a desert scene: dune-crests, dry riverbeds, their courses lined by coolibahs; windmills; the ironwork fences of abandoned stockyards.

I paced up and down, conscious of the silence in the hotel, the cool of the room and the heat outdoors. A pair of Japanese motor-cyclists, who had formed the idea that they might be able to cross the Simpson in high summer, and had only been dissuaded from this suicidal plan by the combined efforts of the hotel's staff, the Birdsville police and the national park rangers, were lounging behind me, gazing in desultory fashion at maps of the landscape they would never see. After some minutes, I heard a voice, soft, distinctly accented, at my shoulder.

'Do you like them?' it asked, in a whisper.

I turned around. Beside me was a man, tall, rangy, wearing the most exiguous scraps of clothing: khaki shorts, a rough bush shirt, its neck ragged, its sleeves hacked off at the shoulders. The individual revealed, rather than concealed, by this attire had a soft face, long black hair and beard.

'I am the artist,' he said, his voice swelling with a note of nervous pride, and, as though to introduce himself, he pointed to the stylised squiggle in the corner of the work I was examining.

'Dieter Jahn,' I said, uncertainly, and my companion beamed.

'You're one of the only people who's been able to decipher my signature.'

'I'm not surprised,' I said. 'And what does the painting show?'

He looked a touch disappointed.

'But it's the creek-line at Annandale. Didn't Nikki tell you? That's where we're going.'

'She wasn't very specific. In fact, she didn't tell us anything at all.'

'That's her way. But she told me about your expedition: Broken Hill and Tibooburra; Sturt and Browne; salt lakes and gibber plains. I hope we can show you what you want to see. It's beautiful country we'll be travelling through. I've been looking forward to this trip a great deal.'

'Then you knew about it before we did.'

'That's not unusual here,' said Dieter. 'In fact I've been waiting to talk to you for days.'

At that point, a young woman, with a face of medieval reserve and delicacy, came towards us, slipped her arm through Dieter's, and allowed a smile to radiate in my direction.

'My wife,' he murmured, with the air of a man almost unable to believe the extent of his good fortune. 'Katherine.'

An hour or so later we drove out westwards through the bleached landscape, our Landcruiser tagging behind the Jahns' mud-stained troop-carrier, while over the UHF radio Johnson had procured for this adventure Dieter began telling us how he first came to Birdsville.

Even narrated in more conventional fashion, it would have made a striking story. Under those circumstances, with Dieter's voice crackling over the radio speaker as we raced along behind his twisting dust-plume, deep into silent country, where pink sand-ridges rose like battlements on either side of us, I remembered scenes from a film that once had seemed to me the only work of art worth taking into oneself: Cocteau's *Orphée*, a bleak fable made during the years of war-time, in which the hero receives mysterious signals, transmitted by radio, and these, he soon discovers, are tidings from the world of death. With this comparison dawning on me, I too leaned over the radio receiver, listening, intent, as Dieter's words came crackling through.

'I was a successful designer,' he began, 'in Sydney, in the world of fashion and textile collections for many years, and that life was full of excitement and rewards and the veneer of success. In those days I felt I was fulfilling myself, and living, even, to some limit. But now, after some time in my new world here, it seems to me that high-powered business life was the epitome of falseness, of fooling yourself and fooling everybody else in the process. I lived happily and deeply involved in that world for a quarter-century, and all its beliefs were circulating in my blood. I used truly to believe that when I designed a new collection it was an event of the greatest importance, that the world around me should be holding its breath. But at the same time there was a nagging sense inside me that all this was nothing, that all the people I was dealing with were con-men, and they themselves understood that, and I was the only one who hadn't quite caught on – and you know, I was on the right track, although I'm a slow learner. It took me decades to work things out, and I had only one ally. I'd always loved the Australian landscape, and that was the thing that rescued me. When I first came to this country, in some corner of my mind I'd planned to stay only for a couple of years and then move on, but I began to go on journeys by myself through the interior; I travelled into northern New South Wales, to Walgett; I went digging for opals in Lightning Ridge – and gradually I fell in love. With the space, above all. At last, when I was at the peak of things, a fault-line opened in my city life. I sold my business. I moved, I cleared everything out. Almost at the same time I found my way out here. I had an exhibition of paintings in the gallery at Delmore Downs.'

'And are we going anywhere near there?' broke in Johnson at that point.

'But no,' came back Dieter's voice, in some surprise. 'We've gone in the opposite direction: that's the bed of Eyre Creek along-side us. We're coming up to the waterhole, and the ruins of

Annandale station, our little oasis in the desert. You wanted to see Sturt's country – sandhills, salt-pans, emptiness – and here it is.'

We set up camp at the Jahns' favourite spot, close by the remains of the homestead, beneath tall gum-trees, almost on the bank of the wide sheet of water. The heat had vanished from the air; the sun was low. After some minutes Dieter and I picked our way along the edge of the stockyard, towards a sand-dune where, as he told me, he liked to sketch the landscape as night fell. I listened to the noises all around us: wind-gusts in the coolibahs, the scold of zebra finches, the creak of ancient fence posts. Only after a lengthy silence did he begin speaking, and, almost without my prompting, he fell into the subjects that were on the surface of my mind.

'There's a softness to the light this evening,' he murmured. 'It's a good time for us to have come. Do you see, on the other side of the waterhole, over there, you can find traces of the old Aboriginal people: flints and grinding-stones. When I first began visiting this spot I sometimes used to take a few, and spend a short while with them, then put them back again. At first I would take them to Sydney, but now I don't collect anything any more. You find relics all along the creek-bed, signs of human endeavour: bones, and weapon-points. It's a hard land.'

'It looks beautiful,' I said.

'Now – yes – in these balmy temperatures. But it can give you a false sense of security. Look at the homestead: how the people living here must have suffered. This is a good example of man's attempts to conquer nature, and nature drawing the boundaries. You're much closer to death out here than in the city; you can feel it bending humanity to its will.'

He sighed, and continued sketching.

'I've always been very close to nature: from my childhood onwards.'

'In Germany?'

'Of course: I came from the East; from a region that was very heavily wooded. When I was a little boy, we went for long walks in the forests. We collected berries in the autumn, and wild mushrooms, too: I miss those walks, those little journeys, to this day. But for us everything was shattered almost from the very beginning.'

Dieter had been a young child in the years of World War II. He told me something of his experiences then: how he had travelled for six months, together with his mother, on the roads of Silesia, westwards towards the Bavarian mountains, constantly under fire, constantly coming across the bodies of civilians, torn shapes, decayed or mutilated, until he would wake each morning afraid the sleeping figures round him might not stir.

After their flight from the eastern front they made their way through unknown country towards the coastline, through air-raid zones, and battlefields, and emptied towns. They reached Bremerhaven, and pushed on as far as the Dutch border, which they crossed almost as the unconditional surrender was being signed.

'I am here in some way because of the War,' he said softly. 'It developed in me a keen sense of the futility of conflict. We saw Germany occupied, divided. Those were the years of pressure, as, looking back, I see them now. I had no hopes. For others, it was the time of beliefs: ideology, revolution, all those things that madden men's minds. Once I had grown up myself, in 1959, at the height of the Cold War, I was enlisted into the Army. I was at a crossroads. I realised I had become a foreigner inside my own country. But by chance, at that time I had already formed an idea in my imagination about Australia. I had read a book called *Flight into Hell*, by a wartime pilot who flew a Junkers and crashed on some secret mission in far northern Australia, and that fascinated me, the idea of a continent that seemed untouched. I made the arrangements: I arrived in Melbourne in 1960, by ship. Almost at once I began exploring the outdoors, hiking in the Snowys, diving in Sydney harbour. I was longing for this pure new country, but only after I came here, to the deserts, did I begin actually to find it.

'This world now is mine,' he said, leaning forward. 'Not the old continent of childhood, but here: the haze in the sky, the late light, when the contrast comes. The wind: if I could paint the wind, when it comes rushing through, or the landscape now, at dusk, when nature exhales. Perhaps all this seems to you a stupid, childish set of things to say, but when I come out here alone and walk out from this waterhole, over the bank, and out, I might as well be the first man who has gone there. I imagine that this feeling, this dream of being the first man on earth, is what drove the explorers on – and one of them, above all.'

'Sturt?'

'Absolutely. This is the landscape he described, and we are at his furthest north. But there is another of them, who is closer to me: far closer, for reasons you can imagine. When I first came here I heard the stories from the old stockmen who became friends of mine. They told me how when they were young they had found the Leichhardt party's camp sites, how they were sure he had passed through the Simpson – passed into it, I would rather say – as I would love to. And I know for certain that, in my expeditions and my wanderings, the time will come when I cross his pathway, like a golden thread across the sand-dunes, and I will find him there before I die.'

Dieter laughed, as if to show that some part of his nature, at least, did not take this declaration altogether seriously.

'That, for me,' he went on, 'is the truth about the desert. Here, in this country, where we are now, on the banks of Eyre Creek, is the centre of the Centre: the point where everything has found its balance, and all the explorers are at rest.'

After a while I left him, and walked up to the shell of the deserted homestead. The wind had died away. The birds were still.

In the sun's last reflected light, the sand-dunes had turned a washed-out ochre, the spinifex was purplish-grey. I ran my hands along the posts and brickwork of the outhouse. Glinting at my feet, all through the sand and cane-grass, were little chips of plates and dark-glass bottles. On the stone work-floor there was a pile of springs and rusted engine-parts. I bent down to touch them. How like the burnt, dead mulga stumps and branches they seemed in those moments, as though all difference between these two worlds had long since been effaced. And what were those shapes before me, at the station entrance-gate, like the ceremonial arches of some ancient tomb? Twisted blades from an old windmill, bent dray-wheel hoops of weathered iron – and in that instant, all the silhouettes and shadows round me, the chimneys and the outhouse walls, the creek-bank, the coolibahs, the dunes and grasses, seemed like the emblems of some distant kingdom, where I had been before, and where, in good time, I would walk again.

Late that night, after many hours talking with the others, I lay down in my swag, and watched the stars above me, and the lightning flashes from the storms on the horizon. Eventually I fell into a heavy, dream-laden sleep.

It was early in September 1845 when Sturt's party, after a month of mazy progress, came upon the Simpson's outlying dune-fields, which they tackled at first almost head-on, the horses picking their slow way among the tufts of spinifex. One morning, while still on the desert's margins, they struck a broad creek, high-banked, full of water: a creek Sturt named, with mixed feelings, after his brother explorer, Edward Eyre.

'No doubt,' he mused, 'it is an important feature in the country where it exists – and if the traveller happened fortunately to cross it at a favourable moment he would have every chance of success.'

But Eyre Creek, like its namesake, and his dream of the inland sea, was elusive: it turned from salt to sweet and back again; it led them on; it flowed then disappeared. Forward they pushed, along its twisting channel, down clay-pan corridors, attempting probes and traverses, eastward, westward, but at every turn they found themselves hemmed in by dunes or by dark, samphire-covered plains. As they advanced, Sturt stared guiltily across at his companion: '*It had pained me for some time to see Mr Browne daily suffering more and more, and although he continued to render me the most valuable assistance, a gloom hung over him; he seldom spoke, his hands were constantly behind him, pressing or supporting his back, and he appeared unfit to ride.*'

By this time, as Sturt well knew, the geographic centre lay almost in their reach, no more than a degree of latitude beyond them, and yet at last they had penetrated 'to a point at which water and feed had both failed'.

Could there be some hope, some faint sign of promise, something to save the expedition in the landscape that lay ahead? Together with Browne, the Captain climbed the highest crest in their vicinity, and from that vantage point the two men gazed out. Before them were tall sand-dunes, in numberless succession, receding one after another as far as the eye could see, the peak of each ridge flame-red, above deep, shaded blurs of sickly purple vegetation. They had come upon a sand-wave desert; a frozen sea.

'Good Heavens!' cried out Browne in horror. 'Did man ever see such country?'

And the Captain said nothing in reply, yet in his memoir he sets down his private thoughts, which were, if anything, more agonised: '*The scene was awfully fearful, dear Charlotte. A kind of dread (and I am not subject to such feelings) came into me as I gazed upon it.*'

Sturt had found his heart's desire: the sculpted ocean of the inland, the sight that he had dreamed of, and feared, and journeyed towards for half his life, and it looked to him in that instant 'like the entrance into Hell'. With these words in his mind, and the extinction of his hopes, and the fulfilment of all that he expected, he turned, and the shadow of his future swept over him: retreat; a decent fame; a long obscurity; provincial, impecunious death.

There is a well-known painting, by Ivor Hele, which depicts Sturt's renunciation in heroic mode. Haggard, yet self-possessed, he glares at the horizon, his face half in the shadow of his bush hat, his body limp yet full of worn defiance, while around him his men and horses droop in the last stages of exhaustion. But I had a different picture of Sturt in the desert as I lay in my swag that night: I saw him on the dune-crest, staring out, one hand shielding his eyes, and beside him stands the Doctor, thin and weak and torn by pain. So frail is he that when the Captain places a hand upon his companion's shoulder, as if to comfort him, the doctor flinches – and Sturt feels once more the despair and separation of all creatures in the mortal world. He looks at Browne, whose life he had toyed with sacrificing in a last wild drive to the Centre, and, for the first time in the journey, for the first time in all his life of looking, the Captain sees himself reflected in another's eyes.

Next morning, the decision made to retrace their steps, they were untethering their weary horses when an encounter took place: slight, momentary, scarcely worth attention at such a time, but it was one that struck the Captain greatly, as he records, for it seemed to him, in abrupt and mocking manner, to confirm the truth of all his imaginings. The sea, the secret water – how near it must have been, how veiled by fate from his poor eyes.

*'Just as we were about to mount,'* he writes, in the most collected of his several narratives, *'a flight of crested parroquets on rapid wing and with loud shrieks flew over us, coming directly from the north, and making for the creek to which we were going – and it was a singular occurrence, just at that moment, and so I regarded it,*

*for I had well nigh turned again. What would I not have given,'* he sighs, like a haunted man, in tones of deepest longing, *'what would I not have given for the powers of those swift wanderers of the air?'*

Before the dawn I woke from these dreams of him, refreshed for the first time in that journey, and almost free from cares. After some while watching the stars fade and light steal into the sky, I climbed from my canvas cocoon, went quietly down to the water's edge and looked out across Eyre Creek to the shadows opposite, where a few wading birds and pelicans had just begun to stir. The sun's rays touched the coolibahs. The light was soft. I swam out, and for what seemed like a lengthy interval floated there, drifting mid-way between the two banks, scarcely conscious of a single thought, until I became aware of a cloud, or trail of smoke, far away from me, almost at a bend in the waterhole. The light shone through it, its colours changed, it seemed somehow to twist and whirl, and as it came closer, I realised I was staring at a flight of dazzling pale-green, yellow-breasted birds – hundreds, thousands of them, budgerigars, swooping, darting near the water's surface. They split in two, they joined together, they danced in my direction – all this in a space of seconds as they hovered, coiling, close above me, their rush of wings came circling, scattering, like a breeze, a murmur – and at that moment, as they swept beyond me, a green wing-tip, in summons, grazed my cheek.

# Four     Strehlow

# I

It was the end of a long haul. I pulled off the Haast's Bluff Road, turned onto a short driveway, climbed from the Landcruiser and gazed around. Red stone ramparts, a sandy riverbed, a gorge, deep blue sky softening in the sunset – and there it was, a low-slung, pitch-roofed station house. Could this really be my destination? I pushed inside, and found myself at once bathed in a wash of reverberating sound: the blues, played so loud the plate-glass windows round me were shaking in their frames. I was standing at the mid-point of a long, bare set of rooms. To one end, before a bar, was a ramshackle table, round which was gathered a group of men, all of them of the most disquieting appearance. There were worn-faced ringers; there was a park ranger, head down on his arms, as though passed out; a pair of Aboriginal stockmen in dark glasses, drinking black tea and playing cards; a knot of bearded individuals in motorcycle leathers – and, at their centre, a tall figure with a proprietorial air about him, grey-haired, handsome, heavily tattooed. Everyone stared at me.

'Is this the new resort hotel?' I asked uneasily.

'No resort here, son. This is a homestead. Glen Helen homestead: capital of the blues.'

'And can I stay the night here?'

'If you're sad enough, if you've got the blues bad enough, and if you cross my palm with folding money we might let you roll out your swag on the verandah. I'll show you.'

The tattooed man led me to a broken, half-concreted belvedere, from which we could see the winding channel of the Finke River, the cliffs high above us turning fire-red, the blackness of the canyon-line beyond.

'Pretty special place, don't you reckon, the West MacDonnells?' said my companion. 'See – no resort. This is the station-house. They built this a hundred years ago. There's resorts at Yulara and Watarrka already – the old Centre's slowly dying. A lot of tough hard white men grew up here, but there's not many characters left now, fellows you'd just sit around and talk to all day. We're losing it, and that's what I don't want to happen here.'

'And you're the owner?'

'The owner! I'm the caretaker; unpaid, but full of freedom. I can do anything I like, except sell drugs. It's owned by Western Aranda Aboriginal groups, very anthropologically important people. I always thought about and dreamed about this part of the world when I went to school. You know, we did things on Lasseter, and he was a hero to me. I saw him in my mind's eye, the prospector who found a reef of gold.'

'So you weren't brought up in the Centre?'

We had wandered, by this time, as far as the river-bed, which was lined by pale-trunked red gums.

'Me? No. I went to school with Paul Hogan in Sydney's West.'

'Well of course,' I said. 'Now that you mention it, I can see the behavioural resemblance.'

'Don't you get cheeky with me, son! You're a long way from home! Those were rough days back then. Anyhow, the time came when my father took me aside. He gave me two hundred dollars and a kick up the arse, and he told me: Danny, when every police-man in Parramatta calls you by your first name and you're only fourteen, it's time to move on. So I drifted up this way, did station work, railway work, hit the Territory. There was a famous old bushman from round Arltunga, and he told me how things were: "You'll never be a stranger round here for more than twenty-four hours," he said. "Everybody knows everybody in the Centre. It's a bit like Peyton Place. Everybody knows who you're jumping, and if you're back-dooring someone." Hey, JC!' he called out, for one of the men in leather had meandered down towards us. 'JC'll tell you. You should be talking to him. He knows the Territory inside out. All the tricks. How to call a dingo. How to bring up an emu.'

'And what does he do: run a motorcycle gang?'

'No. He's the real master of ceremonies. We run a blues univer-sity out here, don't we? Look.' He pointed, with some pride, to his T-shirt, on which was imprinted a bold statement of geographic equivalence, 'London, Paris, New York, Glen Helen NT.'

'Is this the right place for it?'

'Sure. It's got good vibes. We sit out on the verandah together of an evening, and listen to life. We watch the kite-hawks diving, play-ing, sparring with each other, coming back in on the thermals. And when we've knocked off work, sometimes, late at night, we come down here, and just watch the stars. It's easy to lose yourself in the West Macs – to lose your past.'

More details of Danny's life emerged: his time as a DJ in Alice Springs; his marriage; his six children; his wife's early death, long ago; the heart's dimensions; the landscape; memories.

'And you?' he said. 'What brings you here?'

I told them.

'You see,' took up JC. 'It's the music.'

'It is?'

'Sure. The blues relate to life, everybody's life. Rock and roll's good to rage to, but when people pull in to Glen Helen they realise it's the blues that have been calling them in. We've got old Ike Turner songs here that sink deep into you. We've got Leadbelly, and John Lee Hooker: each song pulls in its own.'

'Dead set!' said Danny. 'Everyone comes here in the end. You never know who's going to pitch up. We had the Netherlands Mountain Bike champion the other day. We had the grandson of Central Australia's most famous German missionary. But that's nothing: just the other day, we had the king of the blues himself.'

'Really?'

'True! B.B. King stopped at Glen Helen. Well, you can imagine! When that black bastard walked through the door, I jumped the bar. "Give me your hand, man," I said to him. "I know who you are!"'

'And what was his reaction?' I asked, wishing I could have seen this implausible encounter.

'He understood at once. He could tell he was among his own people. We turned up the volume. We began telling the old stories: friends who died; who cut their throats; the weight of time; all those sweet, bad things in life.'

'Can we just back up a moment,' I interrupted. 'The German missionary?'

'What's the matter?' said JC, in tones of outrage. 'B.B. King doesn't do it for you?'

'Ah, the missionary,' replied Danny. 'Blood oath! We had a tourist group come through – in fact, they should be turning up again some time – and we were talking with them about the area, about its traditions, Mount Sonder, the Gorge, the ochre pits, and one of them had been here before. It turned out his ancestor was the father of Australian anthropology, Pastor Strehlow. Maybe you've heard the name?'

Carl Strehlow and his son Theodor haunt the intellectual climate of the Centre in much the way a pair of soaring eagles, by their mere presence, redefine the sky. The father was born in 1871 at Fredersdorf, a small town within the lake-filled Uckermark of Brandenburg, midway between the Baltic and Berlin. His education led him to the seminary at Neuendettelsau. At the request of the Immanuel Synod, he travelled to South Australia, where he was ordained in the Lutheran church at the age of twenty-one.

His was a driven, self-denying temperament. His religious intuitions were only strengthened by the harsh landscapes within which his life was lived. Soon after his arrival in Adelaide he was dispatched by the church to the Bethesda mission beside Lake Killalpaninna, a hazy salt-pan close to Etadunna homestead, almost midway along the Birdsville Track. Contemporary photographs record an imposing compound, with a church, workshops and dormitories, all thronged by neat-clothed Dieri men and women, though the Aboriginal presence in this corner of the desert has long since vanished and nothing but the foundation-stones of the mission can be seen amidst the sandhills today.

After two seasons at Kilalpaninna, Strehlow was sent to Hermannsburg, on the banks of the Finke River, where he was to remain for twenty-eight years, almost without interruption. To the passer-by he still seems present there today: the long, thick-walled, whitewashed buildings, the bare church and the quiet, unvisited museum galleries call up a mood of introspection, of intensity and prayer. Strehlow's reign at Hermannsburg is well-documented. He translated elements of the Old Testament into Aranda. He convinced his flock, who loved and revered him deeply, to abandon their religion of sacred boards and stones. He devoted himself to painstaking study of the Centre's myths and legends. The fruits of his research were published in seven sections by the Frankfurt Ethnographic Museum as *Die Aranda und Loritja-Stämme in Zentral Australien*, but despite their influence on European ethnography they have never seen the light of day in English and remain largely unknown in the country whose traditions they seek to illuminate.

Late in 1922, after a prolonged period of ill-health, suffering from pleurisy, and in the furthest extremes of pain, Strehlow was forced to leave his charges at Hermannsburg and head south in search of medical attention. On October 10th, his condition fast deteriorating, he, his wife Frieda, his young son Theodor and a group of Aranda helpers set off on an arduous journey from the West MacDonnells towards Oodnadatta railhead. The party wound its way along the Finke, by Palm Valley and the Krichauff Ranges, Strehlow himself lying prone in the back of a horse-cart. The route led them up and down sandhills, along the rock-strewn river-bed, until they reached the scene of the dying man's last agony, a homestead on the western fringes of the Simpson Desert. The stages of this ordeal form the subject of a meditative reconstruction by Strehlow's son, one that has made a deep impact on many of its readers: indeed, I can still recall my own first encounter with Theodor Strehlow's *Journey to Horseshoe Bend*.

I was a young teenager, browsing through my father's study, whose windows looked out onto the green expanse of Rushcutters Bay. At one point in my investigations I came upon a torn, much-annotated copy of the book on his shelves.

'Why don't you take it with you,' my father said, smiling sadly. 'It's all about the pains of childhood.'

'And what,' I felt like answering, 'would you know about the pains of childhood?'

'It enchanted me,' he said in a low voice. 'As soon as I began reading, I felt the narrator take me by the hand: I walked with him, I saw things through his eyes. I felt excited to be alive at the same time as a man who could write like that.'

I took the *Journey* with me, and even then it had a beauty for me, and a charm. Yet I felt myself thrown off balance, mystified. Its sentences wound here and there in mazy fashion. It jumped from Bible tales to Aranda legend. It included conversations on station verandahs, dingo stories, totemic rites; the prayers of the father, the dreams of the son, a son who, at the time the journey was undertaken, was a mere fourteen years old, though half a century would pass before he chose to publish his account.

Somewhere, on some European journey, I lost the book, and it was not until I was once more finding my way into Central Australia that I was moved to hunt another copy down. It led me swiftly back into the heart of the Strehlow world.

'You know the story?' asked Danny, a note of disapproval in his voice.

'Sure. Very well.'

'Dripping with tragedy,' he said. 'Just dripping with it. You want to be careful you don't get too caught up with it yourself. Everyone who sets off on the Strehlow trail goes slightly mad.'

'That's right,' murmured JC. 'Central Australia cut deep into him. A heavy dude. Fallen metaphysics.'

'I'm sorry?'

'Many devils in his universe.'

JC produced a tin of rolling tobacco and began construction of an elaborate, neatly-balanced joint. I looked at Danny.

'I thought you said you weren't allowed to sell drugs.'

'I'm not selling them.'

'Anyway,' said JC, 'it's not marijuana. It's pituri. *Duboisia hopwoodii*, the king of nicotines. All the way from Boulia, down the Plenty Highway, that's where the strong stuff grows. Want to try some? Aboriginal people tend to chew it with a lime admixture. I prefer a more direct route. Here: it's like a .45 Magnum. It'll blow your head clean off.'

He lit up, and promptly collapsed in a heaving, coughing fit that persisted for several seconds. Deep, racking shudders forced their way to his lips, as though emerging from the very core of his organism.

'It sounds like an acquired taste.'

'That's true,' he said, recovering a little. 'You have to work at it, give something of yourself, like any drug. So: Strehlow. Always an appealing figure to my friends on the wild side of life.'

'The Harley-Davidson fraternity?'

'No, those of us looking for divinity and inspiration in the land-scape. We're right in the heart of Strehlow's country here, you know: sunlight, colour, air and warmth. There's the mission, down the gorge. There's that research centre they set up to house Theodor's collection, back at Alice Springs. I've heard they even scattered his ashes along the range-line of the MacDonnells. Sometimes, when I'm out here alone at night, looking up like this as the stars come out, I wish our paths had crossed, and I had more idea what he was like.'

Theodor Strehlow was born at Hermannsburg in 1908, the year his father's ethnographic researches first entered into print. The legend of the son's life has by now eclipsed the father's patient ethnographic work. As a child growing up among Aboriginal chil-dren Theodor was as fluent in Aranda as in his native tongues. His linguistic gifts became clearer still during his time at the University of Adelaide, where he excelled as a classicist. Almost immediately after graduation, he found employment as a researcher into the indigenous cultures of Central Australia: he set out to study what he once had lived. With a dream of 'salvage linguistics' in mind, he embarked on a series of field expeditions, travelling by camel, together with an Aboriginal guide. He looks back upon this period in his last book, the unwieldy *Songs of Central Australia*, which, by virtue of its rarity, has become a kind of sacred object of the modern literary domain.

He journeyed extensively, as he relates, with old Aranda men of high authority, covering some 4700 miles in his first three seasons, often walking behind his camel-string so as to be able to note down more easily the ceremonial sites and legendary points passed along the way. Eight further expeditions which he made in four-wheel drives during the fifties and sixties presented a different set of challenges, for even hardened journalists find note compilation near-impossible while bouncing in a short-wheel-base Land Rover down ungraded desert trails. But Strehlow was somehow able in this fashion to record all he saw, and extend his knowledge of the Centre's sacred landscape. He reached across the valleys of the Goyder, the Palmer, and the Finke, which he had travelled before in such puzzled sadness, through the East and West MacDonnells, even into the western portion of the Simpson desert.

Yet for all its encyclopaedic scope, its romantic tone, its elaborate, theory-laden structure, there is something in this work of retrospect that is inert and dead. Strehlow conceived his *Songs of Central Australia* as the last record of a dying world, and that mood stains all within its pages. The sacred songs become chants of mourning and loss; the civilisation he describes seems no more than an afterglow; even the landscape breeds in him feelings of isolation and of loneliness.

Towards the close of the last ceremonial festival staged by the southern Aranda at Taka, near Maryvale station, Strehlow recorded in his diary – it was the 30th of July 1953 – an obituary for the Centre's Aboriginal world: *'The silence that knows no end is about to close in on this peaceful site. My heart tonight is sad – because there is no hope that this fate can be averted.'*

This conclusion led directly to the events of his later life, a life that mirrored in its slow dissolution his ideas about the passing of the Aranda realm. Strehlow regarded himself not only as the recorder of a disappearing world, but as its last custodian: the rituals, the songs, the magic boards bequeathed him by the old men were now his, and the burden of their gift weighed down on him.

The denouement was swift, and worthy of Homeric legend. Strehlow yearned to establish a foundation that could protect the treasures he had amassed. In a bid to raise funds, he sold his photographs of Aranda ceremonies to a German newsmagazine. Their republication in Australia – something he had not endorsed or anticipated – caused outrage among his Aboriginal friends and professional colleagues.

A few weeks later, on the afternoon of October 3rd 1978, the day of the formal opening of his Research Foundation in Adelaide, Strehlow, while in the act of elucidating Aranda sacred regalia to his guests, collapsed, suffered a heart attack and died. But death has been no more than a point of inflection. Scholars still do battle over him. Biographers dissect him. He remains what he was in life: a brooding, unquiet spirit, a white Aborigine, the poet of the inland.


With such thoughts and pictures before me, I fell asleep upon the Glen Helen verandah, and slept through leaden dreams. Next morning, just as sunlight was beginning to touch the ranges, I heard noises coming from close by. I struggled up. It was a group of four-wheel drive travellers near the boughshed, cooking breakfast on an open fire. One of them came across to me. He squatted down beside my swag.

'I think you were wanting to talk to me,' he said in a softly accented voice.

'I was?'

'Wighard Strehlow – *Naturwissenschaftler*.'

He held out a hand. I gazed at him. He was fine-featured, with short hair and piercing eyes, thin of face, unshaven – though the effect of spiritual intensity was somewhat spoiled by the deposits of scrambled egg which were adhering to his chin, and which, I now noticed, had trickled their way down the front of his desert khaki shirt as well. I hauled myself up.

'They tell me you're writing a book about my family.'

'Who on earth told you that?'

'Danny, and JC as well: the scholars of Glen Helen.'

'I think they might have been exaggerating just a touch.'

'Don't worry. I don't mind. Everyone in Australia writes books about the Strehlows: I've written one myself.'

Wighard Strehlow was a grandson of Carl and nephew of Theodor. His was the German branch of the family, he explained to me over the next few hours. Although he shared the other-worldly inclinations of his Lutheran forebears, they had found in his personality a rather different form of expression: he was a prac-titioner of natural medicine, and a devotee of the teachings of Hildegard of Bingen, the twelfth-century Rhenish abbess, vision-ary and composer. Her doctrines were the inspiration of the Hildegard Zentrum Wighard had founded a few years earlier at Allensbach on the shore of Lake Konstanz, and something of her vivid cast of mind seemed evident in the manner of his conversa-tion that morning.

'Your book?' I prompted.

'I shall send you one. And a copy of my book about Saint Hildegard as well. It is my conviction she was able, unlike anyone before or since, to read God's handwriting in the face of nature.'

'I remember an illuminated picture of her,' I said. 'Sitting in her convent, with tongues of fire reaching down about her head.'

'But that is the image I have chosen for my web-page! This is wonderful – we must celebrate.'

He went off to find some tea and came back with a mug in his hand which he presented to me.

'And what brought you to Glen Helen?' I asked, fishing out as unobtrusively as possible the dead flies that were floating on the surface of the liquid.

'But I am retracing the footsteps of my ancestors, of course. All we Strehlows are troubled by the past. My uncle used to call in here, on his journeys, and look out, and see the same landscape that is before us now. I feel in some way very close to him – and to my grandparents, as well, and all they discovered and set forth.'

'You mean the secrets of the Arandas?'

'Not secrets.' He leaned towards me. 'Truths. All the spiritual strength of the traditional world, all the beauty of Central Australia, alive in the myths and legends they collected, all the lessons that Aboriginal culture holds for the crisis we find ourselves in.'

'Crisis?' I echoed, looking nervously around.

'Self-evidently, yes. Political, ecological, social. Even today, when no one can live the way the Aborigines once lived, there are many things that were holy for them which can be decisive in our lives as well. These are the exact values that Hildegard describes: compassion, patience, courage, love of truth. There is a creation secret of the universe that we still can connect with, and its knowledge can make our world whole. All those traditions and inspirations are present in the work of my grandfather and my uncle. Don't you feel it yourself, when you wake up out here, with these purple mountains all around you, and the sun climbing in the sky?'

'Absolutely,' I murmured. 'Of course I do.'

As I said this, the image of the elder Strehlows passed before me. I remembered a few stray words from *Aranda Traditions*, a small book of Theodor's that communicates a mood of inconsolable sadness. Near the end of one of its essays the anthropologist relates some details of ceremonies, connected with the snake totem, that were once performed near Horseshoe Bend.

At the centre of these initiation-rites were two legendary brothers who, alone among the totemic ancestors, ascended to the sky when their days on earth were done. But now these rites were no more than mirage-like memories. The ascension site itself would have been lost had one of Theodor's informants not been told the secret by a dying man.

In 1933, writes Strehlow, he was taken, with two old men of the southern Aranda, to this site, and shown a large cluster of stones lying in the midst of a bleak desert of table mountains. Out of the huge total of ceremonies, whose performance at this spot, according to tradition, once lasted for more than six months, only a few scattered dramatic pieces were still remembered: 'Everything else had been swallowed up, by time and oblivion and death.'

Some days later, this conversation still much in my thoughts, I found myself headed back to Alice Springs, a town I always approach with a certain anticipatory alarm, for on every visit I come on friends of mine from desert communities, drinking themselves to slow perdition in the dry sand riverbed. It was a soft, clear morning as I drove in, past the Desert Park and railway station, along Larapinta Drive.

I parked in the town centre, close to the corner Todd Street makes with Gregory Terrace, just by the public library, and glanced round, at once hoping and hoping not to catch sight of faces I knew. Across the road from me, behind the plate-glass window of the Papunya Tula Artists Company – the Galerie Maeght of the desert painting school – I could see a knot of tourists gathered round a middle-aged blonde woman who was unfurling large bright-coloured canvases before them, a look of infinite weariness in her eyes.

I waved and went across; I called out enthusiastically. Daphne

Williams, the impresario of this institution, frowned at me as though I had just trespassed on forbidden ground.

'I'll be with you in a moment,' she declared through half-pursed lips, and I leaned back against the whitewashed wall, momentarily overwhelmed, for this casually-bestowed sign of recognition marked the climax of a year's diplomatic efforts on my part.

'I can't talk for too long,' she said in a brisk voice as she came over. 'I've got one field-worker out at Kiwirrkurra who's about to call me back; and there's another group stuck on the road just this side of Kintore.'

'Situation normal, in other words.'

She laughed.

'One day,' I said eagerly, 'perhaps I'll be able to lure you from the gallery. We could go for a walk. You could tell me about the early days. We could even have a quick coffee together at Bar Doppio.'

'Bar Doppio?' she repeated, turning these syllables over on her tongue and sounding sceptical. 'I'm not sure I've ever been there.'

'But, Daphne, if there are European sacred sites, it's the most important one in Central Australia. And it's only two minutes from you, in the arcade. I'm sure you know it – the one with the never-ending supply of German waitresses.'

'And what brings you back here so soon?' said Daphne, deciding to ignore this suggestion, and displaying all the froideur of a countess who feels court protocol has been infringed.

Even in a more relaxed discussion I would have found it hard to put my reasons into words. On the drive through the West MacDonnells I had imagined myself telling Daphne all about the early painted Papunya boards I had seen in the basement of the Darwin Museum; how I had snaked and crawled my way between the narrow storage-racks; how the shapes and colours of the paintings had danced before my eyes, dozens of them, musty-scented, raw, and rough, the number-tags still hanging from their stretcher-frames; or I could see myself engaged in some slow, meditative conversation with her about artists I never had the chance to know. The painters of the first wave, perhaps: Tim Leura Tjapaltjarri, Kaapa Tjampitjinpa, or Uta Uta Tjangala; or I might simply sit, still and silent, in a corner of the Papunya Tula display-room, which seemed to me little short of the Florence Baptistery in its significance, while I watched the tourists come and go, the painters and their families drift in, and the field-workers too, worn, unkempt, exhausted from the road.

'And where have you actually been?' prompted Daphne.

I told her about my trip to Haast's Bluff, and Glen Helen, and my meeting there.

'Strehlow,' said she. 'That's a name one doesn't hear these days.'

'And while I was talking to him,' I went on, 'I had the odd impression that I understood something for the first time, some-thing important, about Theodor Strehlow's world.'

'What?'

'He thought that everything was dying about him in the Centre, that he was the last human being who would ever hold the knowl-edge the old men of the Aranda gave into his hands – but at the same time I wonder if he ever half-suspected, in some recess within himself, that their knowledge, those secrets, all the ceremonial treas-ures, were the very things that were destroying him, that they were still too strong and potent to be seen by outside eyes. And as I was talking to his nephew I wondered if, in the last years of his life, he believed the same thing about desert art as well.'

I expected Daphne, whose life had been bound up for decades with Papunya Tula, and with the painting and the selling of western desert art, to find this idea arcane, or even insulting. She looked at me for some moments.

'Perhaps, if Strehlow thought that, he wouldn't have been the only person who wondered about these things, in secret; in private,' she said. 'In fact, I imagine many people do.'

She tapped the gallery's display copy of a famous monograph by Geoffrey Bardon, the schoolteacher round whom, in the early 1970s, the painting movement at Papunya settlement first crystallised.

'You know this book, don't you?'

'I've looked into it,' I said.

It was a work of the greatest splendour, written in a high, poetic style, as convoluted as the paintings that filled its pages, as bleak as the photographic portraits it contained of the early artists.

'Geoff's been interested in those kinds of things.'

'I'd love to hear him talking about the early times,' I murmured to myself, I realised, for Daphne's attention was beginning to drift away.

I looked round the room, at the piles of canvases, each of them bearing its own freight of symbols, each waiting to be borne off into the world.

'Well, then you should come to the opening of the Papunya Tula exhibition, at the Art Gallery in Sydney,' she said. 'It's not too far off now. We're all going down. I've heard there are plans for a seminar, and for Geoff to give a little speech as well.'

And she plunged back into the sanctum of the inner office, where a gaggle of artists were busy laying siege to her new assistant.


I strolled slowly down Todd Mall, allowing the colours and the pace of urban life to sink into me, and I paused, from moment to moment as I went, to let the crowds flow by. There were European tourists kitted out in desert clothes; ageing Americans, wearing printed tour-badges on their jacket lapels; Walpiri teenagers, hurrying past in tight, fierce groups; old ladies from Santa Teresa community, hawking their canvases to everyone they met. How familiar the Mall's shop-fronts seemed, like stage-sets for some long-running musical where nothing could ever change: the tatty art emporia; the photo-lab with its display shots of enormous trucks and road-trains; the bush museums; the banks; the overpriced travel outlets and bleak takeaways.

I had paused outside Wayne's, that Harrods of the Outback, where a line of new print dresses was fluttering on the bargain rail, when I caught sight of a stockman's outfitters. 'We know Akubras', announced their sign, and the store, true to this promise, was full of bush hats in an array of different styles. I looked around, thinking of Honest John in Mount Isa, and his vivid sense of life. By his account, those air-conditioned premises in Alice Springs would be rather like the Platonic Academy. Each hat represented a distinct philosophy, an approach to the rigours and the challenges of Outback life.

'Any idea what you're looking for?' asked the manageress.

I explained my dilemma.

'I know John Molony,' she said, sceptically.

'Honest John,' I amplified.

'So he says. I know his hats.'

'The most perfect of them all.'

'I don't know about that. I know he's got a thing going about how special they are.'

'And how every hat carries its own obligations: makes demands of its wearer, that he or she be worthy of it.'

I warmed to the subject, for I felt well-briefed: I had discussed these themes on one of my first journeys to the Centre with Jan Hayes, the mistress of Deep Well station, south of Alice Springs beside the red-tinged Ooraminna range. There, one late afternoon, as we lounged on the verandah of the old stone station-house, Jan went through her understanding of these questions, speaking with the measured care an anthropologist might bring to some overview of complex kinship systems, for she had owned a saddlers and out-fitters herself for many years, and watched the rites of hat-selection from a ringside seat.

'In my day,' she had said, 'they had a hat called the "Montana" – that was a splendid piece of work – but as I came to feel more at home here at Ooraminna I changed; my way of looking at things changed, even the accent of my personality changed a little, and I started wearing a "Down Under". There's the "Snowy River", of course, and another style I've often felt attracted to, the "Open Road". But on the stations the general rule is pretty clear: if you're a young ringer you're going to have a high-brimmed hat, and the younger the bigger – a big cowboy hat. The real old stockmen, they'll only wear sombreros, those tall styles that look like reefing sails on big ocean-going yachts.'

'You mean like the huge black hat that Turkey Tolson wears, with silver decorations all about the crown?'

'Who?' said Jan, with a look of surprise.

'The artist Turkey Tolson Tjupurrula, from Kintore. You always see him in photographs wearing a high black hat pulled right down over his eyes.'

'I don't know about that,' Jan had answered, 'but you do get that way you can pick out individual hats. You might see a hat left out on a stockyard hitching line, and you just know – that's Old Mick's, or Damper Dave's. And you wouldn't ever sit on a man's hat: that's a real insult.'

'So?' said the manageress, recalling me to the present with a little shake and a stern, assessing glance. 'Going to buy something?'

'What would you recommend for someone like me?' I parried.

'I don't know you well enough. Everybody's different: people feel happiest with different kinds.'

'But if you really had to pick one out for me?'

She sighed. 'Well, you've got the "Broncos" and the "Arenas", but they're what I'd call a beginner's hat, and they've both become Americanised. We could try you out with a "Brumby". People round here like them. There's the "Cattleman", of course: I could give you one in mid-brown fawn, and you'd be wearing the best-seller in Australia today. But it's a town hat. You could buy it in Pitt Street! It's just not sufficiently extreme.'

She looked at me again, appraisingly: 'And if I'm right, what you want, one part of you at least, is something that's got the wind and dust and heat written on it. One of these, for example.' She picked up and brandished a vast, deep-crowned object, curved, infolded. 'We still sell a few of these nineteen-twenties wide-brims: original design. There are stockmen and prospectors who spend a long time out in the bush and sandhill country – they won't wear anything but this, because the taller they are, the cooler they are, and the wider the shadier as well. I sometimes feel they're like a hat that's come from a different world.'

'Well,' I said, in decisive fashion, 'that's definitely the one for me.'

'Wait on a moment! I said that was the right hat. I didn't say you could have it.'

'What?'

'You look like a reflective kind of person: would that be true?'

'I hope so,' I answered, feeling, by this stage, slightly crushed.

'Buying a hat – I mean, buying a bush hat, an Akubra like this, you need to think of as something like an initiation. You don't want to rush into it.'

'But I could be blinded by the sunlight in the desert.'

'Ah,' she said in triumph. 'Before you can be blinded by the desert, you need to be able to see. I'll keep this hat for you. Why don't you think all these things over, then come back.'

'When did you have in mind?'

'You can look in again, maybe, in a year or so, if you're still around.'


Some days after this encounter, reprovisioned, and with my jour-nalistic tasks fulfilled, I flew out of Alice Springs by light plane, bound north-west, across range country, over the Tanami Desert, to the Granites mine. Beside me was an Aboriginal cameraman from Imparja Television, and as we flew, and the landscape through the windows changed, he craned across me, giving me an occasional apologetic smile. Beneath us in the early sunlight the peaks were coral-red, their flanks glowed green and purple; white-trunked gum-trees rose from the pale scrub and spinifex. I stared down, as the colours and the land-forms washed beneath us – dunes and flat-topped hills, and creek-lines, blurring, knitting slowly into one another. Cloud-banks loomed on the far horizon; peaks and ridges reared up from the haze; we could see Mount Sonder and the last, silent granite outcrops; gorges yawned below us; scalloped rocks; sand rivers; quick, dazzling glints of water. And what were those shapes? Marks of regularity – outstations, perhaps, or homesteads, with roads running by them, almost drowned amidst the waves of sand and spinifex.

At last the cameraman produced a notebook, and scribbled something. He held it up to me: 'It seems more beautiful when you share it.'

I nodded. He wrote again: 'How did they know?'

'Who?'

'The dot-painters. How did they know what it would look like from the air?'

I smiled, and offered no reply. We stared down, like watchers of some secret ceremony, unmoving, our faces almost touching as we peered through the window's rounded frame, for minutes, hours, until the landscape flattened. Its texture changed. The gold-mine's open cuts, and processing plant, and dump-trucks came into view. Our plane dropped down.

At the airstrip an appealing woman, small, and wiry, with red corkscrew hair, took immediate charge. Her name was Marilyn Webb: she was a veteran of remote mining camps, and felt at home, and safe, in the furthest reaches of the desert. Perhaps, as she herself said, this was the result of her isolated childhood, for she had been born on Mount Riddock station, on the banks of the Plenty River, in Harts Range.

Over the next few days we drove across the Granites mining lease, and beyond, down back-trails and haulage runs, to Walpiri outstations, to Rabbit Flat fuel-stop, searching for relics from the first Tanami gold-rush, and as we drove Marilyn and I exchanged stories. She painted scenes for me of her station childhood: the Eastern Aranda women who helped grow her up, whose presence and whose touch she missed to that day. She had learned their language, and gone out gathering bush foods with them: bananas, figs, plums and oranges. Her family were all buried in the Mount Riddock graveyard, and she hoped soon to be buried there herself.

'That's a morbid thing to say!' I protested. This conversation was unfolding at a remote spot on the Tanami Track, midway between the Granites and the next mining camp. We were sitting in the shade of an ancient corkwood. It was close to sunset. There were zebra finches and yellow warblers singing round us. 'What makes you even think such a thing in a landscape as beautiful as this?'

'I don't think it,' she replied. 'I know. When you're brought up the way I was, so much part of nature, you see yourself differently. You don't understand yourself in isolation. I know the shape of my life. It's been a good one. I've travelled to a lot of places, and known interesting people. I've always realised that you have to rely on others: you can't just be an island. It's not the knowing of things that's important, but telling other people about that knowledge.'

I listened to her carefully, and in time the places she spoke of became familiar to me, the stations that her father and her cousins had once owned: Napperby, and Huckitta, and Alcoota by the Simpson. There was a Webb Street in Alice Springs, and a Webb Gully at the Arltunga Reserve, where I went often; and Mount

Riddock, too, its lush grasslands, its old homestead with walls of hessian and logs of desert pine.

'I miss Mount Riddock,' said Marilyn. 'It's still a special place for me. Wherever you go in the Centre, there's links with the past and with the future. But I think about Mount Riddock often – I was given a white-quartz sacred site by the old ladies there. I still treasure that in my mind. I used to go back there every year, for the Harts Range races. My father started them up, with his two brothers and some friends, in 1947.'

'I'll make a point of trying to go,' I said, 'next year.'

Marilyn looked at me with exasperated gentleness.

'I won't be there next year,' she said. 'I won't be at the Granites, or Alice Springs, when you come back again.' Nor was she – and her soft voice, and half-smile, and little shrug, are all that remain of her in my memory today.

Towards the end of my spell at the Granites, one morning at breakfast in the mine canteen, a thick-set, bearded man sat down with a thud beside me.

'You the bloke interested in driving through the desert, west of Centre?' he said, staring at his plate, which was heaped with mounds of mashed potato, fried sausage and gravy-smothered scrambled egg.

'Whatever gave you that idea?'

'It's not a big place, this, you know. Word filters out. You going down the Stock Route, or Lake Dora and the Talawanna? You see' – his voice dropped, almost to a whisper – 'I know those roads a bit. I've been out that way myself: Well 33, Gary Junction, Sandy Blight.'

In fact, Wayne Pengelly, in his long-distance haulage career, had very likely seen as much of the western desert as anyone alive, although this distinction was not immediately clear from his conversational manner, and I was feeling worn, and underslept, and scarcely in the mood for the breakfast chat that began unfolding among the men around me, with its loose focus on the Beatles, the Hollies and their respective song-writing styles. I got up to go.

'I don't think I'll be making any journeys into the desert,' I said, 'not until the dry time comes.'

'But wait,' Wayne followed me. 'Don't you even want to see the vehicles we have out here? All customised for desert haulage? If you're interested in travelling in remote country, they're worth a look.'

Together, slowly, we drove round the plant, the workshops and contractors' camps, past fenced-off pits and crushed piles of rock, and as we went something of my companion's story emerged: how he grew up round trucks, in Toowoomba; his trip into the Territory as a young man; his work on the Stuart Highway, and hauling manganese from Woodie Woodie; his time at Macarthur River, near Borroloola, where he piloted the world's longest road-train.

'You're a celebrity,' I interrupted.

'I don't know about that . . .'

We turned down a shallow incline into a red-dirt trucking yard, across which diesel cabs and ore-carriers were parked in maze-like rows.

'. . . Although there is a stuffed penguin as a little nod to me, along the turn-off road to the Callie open-cut.'

'A stuffed penguin?'

'Yes. Pengelly – Penguin. Here we are.'

He braked, and jumped out. Before us was a radiator grille of alarming proportions, the height and width of a grown man. Exhaust stacks like castle towers rose above it on both sides; a train of ore-carriers curved away into the distance behind it, the wheels and red-stained mudflaps forming shapes and patterns in the angled light.

'What do you think?'

He hauled himself up onto the front bumper.

'It's magnificent,' I said, rather unsure what the right response to such a question would be, for the machine towering above me looked more like a heraldic monster than a means of transport. 'And what is it exactly?'

'A six-hundred horsepower Kenworth C510. That'll take you wherever you want to go!'

'I'd have to say I was thinking more of making the journey in a Landcruiser.'

'My time out in the desert was all with trucks,' said Penguin, wistfully. 'Nowadays, it's mostly the run to DBS, down the bitumen.'

'DBS?'

'Dead Bullock Soak – the new mine. But I used to go everywhere, across the sand-dune country, down the tracks to exploration oil-rigs, running fuel into the remote blackfella places, from Kiwirrkura all the way across to Sandfire. I've been to Port Hedland every way that you can go from Alice Springs, except by air. I've been up and down the Tanami Track to Halls Creek and back that many times and not passed another car the whole way. You get to know the road; you see the lights. I used to leave Alice just after tea and be in the Kimberley at dawn. Or you can always stop at dusk: I like rolling the old swag out at night-time, and looking at the stars. You don't know how many there are until you get here and it's pitch-black. Maybe there's two or three of you, driving together. You pull up, make a fire; you talk: where you've been; what you've done; who you know.'

'And you never get stuck?'

'Stuck? I've been stuck, bogged, everything, and I've survived. You could say the desert's like the sea. It looks tame, but it's deadly. At Oakover River once I was stuck on the dry side for eight days, and all I had was what I was standing in. It was Easter, I'd promised I'd get home to see my kids. I don't mind the odd adventure. The best job I ever had was out at Woodie Woodie. I absolutely loved that job – the road was so bad you didn't know what was going to happen, where you were going to have to stop and help someone chain up an axle. Top drivers, out there at that camp – there was even a sheila at Woodie Woodie, she was excellent. Good-looking, too!'

'And what is it about the desert? What do you feel when you're out there alone?'

'Feel?'

He smiled and shook his head. I asked again.

'I could pretend I don't know what you mean. Look!'

He waved his arms, to indicate the scene around us: ore-trucks were rumbling past. Mine-dust blew into our faces. Men in hard-hats hurried by.

'I'm a road-train driver, not a philosopher, but I do know, when I drive out in that silent country, it has a rhythm all its own. When I'm out there sometimes I'll switch the music off, and keep going, hour by hour.' He leaned forward at this point, intent. 'And some-times, in those places, you can tell you're not alone.'

'There's someone with you?'

'Not someone. Maybe something. When you're out, hundreds of kilometres from anywhere, you hit a patch of light, a stretch of landscape, a range of hills – and you just know. It's best if you make a trip yourself: it's not the kind of thing you get near with words. Maybe I'm talking about those Aboriginal spirits, maybe ours – some old-timers, maybe, far from home.'

He shrugged. There was a commotion near us; foremen and maintenance men in overalls hovered close by.

'I think time's up,' said Penguin, with the air of a man turning his attention to serious things. 'How about a quick run with me out to the mine and back?'

———

Some weeks after this set of travels in the desert I retraced my steps to Sydney and to the familiar upheavals of journalistic life – but almost as soon as I was there I felt the landscapes of the Centre sharply present before me, more so than when I had been walking through the ranges and the gorges of the MacDonnells, or climbing by myself up the ravines outside Arltunga, in the shade of ghost-gums and paperbarks. Chance conversations in the Todd Mall came back to me; I saw myself once more in Docker River, or Yuendumu, and I could only smile, and give a private laugh, so fervent were these re-creations in my mind. I was building a world inside myself, just as I had been all my life: alpine summits, out of reach, half-lost in cloud; rock formations in the shape of ruined castles; distant, haze-filled valleys.

For some while in the first months of that year, my time was consumed by the jousts and shadow-play of politics. There were no more frontier tales or bush assignments: I travelled only to regional towns and between south-eastern capitals. Election stories, campaign sketches, great debates. In spare half-hours in motel rooms I ploughed my way through nineteenth-century memoirs and records of the inland; and from time to time, by chance, I would catch some film or news clip from Alice Springs, some glimpse of red peak and spinifex, and feel a softness in my eyes.

At last, one week in late June, a red-letter day loomed in the calendar: the last afternoon of the preview exhibition which the auction house of Sotheby's holds before its sale of Aboriginal art each year, a sale at which new records are set with metronomic regularity.

I had arranged, as usual, to meet my friend Vivien Johnson – the foremost scholar of the desert painting school – at the exhibition, which is always held in the same barn-like gallery high up in the firm's Sydney headquarters.

This annual rendezvous of ours has long since assumed a talismanic importance in my mind, in part because it was Dr Johnson who first opened up the Centre for me through her conversation, but above all because Dr Johnson herself, a woman of almost painful reticence and beauty, seems to come most fully to life before those crowded walls of dot paintings. I hurried in, trailing bags and computer cases behind me, for I had come straight to town from Mascot Airport. I was late, grievously so. I found her, gazing up at a slender, shard-like piece of painted board.

'Forgive me,' I said, and she, with only a vague quiver of the eyes, and the faintest half-smile of acknowledgement, went on looking.

I strolled about the exhibition gallery, absorbing this rebuke, and accustoming myself to my new surrounds; and though I was quite familiar with the ritual of discovering new masterpieces, though I was uplifted by the mere presence of the paintings on the walls around me, and knew some of them already, since the same works tend to circle through the sale-rooms like cursed objects on some nomadic journey, gaining in value with each passing year, still I was startled by the mood that I felt take hold of me, a mood both sharp, and sombre. It was as though the sadness that breathes inside the paintings of the desert had seeped into my heart.

I watched the collectors drifting around me, well-dressed, with assured expressions on their faces; and in those moments I pictured the artists as well, those I had come across, old men living in the town camps in Alice Springs, and those long dead. What thoughts might occur to them, I wondered, could they glance down from their ancestral domain and see a long room full of their tiny, light-filled squares, all their bushfires and their precious water-dreamings stretched out before a throng of western eyes?

'So,' said a crisp voice at that instant, from close beside me. 'What's the verdict on this year's harvest?'

I wheeled round. Before me stood a young man, cherub-faced,

smiling quizzically, his long blond hair combed back. Tim Klingender, the auction house's resident expert on Aboriginal paintings, their meaning and their symbols, their acquisition and their disposition, occupies that ambiguous zone where art and money meet and interpenetrate. Something of their interchange is reflected in his shifting manner, in which, at different moments, can be read both grace and prudent wisdom, candour and a measured degree of self-restraint. One of the more intriguing indices of his private journey was the evolution of his distinctive sartorial style.

That afternoon he was wearing a handsome, up-to-the-minute dark suit, reassuring in its cut and elegance. I fell in beside him. We walked the length of the gallery, talking over the questions that were uppermost in his mind: the wonder of the works he had spent the past months assembling; the excitement at their discovery; the negotiations, swift, dramatic, that had led to their consignment to the sale; the artists he knew, whose life and strength was ebbing; his sense that the movement was entering a new phase.

'Is that your tactful way of saying that it's over?'

'My God, no! No, of course not!' Tim looked horrified. 'Don't say that! That would be a dreadfully conservative view to take.'

He shook his head, as though unnerved by the very idea, while at the same time secretly attracted by it. He smiled at me and assumed an Olympian air: 'Inevitably, you see, with Aboriginal art, with the whole Aboriginal world, there's always a temptation to look back to a golden past, when tradition was purer, painters grander and more ceremonial. And it's true I find it hard to look at works like these' – he gestured in a sinuous fashion – 'works from the first days at Papunya, and not feel there's a kind of electric splendour to them; not love them more, because those times are vanished. Don't you think that?'

By way of answer, I told him something of my recent travels in the desert: Balgo and Fitzroy; Kintore, Lajamanu; and at each placename, and the mention of each artist, sagely, indulgently, he nodded.

Dr Johnson, at this point, drew in her tentative way towards us.

'Vivien,' called out Tim expansively.

He embraced her; they began talking. I hung back, as though present at some conversation of Panofsky and Warburg, while their ideas swirled unchecked here and there: the dotted markings upon an early Johnny Warangkula; the brightness and the strength of Old Walter's fresh-discovered work; squares, and the coming of TV to the desert, and Ronnie Tjampitjinpa's style; attributions, symbolic meanings, the most gem-like, scandal-laden gossip – until a client came into view. Tim, reassuming his professional mask, strode off, and I was left with Vivien.

'We meet again,' said she, smiling ecstatically, but looking almost on the verge of tears.

'What's the matter?'

'You know how much these paintings mean to me,' she said, and shrugged almost in apology.

And I did: I had over time pieced together much of her unusual story. She was brought up in New South Wales, in a quiet, conventional home, but even as a child conflicting impulses warred inside her. Her precise and intellectual temper was matched by a love for all that was elusive, instantaneous, on the verge of disappearing from human sight. As a young woman she was strongly drawn to Sydney's independent music scene, and in particular to that short-lived cult band, Radio Birdman, whose concerts she haunted, whose members she knew, admired, and, perhaps, adored. A full decade after Birdman's demise, already married, with young children, and enmeshed in a university department, she published an unusual study of the band, at once academic paper, nostalgic tribute and eye-witness report. By this point in her life, she had already heard the siren call of Central Australia, as is plain from the introduction to her account of Birdman, whose abrupt fall into obscurity had deeply troubled her: '*It is as though we are all observing an Aboriginal Australian practice of not speaking the names of the dead until the pain of their memory has faded. But the tribal rule of silence does not apply absolutely or forever. There comes a time when the dead one's spirit has at last completed its passage back to the Dreamtime and their name can again be respectfully spoken.*'

So it was with the artists of the Western Desert who had been her friends, and whose works she collected in the most frenzied fashion for many years, while compiling a biographical dictionary of their lives and their ancestral connections, a work that remains the standard reference today, and that seems, in retrospect, to have been both the fulfilment of an obligation and a race against swift-footed death, so frequent, since the dictionary first appeared, have been the funerals in the far reaches of the desert.

At some point in her career as art historian and connoisseur, she began to feel her ownership of Aboriginal paintings as a burden, almost a physical weight upon her shoulders. Although she was not a person of great means, she resolved to offer the finest pieces of her collection to the Art Gallery of New South Wales. An exhibition was held to mark the moment; a brief note of hers goes some way towards explaining this decision.

'*At the time,*' she writes, when she first encountered desert art, '*I was so full of passionate conviction about the purchase of every single painting, though with the passing years I am still struggling to articulate my part in amassing a collection of these works that once numbered in the hundreds. Long association with people from the Western Desert has however taught me that individual intentions may be largely irrelevant to the imperatives of the Dreaming. These, I now realise, I have all along been enacting through my interventions in these paintings' destiny.*'

Was she enacting them now, I wondered? Were we both? I kept pace beside her and she told me about the books she planned to write, and write with urgency, for she was fragile, time was running, and there was a drive in her to record, to assess, to classify. There would be a book about the fraught domain of indigenous copyright; a second version of her dictionary; a historical account of the whole Papunya school, and that unfinished book was itself proliferating in her mind, for the subject needed many volumes. One, almost as preface, for the imaginary museum . . .

'What museum?'

We had paused in front of a small, square painting: it brought back to me the view from the plane window above the Tanami.

'If it was up to me,' said Vivien, her voice falling almost to a whisper, 'I'd be an art detective, and hunt down all the paintings made at Papunya in the early days, all the boards.'

'But you said there were hundreds of them.'

'Maybe a thousand, that's right. I'd collect them all back from the corners of the world where they've been scattered, and from the private homes and galleries and parliaments and courtrooms across this country too, and I'd build a special home for them.'

'Where?'

'In the desert, of course – where they come from, and where they belong. It would be the most magic place, the most beautiful place in all Australia. It would be the key.'

'The mystery at the heart of the continent?'

'We'd be giving back to the people of the Centre what they first offered to us, as a sign of who they were: what we pounced on, and bought and sold, and hid away in dead storerooms.'

'But Vivien,' I said, uneasily. 'Have you mentioned anything about this idea, or your feelings about the art market, to Tim, or any of the dealers and gallery curators?'

'I think they know exactly where I'm coming from.' She glared at me with a sudden, wild determination, and behind her glasses her blue eyes gleamed like rare jewels in a museum's display case.

'Just look around you,' she hissed. 'Look at all these masterpieces hanging here, calling out to us. I can't believe the walls of this gallery aren't bursting into flames.'

The next morning, as if sent by desert spirits, a large parcel, post-marked from Allensbach in Germany, arrived.

'Hildegard Zentrum', read the writing on the label. 'Sender: Dr. Rer. Nat. Wighard Strehlow, Heilpratiker'.

Inside, nestled in a bed of bubblefoam, were two smaller pack-ages in brown paper, and a brief explanatory note, typed on stationery emblazoned with a blooming rose: 'I am happy to send my books about Hildegard of Bingen's medicine – and my appreci-ation of Carl Strehlow, who is, unfortunately, not remembered very well anymore both in Germany and Australia.'

I tore open the larger package, marvelling as I did so at Wighard's signature, which bore a strong resemblance to an ascend-ing scale of alpine slopes.

*Wüstentanz*, announced the cover of the book before me. *Australien spirituell erleben.*

I gazed out through my window at the smog clouds and the squalls of rain across the harbour. With a sense of unease I flicked the volume open, and began leafing through its pages: as soon as my eye fell on the illustrations I snapped it shut.

The book, which I investigated more carefully and with much greater circumspection over the weeks ahead was, as Wighard had claimed, a portrait of Pastor Strehlow, and not merely of his life's events, but of his research and his indigenous informants: their hid-den world; their myths and legends, their songs and tales. Interwoven amidst these complexities were biblical quotations, and extracts of verse by Hildegard, sub-chapters describing desert food-plants and bush medicine; line-drawings of carved tjurunga-boards, and opposite, for comparison, the electron-microscope image of a human cell.

However, it was not these peculiarities that made me close the book that morning with such anxious haste. Scattered through it were colour photographs of pinpoint clarity, and they showed, in unsparing detail, senior Aranda men, in head-dresses and body-paint, visiting sacred sites, performing dances and initiation ceremonies. I hid the book away in a back cupboard, more out of fear – for I have always been mildly terrified by religious ritual – than from mere dull respect for the beliefs of another culture.

It stayed in that hiding place, wrapped up in its parcel, and playing on my mind. A few days later, the time came for another trip to Alice Springs, where native title stories beckoned. On impulse, thinking I might do research of some kind at the Strehlow Centre, I got down my copy of *Wüstentanz* and took it with me.

After some while in the town I paid a visit to a consulting anthropologist I knew, a man of the grimmest post-marxist opinions. Had he ever heard of Wighard, or come across the book?

'Christ,' he said, sitting up in his chair. 'It's not in that silver brief-case, is it? You didn't bring it here?'

'No – no, of course not,' I answered, uneasily.

'Thank God for that! I wouldn't want to be within a hundred miles of that thing. What's it called again – *Dances in the Desert?*'

'Something like that – and why not?'

'Don't you know? It's got the same kind of photographs Strehlow sold to *Stern* magazine – the ones that caused him so much grief and unhappiness.'

'And they show secret material, and shouldn't be viewed by outsiders?'

'They're just bad luck, like everything to do with the Strehlows.

If I were you I'd get rid of that book at once, or at any rate, be careful where you read it – and in what frame of mind.'

Frame of mind? But I was always, in those days, in an agitated mood, sleepless, on edge, drawn to stay on the road, travel further, deeper, as if towards some imagined stillness at the heart of the continent. Over the days ahead I traced out a route down back trails, between stations and dilapidated roadhouses, north-west at first, from Tilmouth Wells to Lake Bennett, then round in a great circle across the highway to Harts Range, with Arltunga as my goal; and at night-time, in the humid silence of some accommodation block, or by the flickering light of a campfire, I continued my journey through *Wüstentanz*, across which, inexorably, as I advanced deeper into the text, the shadow of Wighard's star-crossed uncle seemed to fall. His book was in great part a rendition of Theodor's masterwork *Songs of Central Australia*, stripped down and simplified, and rendered into a grand, heroic German. The effect, on those winter nights under star-filled skies, was unnerving in the extreme. I would pull up at sunset, after a day's slow drive: perhaps I had passed no cars at all; perhaps a pair of cattle-laden road-trains. I would begin to read, and find myself at once transported to the realm of Tristan, or the Nibelungs. By the time I turned off the Plenty Highway, and ground across the Hale, past Ambalindum and Claraville, and Arltunga's rooftops came into view, I was feeling more like some medieval knight than a modern traveller – a knight whose grail was somehow oddly bound up with rain-making ceremonies, and with bat and emu cults.

After much calling out beside the hotel's front gate, and sounding of the horn, I tracked down Arltunga's solitary owner, Christine Knox: she was in the far corner of the red-soil paddock, consulting her weather instruments.

'Hello there,' she said, smiling gently, as though surprise calls in the middle of the off-season were all part of the magic of the desert day. 'It's lovely to see you again. I'll just be a moment longer. I've got to do my ground temperatures.'

Some while later, sitting round the hotel's pot-bellied stove, Christine gave me her news bulletin: all quiet in the Cavenagh foothills; a few geologists around; movement at the ranger station. I listened, soaking up the strangeness of human company.

'And what have you been doing with yourself?'

I told her.

'You always liked driving, didn't you? Ever since I first met you. I know the appeal. I'm a road person myself. I'd happily just jump into the troop-carrier and set off right now for Darwin. It wouldn't bother me at all. And what did you do with yourself, all that time on the road?'

I gave her a quick version of the Strehlow story: Hermannsburg and Horseshoe Bend; Wighard at Glen Helen.

'Perhaps you've seen his book?'

I reached for my briefcase and began to pull it out.

'No – and you better leave it in there. I've never seen anyone with it, although we do get a lot of Germans up this way, when the hotel's open. I remember all the story very well, about the photographs – that was big news in the Territory, years ago.'

She shook her head. We spoke on: how happy she was, alone in the bush; how strange the weather had turned, those past few days; all the wildflowers I might see, if I went up into the ranges; the prospectors, a strange bunch, who were marauding about.

'Strange?'

'There's one who uses metal wire, and believes he can tap into the powers of the cosmos. He goes out, sometimes, completely covered by a rubber suit made from car tyres, with a rubber helmet, and homemade rubber boots.'

'To insulate himself from earthly distractions?'

'That's right. I've never seen him, but I'm told he's got a camp up in White's Range, near the old mine, and he believes the universe is full of higher beings, with whom he's in continuous dialogue. I think I'll put you down by the creek-bed, in the old cabin, if that's all right?'

I left her to the weather details, and drove down to my quarters, just by a line of ancient gum-trees. It was close to sunset. There was a blush across the ramparts of Mount Gordon. The sky was pink and mauve, and flecked with high trails of cloud. That night, by torch and candlelight, I finished off my reading, and I glanced once more at the Strehlow pictures: old men, engaged in blood-letting; old men climbing into hidden caves, handling sacred boards; or kneeling, at the end of their ceremonies, gazing at each other, embracing.

With sadness mounting, reduplicating, I turned the pages for a last time, and gazed at the final photograph, which I had barely taken in before: it showed a desert plain of rock and spinifex, the horizon formed by long flat-topped ranges. In the foreground were two men, one standing, one kneeling, their eyes cast down, in the midst of a stony forest, a cluster of raised, cairn-like stones.

'*The place where death came to the world,*' declared the caption. I knew what it was, and where: it was Rowanawana – the ascension site in Aranda Traditions – the sacred place, where the snake ancestors rose into the sky, the monument whose site had almost been lost.

It was surely lost now, I thought to myself, changed beyond all recognition, drowned in the past, and washed away – even though the stone cairns, or what was left of them, were close to where I lay that night in my cabin. All Strehlow's country was: Maryvale, and Tjikara, and Horseshoe Bend, across the ranges, almost in my hands.

At some point while I was sleeping, the weather broke. I opened my eyes. The rain was drumming down on the tin roof. The sky was still half-dark. I went outside: rust-coloured water filled the ruts along the road. I struggled up to the hotel building. Christine turned around: 'What have you brought with you?' she said, accusingly. 'We've had some wild storms here before – mini-tornadoes, direct lightning strikes – but not like this, not at this time of year. It's unbelievable. If it keeps up this way, the creek will be running by tomorrow. And did you see the water pouring off the ranges? We'll be cut off soon. Better get used to a long stay.'

## II

Later that year, during the deceptive weeks of spring, a time when Sydney, for the briefest interval, seems almost to have a European look and feel about it, I flew back into the city at the end of some protracted assignment, and as the 727 came ghosting in that evening, the light upon the Opera House brought far-off scenes to mind: Triestine palazzos, with shade slanting across them; yachts and fishing boats, at sunset, bobbing in the golden harbour at Sanary; the purple Simpson, its sand-dunes edged in darkness, receding in grid-like waves to the horizon's line.

In the apartment, I flicked on my messages; there was one from Dr Johnson, clipped and brief: 'If you're back from your desert exile,' said her voice, 'remember the Papunya exhibition. It's the seminar this weekend. The whole Aboriginal art establishment will be there.'

Next morning, as instructed, I set off through Hyde Park for the Art Gallery of New South Wales, and even from a distance I could see a crowd waiting outside its entrance, spilling onto the pavement and the gardens of the Domain, a crowd of unusual composition: young men and women in dark shirts and suits; scruffy Outback types in jeans and jumpers; puzzled throngs of Japanese tourists;

students; television crews; anthropologists; and a handful of over-coated artists from the Central Desert, gathered, as I could now see, like some protective guard round Daphne Williams at the very top of the steps.

I was making my way towards them when, from behind a column, a striking figure emerged.

'JC from Glen Helen,' I said, a touch anxiously, for he was wearing the most elaborate, not to say alarming, attire: full leathers, a metal-studded neck choker, a red bandana, a ripped T-shirt bearing the image of a storm-lashed Uluru.

He beamed.

'You remembered.'

'You're not the most forgettable person I've come across in remote Australia,' I said. 'And there's not too many people wandering about this city in gear like that.'

'You like it?'

He swivelled round. On the back of his jacket was an intricately inlaid death's head emblem, and around it, picked out in worn, frayed letters, the legend: *Coffin Cheaters Motorcycle Club, Kalgoorlie WA.*

'Is that a current affiliation?'

'Some things never entirely leave you – but I'm on a different vector now.'

'And what are you doing here?'

'I'm here to see the man, of course.'

'The man?'

'Geoff Bardon. I'm a collector. Early Papunya boards – I've got ten of them, all early consignment, all documented.'

'And you keep them at Glen Helen?'

'Are you joking? Have you seen the security at that place? No, they come with me on the road.'

'You take ten priceless, fragile paintings with you on a Harley-Davidson across Australia?'

'Sure. I love them. They sustain me. I'm their custodian. I've been looking after them for years. They don't mind travelling – they're depictions of dreamtime travels, not out this way, it's true, but their dream-lines reach back where I'm going.'

'And where's that?'

'I'm on a run to the Pituri country: Mernie sandhill, out beyond Cacoory ruins, off the Eyre Developmental Road. Maybe it might interest you, sometime, to come along. It's a very historic part of the world; there are even people who say that's where Leichhardt and his party finished up. It's beautiful: red sand, blue-grey mulga; the five most poisonous snakes on earth. It's the only place where you can find them together.'

'That must come in handy, but what's Geoff Bardon to you, that you drove all this way to hear him?'

'Don't you know that passage towards the end of his book, the Shelleyan echo: "I believe it is in the furthest reaches of the human imagination that our country lies, and there we must seek it out, like poets of a coming age." Don't you remember? "The Western Desert painters, almost by an incredible act of fate, have given Australians a way into the continent." Those are words that mean a great deal to me – and besides, I'm sure you know his story.'

'Not at all.'

JC dropped his voice low. He bent towards me. He was quick and elliptical; he told the fragments of a tale. What he left out was worse than what he said: crisis, despair, treatment; long, silent recovery.

'This would be the first public appearance Bardon's made for years – at least to speak in detail about the paintings. It's as if Thomas Pynchon were to turn up suddenly at some meeting of the Modern Language Association. Listen, I'd love to keep on talking, but I want to grab a seat right at the front.'

He turned to go.

'JC,' I called out. 'About the boards!'

'Yes?'

'You were just putting me on, weren't you?'

'Just tricking, that's right.'

'You're sure?'

He laughed: 'You'll never know. Isn't that the whole point about the early paintings – secrecy, and power? And these ones are the most secret, and most perfect of them all. Perhaps one day I'll show them to you, if you drive out to the sandhills – but only at sunset, of course.'

Sunset, I wondered, and I was about to ask.

'Best time for witch-doctoring. Don't pretend you're not curious. So: you coming in with me?'

Slowly, almost reluctantly, as if pulled by a tide, I followed him, through the domed entrance-hall, down the escalators, deep into the building's lower reaches.

By the time we found the entrance to the lecture-theatre, which was itself in recessed shadows, like the passage leading to a catacomb, the tiers of seats inside were full, the lights were dimmed, the seminar was under way. We leaned against the back wall, side by side, and stared down into the darkness, as though we were peering into the bowl of a vast aquarium, full of rare, luminescent lifeforms. As my eyes adjusted I began to make out faces and silhouettes I knew: there were the enlightened connoisseurs one saw at Sotheby's, their exhibition catalogues ostentatiously open on their laps, and gathered round them, like little schools of pilot fish, were rows of gallery owners and critics, and art world bureaucrats. At the centre of the auditorium I could see a scattering of politicians, and indigenous leaders alongside them. In their midst was Daphne, and Dr Johnson near her, and the grandees of the auction trade. At the very front, bunched together, wearing bush hats, were the objects of their enthusiasm: the artists of Papunya-Tula themselves. The speeches had begun. There were introductions; they seemed endless.

Anthropologists and curators jumped up and made their way to the stage, and spoke, bathed by spotlights, as though they had stumbled into the beam of some intrusive deep-sea exploration probe.

'Witch-doctoring?' I whispered in JC's ear.

'Haven't you ever had any strange times in the desert?' he replied, in a stage whisper, and a couple of faces in front of us glanced round.

'No.'

'Then you haven't been out there long enough. Don't you ever ask around about that kind of thing? Don't you ever talk to Aboriginal people? They'd set you straight right away.'

'And have you ever seen anything, yourself: anything unusual?'

'Are you joking?' came back his voice, soft, and in that darkness, oddly hypnotic, so that after a few seconds I stopped trying to listen simultaneously to it and the words coming from the hall below. 'Every day out there's a day close to the edge. What do you think Bardon was into? What do you think the painting of the desert's all about?'

'Well,' I whispered back, 'form, and ceremony, maybe, and pattern – their place in human life.'

'It's about fear – fear, and danger. The abyss. I've been out near Mount Conner, when the ice-spirits are floating in the air. I've driven out from Balgo towards Lake Gregory, and felt the coming of the dog-men. Once, when I was working on a geo-survey from Alice Springs, at Taka, down near Maryvale, I went out from camp alone one night, into the western Simpson – deep into the devil-devil country.'

'And what happened?'

'I went a long way through the desert. I found an isolated peak among the sand-dunes. I began to climb it, and the devil-forms came rushing, screaming past me. They wanted to uproot my mind: it was the universe's challenge.'

'Shh!' scolded a woman just beneath us, turning round. 'Quiet!'

'Quiet yourself,' said JC. 'Can't you see Geoff Bardon's about to give his talk?'

A thick-set, ungainly man, grey-haired, was clambering up onto the stage, breathing heavily, perspiring.

'Is that really him?' I whispered.

There was almost no resemblance between this individual and the tanned, wry teacher shown in every book on desert art.

'It's certainly someone who's seen what I was just telling you about,' muttered JC.

The grey-haired man clutched at the podium, and cleared his throat. We fell silent. He began to speak and, by some alchemy I am at a loss now to explain, it seemed in those moments as if the first, far-off days in Papunya settlement were being recreated before us, lived anew in all their intensity. It was not through the skill of the performance we were witnessing, nor the splendour of the rhetoric, for it was clear at once that Bardon could barely speak at all; indeed it was almost more than he could do to repeat the handful of words he had typed on a page before him – excerpts, as he told us, from his memoir, his work in progress, which he had been struggling over, redrafting, revising, for many years. He stammered as he read them; he hesitated; he lost his thread; there were pauses of the most tragic intensity – and all the while I gazed down, transfixed, with the same unease one feels on watching a crushed insect writhe upon the ground.

'Sand and dust,' came his voice. 'Sand and dust. I ask you to con-sider these words as markers and limits of our knowledge of what we are' – and his thoughts, like the scurries of some desert wind, flowed on, faltering, breaking.

He glanced round. A photograph of him as a young man flashed up on the projection screen behind him: it had been taken in the desert, amidst the painting men.

'I was engaged,' he said, 'without then knowing it, in a spiritual biography of myself.' These words emerged in a near-whisper, his voice lilting upwards at the end of every phrase.

Briefly, sighing with each pause for breath, he painted pictures of the artists he had known, and been closest to: their smiles, their looks, their movements, Mick Namerari; Charlie Tarawa; Uta Uta, Tim Leura; Kaapa. Tears were standing in his eyes; he spoke their names like those of saints.

Sharp, agitated whispers were beginning among the audience.

'I can't bear this any longer,' I whispered to JC. 'It's as if he's crashing and burning in front of us.'

'But that's the way it has to be,' came the voice close by me. 'Don't you understand? That's what life is for him. That's what the painting movement was. This is his ordeal – his danger.'

I gazed down, feeling complicit by my very presence, and with each phrase the speaker on the stage below swooped nearer, nearer to disaster, until, just as it seemed he would dry up, fragment, collapse in public, suddenly, without warning, without even a second of adjustment, his manner changed: his words became smooth and calm; his look was one of triumph.

What were the early paintings, he asked, and at once he gave his answer: they were mind-maps, of course, a system of mind-maps across the whole continent. The artists at Papunya had made the invisible visible. How grave, and beautiful, the faces projected behind him were, and how grave he looked himself, as he won his battle there before us, his eyes wide, his forehead damp with sweat.

'It was a great honour to work with these men,' he said, and his hands gripped the lectern. 'It was a great honour to speak here today. My time up there, in Papunya, was one of rejoicing and joy. The painting movement is now a vast unstoppable force of conscience which has emerged so as to forever change the history of the world.'

He fell silent. He made his way off stage. Uncertainly, applause began.

Outside the auditorium, I turned on JC.

'I can't believe you made me listen through that! You didn't say a word about what it would be like. I felt like some voyeur in a psychiatric ward!'

'You've got a lot to learn,' he said. 'And I didn't make you do anything. As a matter of fact, I thought that was one of the most transcendent, most beautiful things I've ever seen. Just like the man said: it was a privilege to hear him. I'm going to ride on. Coming with me?'

I laughed.

'What's the matter? I thought you wanted to see the inland.'

'Let me just explore the modalities of the offer: you want me to leave everything right now, forget my life, and ride with you on the back of your motorbike all the way from Sydney to the eastern sand-hills of the Simpson Desert, which you've just told me you think is haunted by primeval spirits, in order to harvest a form of nicotine plant that induces spasmodic fits in everyone who smokes it?'

'Something like that, although I keep telling you smoking's not the standard route of ingestion. But I wouldn't have given the idea quite your spin. I'd put it this way: when you're in the open while you're travelling the bush, everything's different. I'm giving you, for the first time in your life, your sheltered, idea-filled life, a chance actually to feel the landscape – to have its shifts and changes on your skin. You wouldn't forget the journey, that's for sure. We could go up along the Warrego, past Barringun and Cunnamulla, where they breed the hardest polo ponies in the world, through Carpet Springs, into the Channel Country, up the back roads, and the ranges, to Toompine, and Quilpie.'

'I've been that way before,' I interrupted.

'You've got no idea what it's like up where I'm talking about.

There are tracks I go on that no one's seen since exploration times: deserted homesteads, landing strips from World War II, just mouldering away. I could drive almost from here to there without seeing another soul.'

'Sounds tempting – but you know I can't. I can't just shrug my shoulders and drop my world.'

'Why not? Is it so worth keeping? Doesn't what I'm saying sing to you? Don't you hear the music in it? All that country's out there, waiting. You can't stay away from it for ever.'

'JC,' I said, helplessly, and, to my amazement, I felt a deep, heartbreaking regret.

'Relax! This was one time for you. Maybe there'll be another. Like Mountford said, it's all in the stars. The land will claim you, in its way, and in its style.'

We were outside by now. We had walked together down the tree-lined driveway of the Domain. JC stopped beside his Harley-Davidson, which he had left propped against the railings near a statue of Robert Burns.

'A favourite of yours?' I asked.

'Well, he was interested enough in wildlife. Wait up a second: I've got something here for you.'

He reached into one of his saddlebags and fished out a slim, dog-eared pamphlet: on its cover was a red and ochre-shaded design.

'There you are.'

I glanced down at it. The title was in tiny print. I read it out loud: '*Agencies of Social Control in Central Australian Aboriginal Societies*. Sounds fascinating!'

'Dead right: check it out, funk-soul-brother!'

'That's very kind of you,' I was about to say, when my eyes fell on the author's name, in tiny letters: 'T.G.H. Strehlow'.

'More Strehlow!'

'Is that a problem?'

'No, it's just that I've read through quite a lot of him this year –
and anyway, how did you know you were going to ever run into me?'

'But I came looking for you.'

He brandished the pamphlet, and passed it like a baton into my
hand.

'Read it. Every word. He's playing from the same deck as
Bardon. He's been down to the abyss. You'll find something in there
you need, and want.'

He jumped onto the bike, and started it.

'Another thing,' he called out above its roar. 'Don't forget your
friends. You were almost a regular out at Glen Helen once. Come
back and see us again.'


A few weeks later, at the tail-end of a long journey through the
Western Desert, worn out, ragged, half-blind from heat, and glare,
and dust, I took JC at his word.

It was close to sundown when I pulled up at the homestead. The
building had an even more ramshackle look about it than on my
previous visits. I paced round, and called out. An unexpected sense
of satisfaction filled me: I had just driven alone, without mishap,
through the range country between the Petermanns and Kintore,
and on to Haast's Bluff, and all that elusive landscape seemed to fit
together for the first time, and form a pattern in my mind. I
knocked, and listened. No blues; in fact, silence. I called out again,
then, after some while staring up towards the peaks as they shone in
the last light, I went round the back, tried the wire-screen door,
forced it slightly open and slid through the gap inside. There was a
growl from the far end of the suite of rooms.

I stopped. Chairs were piled upon the tables. The window blinds
were all pulled down. A lone man, young, clean-shaven, with
handsome, even features, was sitting at the bar, a glass and a bottle

of whiskey before him, and on the bar itself, panting, and glaring at me through the shadows, was a large, sandy-coloured dog.

'Good evening,' said the man, regarding me coldly.

'Danny?'

'He's not here any more.'

'Where is he, then?'

'How should I know?'

'And JC? I'm here to see him.'

He shook his head: 'Ditto.'

'And who are you?'

'I'm the owner – or the caretaker. Does it really matter? It doesn't change anything.'

'No, but I had friends here.'

'So you felt you could just break in? You're not on very firm ground, are you?'

'And what have you done with the music?' I said, perhaps a shade too combatively. 'Where's the famous Glen Helen jukebox?'

'Well,' said the man, as if turning the question over.

He stood up, and the dog jumped down, landing noiselessly upon the floor beside him. He came towards me with slow, distinctly menacing steps; the dog bounded forward, and began nuzzling at the seam of my trousers.

'Tanami!' said the man, reproachfully, but also indulgently.

'Is he, by any chance,' I asked, with mounting unhappiness, 'a dingo?'

'Alsatian–dingo cross: very interesting animals. Full of instinct: highly-strung, but with many of your wild dog's best characteristics. The coat, for instance: feel how rough and wiry the hair is. And no smell – I like that in him. And very inquisitive, not too finicky. It's always good to know the dog you hunt with would eat you if you were dead.'

'It must be very consoling.'

'And was the jukebox that important to you?'

'Yes,' I said, defensively. 'It's the best one in Central Australia, or it was.'

'Define best.'

'What?'

'Explain to me the qualities that go to make up a satisfactory jukebox.'

The dingo, by this stage, had worked its way, growling, slathering and yelping, up to my waist, and was now beginning, a little tentatively, to chew my new belt of plaited kangaroo-skin.

'I don't know quite what you mean,' I said, taking a step back, with the dingo still attached to me.

'Would you say the jukebox at Erldunda was a good one, for instance?'

'Well, I'd nominate one I saw once at Meekatharra,' I answered gingerly, 'or maybe the one in the hotel at William Creek.'

'William Creek! Now there's a jukebox to write home about. Tanami – down! Don't mind him; he's just playing.'

The atmosphere changed abruptly.

'You're not bloody wrong! William Creek. I remember the first time I flew in there – I've got a pilot's licence, and a few planes. I put down, and walked into that front bar, and there were tracks from "L.A. Woman" on the jukebox! Can you imagine? All that desert country was transformed for me, everything. The colours and the sandhills and that dreadful whiteness on Lake Eyre, it all made sense. Music shifts things. It's the key. That's why traditional people listen to West Coast music so much.'

'They do?'

'Absolutely. Grateful Dead, Quicksilver Messenger Service, Steely Dan – you just can't move out in the Western Desert without your California classics. And look at Top Springs, on the road to Kalkaringi: what a scene they've got out there.'

This disquisition went on for several minutes.

'Right,' I said, at the first moment's pause, and I began to back away. 'I'd better be pushing on.'

'Don't you want your message?'

'What message?'

'JC told me to tell you to head for Adelaide. He said something very important for you was happening there. It's where your life-path was leading you.'

'But that's where I'm going on this trip. Is he there now? And how do you know the message is for me, anyway?'

'There's not that many people who'd drive out to a closed road-house in the quiet season looking for an obscure, fantasy-minded, drug-ravaged ex-Hell's Angel.'

'Coffin Cheater.'

'Whatever.'

'And did he say anything else? What's happening there? Why?'

'He just said it was vital you be there by the fifteenth of October, before close of business.'

'But that's tomorrow, and it's almost two thousand kilometres away.'

'Better get your skates on, then. You probably won't be going on a West Coast detour to William Creek, will you? Shame.'

I drove through the night, at full speed, cruising past the bright-lit road-trains, swerving round torn carcasses of kangaroos and cattle stretched out along the highway, and Marla Bore and Coober Pedy were already far behind me when the dawn began to show. I was in the midst of that drear, treeless South Australian plain that broke so many of the first explorers' hearts. There was Woomera, and the Tarcoola Track, the salt lakes shimmered invitingly to the west-ward, the jumbled skyline of the Flinders Ranges came in view. I watched the railway's progress, and the power lines. I sped on, my thoughts reduced by this stage almost to nothing. I was transience, and movement: dreams, hopes, memory slipped away. And what, precisely, was I driving for, I would ask myself in disjointed fashion from time to time, as the distance markers loomed, then fell into the rear-view mirror's shadows. Who were my helpers, and my guides? Drifters, strangers, the loose change and flotsam of the Outback. And what was that ahead of me, beyond the flat-topped mountains, glinting? Tall chimneys, a smoke-plume, turquoise waters, still and calm. Port Augusta and Port Pirie came, and Mount Remarkable, and Dutchmans Stern. The skies clouded over. A lightning storm began. My destination loomed: straight lines; a street grid; a cathedral spire.

Only in the city centre, once I had slowed to a conventional speed and the façades of King William Street enclosed me, did a sense of the displacement I had just subjected myself to take hold. I parked and, rather unsteadily, walked along the riverbank, past the university and museum, towards North Terrace. It was already late in the afternoon. The pavements were glistening. A broken storm-front veiled the hills.

And what now, I wondered. I crossed the street and strolled on, until, much like a drunkard who fetches up in the back bar of some discreet hotel, I found myself close by the premises of Michael Treloar's Antiquarian Bookshop, a business for which I had grown to feel an almost personal responsibility, so great were the fractions of my income I squandered on its rarities. This conviction had mounted, in recent months, to such a pitch that guilt would eat at my heart during those rare spells when I failed to match the standards of my past extravagance. I took a deep breath, and went in.

'Wow,' said Michael, who, most uncharacteristically, was sitting at a desk in the front of the store, examining some sliver of manuscript. 'You look awful.'

'I've just driven from Glen Helen,' I said, listening with interest to the strangled sound emerging from my lips.

'Glen Helen, NT? That would explain it. I'm not surprised, though. I thought you'd pitch up here today.'

'Why's that?'

'The Strehlow Collection sale, of course,' he answered, looking at me in some surprise.

He nodded sagely, as if to underline these words, and his mane of greying hair trembled behind him like the spray on a waterfall.

'That's what you're here to see, isn't it?'

'In a sense.'

'I went this morning.' His voice dropped to a confidential, somewhat conspiratorial tone. 'It's a sight for sore eyes. In fact, you could say it's one of those spectacles that makes you imagine you've slipped for a brief second into heaven on earth – if you're a bookseller, that is. Treasures everywhere, most of them unrecognised and barely catalogued.'

'Was there anyone in a leather jacket there – a Coffin Cheaters jacket?'

'What? You think Ted Strehlow was part of some undiscovered gang subculture? Maybe you've been on the road too long. They've extended the public viewing. Tomorrow's the last day. You should make sure you go and have a look. There's no problem seeing the exhibits: the galleries are empty. For a connoisseur of melancholia, it's a once in a lifetime event. The sadness, and the sense of ending, of dispersal, sit very heavy. By the way, I've put aside a few things for you.'

He reached into a glass-fronted cabinet before him and produced a dark-bound, brick-like book, which he balanced, with some difficulty, on the palm of his hand.

'*Songs of Central Australia*,' he announced, in triumph. 'An association copy.'

'Going cheap at three and a half thousand, I suppose?'

'How did you know?'

'All I have to do is double the price you gave in last month's catalogue.'

'Well, maybe there's hope for you yet in the book trade. And what about this? I've got some genuinely off-road Strehloviana for you. Here's a school primer, in Aranda language, of course. Or *Nomads in No-Man's-Land*, in mint condition, or here, the *Camel Trip into Blood's Range and the Cavenaghs*. It's not so valuable, but it's very obscure indeed!'

'Is there a difference at all in your eyes between those two things?'

'Now you're getting onto my home territory. Don't tempt me.'

With a flourish, I produced the Strehlow pamphlet, which was rolled up tight in the back pocket of my jeans, and held it out to him for inspection. He leafed through; his eyes widened.

'Where did you get this? You haven't been looking after it. And what's the title? *Agencies of Social Control*.' He laughed.

'You've seen it before?'

'I've heard about it, round the traps. What's it like? Have you read it?'

'Not yet, but I shall this evening.'

'You always have to be careful, I find, with Strehlow,' Michael continued.

He got up, still reading, and strolled about. He flicked through the pamphlet's pages several times. He held it up against the light: 'Potent stuff! I'm not too sure about the stain on the back cover, though. It looks like engine grease.'

He pressed the booklet to his nostrils, which flared elegantly. 'It is engine grease! I didn't realise you were such a bush mechanic. Do you do all your reading underneath the car?'

———

I made my escape, and drove round the parklands once again, watching daylight fade over the Spencer Gulf. At last I checked into a hotel I knew at the rough end of Hindley Street, went upstairs and collapsed on the bed in my little first-floor room, expecting to find myself exhausted: but, as often happens at the end of arduous journeys, I felt uplifted and renewed.

I picked up the pamphlet and dutifully plunged in. After several hours I had forced my way through much of its text. I had the sense I was experiencing, in printed form, some hard, dry stage traced out by Leichhardt, or Sturt, or Ernest Giles: paragraphs like sandhills; arid, endlessly-receding tracts of verbal spinifex. There were no clues to where the paper had been written, for whom, or why. It seemed a set of ethnographic observations, thrown together almost at random. I struggled. For some while I wondered why JC had pressed it with such eagerness into my hands. Then, midway through the evening, I struck a passage that I realised I had been waiting for, as the heart waits for a bullet, or the neck for a blade.

At this point in his argument Strehlow, almost unwillingly, turned to the harshness that he had found in nature, and the helplessness of man before its moods: not only Aboriginal mankind, but sophisticated, city-bred white men also. As was his way, he provided brief cameos to prove his claim. Fear of lonely places, and of the unknown, so he believed, had been a deep influence on human conduct in the world of Central Australia. Sometimes it had taken all his powers of persuasion to get native men to come with him to their old, deserted homes, so great was the terror that enveloped them as they advanced into the uninhabited wilderness. On one journey, in the Petermanns, a range system that still breeds a sense of desolation in the casual visitor, Strehlow, together with three Pitjantjara guides, travelled for weeks without meeting any living creatures, until his companions were brought by this expanse of empty country to a pitch of terror. They would start in their sleep, or wake from heavy nightmares; at last they refused to go on. Old white bushmen, of the kind who lived in Alice Springs before the railhead reached the town, were just as superstitious in their outlook.

These ideas were touched on once more in Strehlow's account of an expedition he made to Ayers Rock, a four-day haul across a hundred miles of waterless country. The camels strayed; the Aboriginal guides went off to fetch them back; the white members of the party themselves became restless, and full of fear.

Strehlow recounts an experience he attributes to his fellow-anthropologist, C.P. Mountford, though he was not in the habit of describing others' feelings, and it may well be it was his own. The party had made their way successfully to Uluru, which was at that time a very different place from the jamboree one finds today: '*We were at the base of the vast silent rock, and not a beast or bird had been sighted by us for over two days. The only sound that night was the moaning of the wind around the titanic monolith. One member of the party ventured out into the caves at the base of the rock in order to copy some of the native drawings in them. Several hours later he returned to our lonely camp fire. He had done little work. Draughts had kept on extinguishing the flame of his carbide lamp, and he admitted that it had been an eerie experience sitting there on his own in these ancient caves, where the wind was producing weird sounds, sighs, moans, and hissing noises. He did not go out again during the next two nights.*'

In fact, Strehlow continues, expanding his theme, such anxieties as these are natural, for fear has been the hidden, unacknowledged wellspring of much in mortal life. In the western world, of course, there has been a gradual diminution of its role, and a fading of the religious instinct, for man in large cities becomes confident, even arrogant. He feels himself the measure of all things, the captain of his own soul. But at the time when Strehlow was writing, confidence in Man as master had been broken by the course of two world wars. It is hard, in these sentences, not to hear a note of mourning for the vanished jewels of Strehlow's ancestral culture coming through, mingling with his lamentation for the demise of the Aboriginal world. In particular, he writes, the last war has shown 'how easily great cities could be reduced in a few days to disorderly masses of broken rubble' – until memory, and grief, and words, are all that remain.

I fell asleep under the impress of these ideas, slept heavily, dreamed intensely, and woke surprised to find myself in sunny, carefree Adelaide, rather than the bombed-out ruins of some Germanic citadel. That morning, I made my way to the auction-house in Leigh Street, close by. The premises were just as Michael Treloar had described them: hushed, lugubrious, dark, drenched in an almost comically excessive atmosphere of gloom. A black-suited attendant, poised by the doorway, handed me a catalogue and ushered me upstairs.

'Do you need any help?' he murmured solicitously after several minutes poised by my side. 'Anthropological explanations, perhaps? Suggested valuations?'

Strewn about the exhibition rooms, in no apparent order I could discern, were paintings, ancient photographs, film projectors, tape recorders, boomerangs, stone ornaments. I walked round, feeling like an intruder in an ancient tomb.

'Is there anything in particular that you're interested in?'

I scanned the catalogue:

'It's certainly an eclectic choice.'

'Absolutely,' said the attendant, sensing in this reply a chink of conversational promise. 'Our experts had a bit of difficulty preparing the sale-list. I'm sure you can imagine.'

He seized the catalogue from my hands: 'Just look. Manuscripts; flasks of sand from Central Australia; a ball of human string, collected by T.G.H. Strehlow, circa 1930. Or this: two splinters, Pitjantjara, sucked out of a patient's body by a medicine man. You don't come across lots like that every day of the week!'

'Has there been much interest?' I asked, taking a step back from this figure, who had now attached himself to my elbow like a gargoyle, and was seeking, by repeated gentle tugs and nudges, to propel me towards the display cases at the far end of the galleries.

'These are great rarities, of course,' he replied. 'But there's no ready market for them: nose-bones, head-dresses, eagle-plumes. I think I can tell you, in confidence, the buying public hasn't shown that much enthusiasm yet. We can't help feeling that people are intimidated by Strehlow's name, and all the controversies surrounding him.'

'And what about that,' I said, pointing to one of the exhibits. 'Wouldn't you be intimidated by that?'

'What is it? Lot 227. Let's look it up: Kadaitcha, Symbolical Feather Boots, last used in the ceremony of the blood avenger Aremala in 1870 . . .' He tailed off. 'Yes, I see where you're coming from. But you have to be careful not to let these things take you over, don't you reckon? They're objects now. They're like works of art. It's not as if they have any active meaning in this world of ours.'

He stepped over to the window, somewhat theatrically, and pulled the shade-blind back. Sunshine flooded through the room, but his gesture only succeeded in making the lots, in their numbered rows, seem more like a collection of recovered contraband.

'Go on,' said my new companion, in a voice of encouragement. 'Take a good look. You can handle them. Anything you want. I like the religious items, myself.'

He picked up a tattered volume, and held it before my eyes.

'The New Testament, translated into Dieri. Do you know the country round Lake Eyre? The Birdsville Track, Killalpaninna?'

'To some extent.'

'This was for those people. If you consult your catalogue you'll see that, quite soon after its publication in 1919, they were almost all wiped out by the Spanish Flu. And how about this photograph – happy days at Hermannsburg?'

I walked ahead of him, his words resonating like lines from some bleak chorus inside my head, over and over, until a strange thought came to me: it seemed in those few seconds as if it was not these objects alone, but all the secrets of Aboriginal Australia – its past, its myths, its dreams, its hopes – that had been picked through, dismembered, put up for sale.

Then, from behind a flimsy curtain drawn across a corner of the gallery, there came a sound: a deep, hawking, throat-clearing cough, followed by low, gruff whispers.

'What's that?'

'Oh, that's the restricted area, over there. I'll show you.'

'Restricted?'

'Ceremonial things. But that doesn't mean you can't go in. We've got a delegation from the Central Land Council doing a quick inspection, checking to make sure there's nothing that they want.'

He led the way into a recess that was even dimmer and dustier than the main exhibition area, and waved a proprietorial hand.

'See – the crown jewels, we call them!'

I looked round. The walls were covered with mounted photographs, in colour. I recognised them instantly. They were the illustrations from *Wüstentanz* – Aranda elders, ochre-painted, feather-decorated, embracing, sitting quietly with their sacred boards.

Close by us, oblivious to our presence, bent in the half-dark over one of the photos, pointing, murmuring, was a group of elderly Aboriginal men. They all wore baggy, threadbare jeans and long hooded jackets. All of them, I now saw, were crying. Every few seconds they wiped the tears from their cheeks. One began to sing, gently, in a soft, wavering voice. At his shoulder a younger man, white, with a thick beard, in even scruffier clothes, listened.

'You all knew him – the bloke in the photograph?' asked the white man after a few seconds.

'We knew him,' came the reply, punctuated by deep, rasping coughs. 'Old fella, him – long gone.'

I looked away. The attendant was staring at me uncertainly.

'Are these the pictures that were published in *Stern* magazine?'

'I don't know anything about that,' he said. 'They come from an exhibition that was held in Stuttgart, in the eighties.' The name of that gilded, museum-rich city shone between us like a blade. 'So? What do you think? It's the inner sanctum, isn't it? You could almost say we're standing at Ground Zero of the whole Aboriginal world.'

I saw the fireball, seething, roaring, spreading across the sand-dunes and the plains.

'Ground Zero?'

He laughed lightly.

'Yes. Isn't that what they call the place where everything begins?'

# Five  Giles

# I

On April 23rd 1874, nine months into his second expedition, and deep in unknown desert, the explorer Ernest Giles made out a blur of broken ranges dancing before him on the horizon's line. Giles reined in his horse. He gazed westwards. It seemed clear to him a change of country was at last at hand. He could see spurs and ridges, notched, irregular outliers, he immediately assumed, of grander, more mountainous terrain. The rise he stood on could itself almost be called a rocky prominence. Water might run in such country during rains, while between him and the hills, no more than thirty miles distant, the landscape stretched down into a valley – long, inviting, dark.

At that moment, from behind him, Giles's companion, Alf Gibson, called out. Unwelcome news: his horse had knocked up and was on the verge of collapse. The two men, in truth, were not poised on the brink of breakthrough, though they had pushed far into the wilderness of spinifex that bears Gibson's name today. They were a hundred miles beyond their waiting colleagues at the support depot, in burning, blood-red sand-dunes, without shade, or sufficient water, or supplies; and now, with only one good horse between them, they could not risk the high ground beckoning; they could barely hope to fall back on their steps.

Poised, amidst silence, Giles glimpsed what lay in wait. He was a creature free from sentiment, a solitary, self-dependent man. To his companions on that expedition, he seemed as hard and sharp as mulga. His stamp came from far away, and years before – from London, from the cold classrooms of Christ's Hospital, where he had been schooled as a boy, following in the steps of those two wounded souls, Charles Lamb and Samuel Taylor Coleridge. Half-fledged in literary sensibility, shot through with romantic tastes, he trailed out to Australia in his mid-teens, in the wake of his family, found work in the Melbourne post office, made his way north-east, to the thriving town of Castlemaine, then – nothing. Giles all but vanishes for a decade and a half into the Outback, into the station country of the Darling: perhaps far southern Queensland; perhaps western New South Wales. There are sightings of him at Menindee – he forms a friendship with his old schoolmate, William Tietkens. His enthusiasm for exploration gathers strength, fanned by words as much as by experience, for, as he himself recounts, '*I had been a delighted student of the narratives of voyages and discoveries, from Robinson Crusoe to Anson and Cook, and the exploits on land in the brilliant accounts given by Sturt, Mitchell, Eyre, Grey, Leichhardt, and Kennedy, constantly excited my imagination.*'

He only emerges into Australian history in 1872, at the head of a small private expedition – but these shadows that surround him seem entirely right. Unlike his precursors and his contemporaries, Giles was not a man of science, he was not a soldier, nor a survey official, nor the emissary of a colonial government. His story has no hidden contours. There was no romance to be exorcised, no psychic tension casting its symptoms onto every range and creek-bed. He had no circumstances; no flaws of character. He was the freest, the most literal, the most disturbing of all the explorers. '*An explorer*,' he wrote, '*is an explorer from love – and it is nature, not art, that makes him so.*'

His being comes through sharply in his words. He lives, he breathes, he seems to stand close by his reader, speaking, whispering, leading forever on, just as he stands in that instant in the desert, face to face with defeat and its expanding consequences. He sees the pattern of the future; his dream of exploration dies before him in the act. The rival expedition parties already in the field, ones larger than his own, and better financed, will now prevail: convivial, well-connected men, like John Forrest and Colonel Peter Warburton, will be the first to cross the final emptiness upon the map. The landscape will be theirs. All Giles will be left with, for decades to come, is words and memory, and his desire: desire unquenched, unfulfilled, feeding in bitterness upon itself.

In his journal of the expedition, which is closely based upon the campfire jottings that he made each night, Giles skates over this realisation in a single sentence, then lapses into a highflown, stilted snatch of verse: 'At this moment I would even my jewel eternal have sold for the power to span the gulf that lay between.' But such a transaction was the one thing that could not come to pass, God and the Devil both being excluded from his philosophy.

'There is no doubt,' he concludes, 'that these ranges shut out from the view other and higher ones to the west.' Giles calls out to Gibson. He looks again; they prepare to turn. First, a name is needed, and a suitably elevated one, for the hills beyond his reach.

Like his fellow-explorers, Giles was an inveterate christener of landscapes: most of the Germanic mountains strewn through the Centre are his, bestowed from a shortlist he had from his patron, Baron Ferdinand von Mueller, the Victorian Government's eccentric chief botanist. Sometimes he would give vent to his classicising enthusiasm or to his poetic imaginings: and one can still trace his path through the desert, from Mount Udor and the Vale of Tempe to Glen Helen and Titania's Spring. Sites of utmost significance, though, he preferred to dignify with imperial labels, and so it went, that hot mid-morning among the sandhills. 'In honour of their royal highnesses, the Duke and Duchess of Edinburgh,' this furthest-sighted feature would, he decided, become known as 'The Alfred and Marie Range'.

I still recall the first time I read those words. I was on a transcontinental flight, bound east to west. We were passing over the western desert. The cloudscape had given way. Far beneath, as if somehow magnified by the haze, rippling lines of red sandhills stood out, the corridors between them darkened by swathes of scrub and timbered creek-lines. I put aside my copy of *Australia Twice Traversed – The Romance of Exploration*, a book Giles published late in life, which holds the narratives of all his major journeys. I stared through the aircraft window's convex glass. Was I gazing down, I wondered, at the same low ranges Giles had seen? Were those swirls and drifts of dark across the landscape shadows cast by cliffs and mesas, by half-known ridges and breakaways? The book fell open at its title page, where Giles, I now noticed, had attached a quote from Bunyan underneath his name: '*Go forth, my book, and show the things/ Pilgrimage unto the pilgrim brings*.' I smiled to myself. I shook my head, and made my way back into the story. Two days before their furthest west, as Giles recounts, Gibson and he had fallen into early morning conversation while they rode along. Giles, who was much caught up in the doings of his predecessors, remarked to his companion that the day was the anniversary of Burke and Wills' fateful return to their depot at Cooper's Creek. But Gibson was young, and had no education, and knew nothing about this tragedy. Giles gave him a brief account, and mentioned in passing that Wills had a brother who also perished in the field of discovery, for he had been lost in the Arctic with Sir John Franklin on the expedition that sailed in 1845.

'Oh, I had a brother who died with Franklin at the North Pole,' said Gibson, who was, as Giles remembered, in unusually jocular mood. 'How is it,' the young man went on to ask, 'in all these exploring expeditions, a lot of the people go and die?'

'Well, I don't know, Gibson, how it is,' the explorer answered, in sombre fashion, like a novelist who senses the emerging pattern of his tale. 'But there are many dangers in exploring that may at any time cause the death of some of the people engaged in it besides accidents; but I believe want of judgement or knowledge or courage in individuals often brought about their deaths.'

'Well, I shouldn't like to die in this part of the country, anyhow,' came Gibson's quick reply, and the subject dropped.

This exchange, so rich in resonances, stayed with Giles all through the long return. After a short way, as both men had feared, Gibson's horse failed. They coaxed it another mile before it lay down in the sand and died. The two, with their lone surviving mount, made their way a little further, walking and riding by turns. At last Giles called out to Gibson. They stopped. They drained the water they had left, a thimbleful for each of them.

'Look here, Gibson,' Giles said. 'You know we are in a most terrible fix, and only one horse; therefore only one person can ride, and one must remain behind. I shall remain, and now you listen to me . . .'

It was a simple enough plan. Gibson would go on to the water-kegs which they had left along their outward route, water the mare, rest an hour or two, then head on by dark. At dawn, the ranges he was bound for should be in view. He would be safe. 'Stick to the tracks' – they were clear in the red sand; they would lead him home. At camp, he should send out a rescue party, with water, to come for

Giles. Gibson asked for the compass so he could steer by night. Giles gave it to him; and off he went. Through some instinct, as Gibson receded, Giles called out once more: stick to the tracks! And watched, staring through the sunshine, while his companion was borne slowly out of human sight.

The plan was not designed to claim Gibson. It was more like an act of sacrifice, a death sentence passed by Giles upon himself, as though in requital for his failure. Extinction in the desert was always in his mind; at times, the desert served him as a realm of after-life, a zone where he might encounter forlorn souls, like Leichhardt, that 'lost Pleiad' for whose traces he was ever on alert.

Giles began his solitary trek. No rescue party came for him. In his narration of his journey, the days and nights pass like a dream. His head spins; he faints; he trudges through stands of spinifex as tall as himself. He makes the water-kegs; he finds and pounces on and eats a baby wallaby, 'raw, dying as it was, fur, skin and all – the delicious taste of that creature I shall never forget.'

On the sixth day he reaches the ranges and the waterhole; after two more days, at dawn, he walks into his camp, and wakes his men, who stare at him as though 'he was one newly risen from the dead'. But Gibson? The returning horse's tracks, as Giles to his horror and alarm had already seen, diverged at mid-point from the outward route. What of him? No sign. Next morning, Giles set off anew at the head of a search team, quartering the desert, looking for the man lost instead of him – but in vain.

*'Here we were isolated from civilisation, and hundreds of miles from our fellow creatures, and one of our small party had gone from us. It being now nine days since I parted from him, it was not very likely that he was still in existence in that fearful desert, as no man would or could stay there alive; he must be dead, or he would have returned, as I did, only much sooner, as the mare he had would carry him as far in a day as I could walk in a week in this country.'*

Failure. Disappearance. Death. This ordeal forms the heart of Giles's expedition narratives. His fame as a bushman rests on that delirium-tormented return, which is described in *Australia Twice Traversed*, in the most racing, tumbling, impressionistic prose.

It is also the climax of the biography of Giles by Ray Ericksen, a book I heard of long before I found my way to it; a book that advances several striking propositions: that writing and exploration were inseparable instincts in Giles; that his response to the landscape was at once analytical and imaginative; that exploration, at its peak, can be considered as an art form; and that, in the Australian record of continental discovery, masterpieces have been accomplished.

When my interest in Giles was dawning, I was given a phone number for Ericksen. I rang. We fell into guarded conversation. I asked him, at some stage, about his subject's view of Aboriginal Australia.

'Have you actually read my book?' asked Ericksen, in a chill voice.

'It's out of print,' I parried.

'Why don't you have a look at it first before you call again – it's got your answer in it.'

'And what does it say?'

'That the attitude of Ernest Giles was hard, and inflexible: it was an amalgam of dislike without respect, of distrust without fear, of contempt without interest, of pity without grief.'

'Is that a quote from your book?'

'Maybe.'

'It's a harsh judgement,' I said.

'I'm no harder on Giles than I am on myself.'

'And do you like him, as a man?'

'I loved him,' he said, and hung up, leaving me surprised by both his choice of verb and tense.

Months later, in high summer, on an early-morning wander

through the shops of Double Bay, I found a tattered copy of Ericksen's book *Ernest Giles – Explorer and Traveller*.

I leafed through it, laid it aside, and went out once more into the city sunshine. Around the middle of the day, I was browsing through the newspapers in abstracted fashion, from back to front, absorbing next to nothing of what passed before me. I was about to turn another page. A sentence reached through; without quite knowing why, I paused: 'A true-blue Australian,' I read. 'He delighted in confounding experts. Non-conformist, unconventional, solitary, he chose his own path in life. He was fascinated by the journey, with all its troubles, delights and contradictions.'

I smoothed out the page and glanced up the column, skipping a paragraph or two, feeling a pull from the words before me.

'His first book, *West of Centre, A Journey of Discovery into the Heartland of Australia*, is his account of seven months spent travelling alone by Land-Rover in the country explored by Ernest Giles.'

On some instinctual level, long before I saw his name, I realised I was looking down on the obituary of Ray Ericksen, who had died on New Year's Day.

With a sense of obligation, the precise nature of which I would have been hard-pressed to describe, in the weeks ahead, while on the road, I made my way through the Giles biography, absorbing it in tandem with the explorer's journals, until I felt myself quite saturated by the fall and dazzle of their desert light – and I decided that regardless of the season the time had come for me to head out, alone, into that country.

It was at this point – I was then in the East Kimberley, in Kununurra – that my path once more threw me together with the elusive Grahame Walsh. I recognised his four-wheel drive, parked askew in the forecourt of a budget motel: I raised my idea with him, for he was at that stage the only man I knew who was familiar with all the tracks and highways of the desert.

'Ernest Giles,' repeated Grahame, frowning, and shaking his head. 'A wild individual. I don't know that I'd want to be out now on his trail – although I have been with him, and traced his steps. He was the first European to find the rock art there – have you seen it, on a sandstone outlier, just by the Tarn of Auber rockhole? No? He's a bit flowery and romantic for my tastes, but I suppose he is a fully paid-up dweller in the realms of the unreal.'

'He was a scientific explorer,' I protested.

'You think so? Show me.'

Grahame leaned over and took my copy of *Australia Twice Traversed*.

'Don't be led astray by all those Latin name-lists of plants and trees at the back. How about this: "I trust it will be believed that an explorer may be an imaginative as well as a practical creature." See: he believed he was writing the landscape, singing it into being as he went. Exploration was his fiction. He was the hero of his own story. He was in hyper-space! Although I must confess, there are times, out in the King Leopolds, with the thermometer over forty, when I almost think he was on to something. Listen: "Strange as it may appear, it seems because the tales of Australian travel and self-devotion are true, that they attract but little notice, for were the narratives of the explorers not true we might become the most renowned novelists the world has ever known".' Grahame laughed. He snapped the book shut: 'Clear enough for you? He was a frustrated author, just like everybody in the desert. To be at the top of the best-seller lists: that's what he really wanted.'

'Well, never mind that,' I said. 'You remember those ranges he fell short of, in the Second Expedition?'

I explained my plan.

'Honestly? I'd come with you, but most of the country between here and the Gibson Desert's under water. The cyclone season's kicking in. Forget about it. You've been in Giles territory before, anyhow.'

'I have?'

'Sure. Round Tibooburra. He spent years out west of the Darling, and along the Cooper. He even camped at Depot Glen, in fact he was the one who found the remains of Sturt's boat, smashed into pieces and washed down Evelyn Creek. And you've been to the Eastern Goldfields: that's where Giles finished up. Can you imagine it – the most untamed of all the explorers, marooned in the back-blocks. He was still working as a clerk in the mining inspector's office in Coolgardie when he died. Poor bastard! He wanted to be buried in the desert, at Ularring rockhole, but they just stuck him in a box in the local cemetery. He's still there now.'

'I'm glad to hear it.'

'There's a flash new monument on top of him, of course. You can see it from the main street – it stands out like the balls on a Kimberley cattle-dog. You'd have to think he ran into Carnegie out there: and that would make him the bridge between the first and the last in Australian exploration.'

'It's an attractive idea.'

'The same way he's a bridge between Europe and Australia.'

I looked back, more sceptically.

'Don't you see,' said Grahame, 'the reason Giles loved the desert landscape so much – the reason he saw all those cathedrals and tem-ples there – is that he was looking at it with European eyes. He was watching it, staring into it as if it was a thing of beauty all through his life.'

Noise rose around us in the bar.

'Don't even think of driving out from here,' said Grahame, as we parted. 'And stay off the Stock Route as well. The best track's through the Pilbara: Newman, Jigalong, Lake Disappointment. Captivating country down there. You could take tomorrow's flight to Hedland – the North-West milk-run. It's worth doing once in your life. Those planes aren't like other aircraft. And if you're really so mesmerised by what Giles found in the sandhills, why don't you read the Journal of the Fifth Expedition?'

The Fifth Expedition? I settled into my seat on the Ansett service to Port Hedland, and plunged into my research. As Grahame had hinted, it was an unusual flight. The plane was a turbo-prop, half-empty, with a few rows of overall-clad miners hunched together in the back. So small was the aircraft's scale that a kind of intimacy was forced upon the passengers; and there was another peculiarity I had not met with before outside the Soviet bloc: the front seats, perhaps in some concession to the idea of business class, were arranged facing each other, across a narrow table of laminated wood.

I was in the first row, looking backwards. The traveller opposite me, his face half-obscured by a large tan-bark Akubra, fell asleep almost as soon as we had taken off. We levelled out. Through the window I could watch the receding procession of storm-clouds. Rain fell in thick nets from their bases. Lightning played. We crossed the flat coastline of the Cambridge Gulf.

I rejoined my explorer in his book's back pages: it was the mid-June of 1876. By this stage of his travels, as Giles well knew, the peak of his achievements was past. A note of speculative sadness hangs over the account of his final expedition, which in fact was nothing but the return leg of his successful crossing of the southern deserts. He was still troubled by his bout of ophthalmia. He had new personnel. He was dependent not on horses but on camels, those 'creatures possessed of marvellous powers' – and this change alone was enough to transform the rules of his engagement with the desert.

Horses, in Giles's eyes, were noble, sharply individuated beings. They had an aptitude for tragic failure, they were beautiful, he felt a bond with them. They have clear personalities in his narrative, and are often better drawn than the men. Indeed, if Giles killed and smoked them, and fed on them throughout his first two journeys, it was only because he viewed their flesh as a sustaining, sacramental bread – but this love of his gives way in the final, camel-borne crossings of the continent to a gentler, more domestic variety of affection.

Camels, with their mazy motion and their unflustered progress, took much of the danger out of desert travelling, and most of the heroics as well – though Giles, with his gambles and his pushes into dry terrain, and his belief that water could best be found by chance, tried constantly to reintroduce the fatal thrill.

On the 18th of the month, after ten days advancing through the plains and dune-fields, he records his arrival at 'a little trifling water-channel, with a few small scattered white-gum trees, coming from a low stony mulga-covered ridge'.

The party dug out a well, much like the native wells which dot this stretch of desert even today: harsh country, deep and still, that merits lengthy contemplation, a domain of shot-lines, and abandoned drillers' tracks, and painted, half-forgotten caves. But the landscape was mute for Giles, and filled with little more than melancholy: the expedition's favourite camel, Buzoe, collapsed at this well and died. 'She is old and worn out, poor old creature,' Giles lamented. 'She had always been a quiet, easy-paced old pet.'

He then did what he would never have done to a horse – he laid out her carcass for the scavengers and desert birds. He named this soakage 'Buzoe's Grave', and the name remains on survey maps. It lies hard by Ngarinarri, the claypan where, a century after Giles's passage, the last two nomads of the desert, Warri and Yatungka, were found. The pair were kindly rescued from their drought-struck homelands and transported to Wiluna, where they survived for two scant years.

'The region is so desolate that it is horrifying even to describe,' Giles declares with relish. If God's eye could have looked down on the party, moving slow and snake-like, it would, he felt, have been with pitying admiration, *'as it forced its way continually on; onwards without pausing, over this vast sandy region, avoiding death only by motion and distance, until some oasis can be found. Slow as eternity it seems to move, but certain we trust as death; and truly the wanderer in its wilds may snatch a fearful joy at having once beheld the scenes, that human eyes ought never again to see.'*

Despite his troubled dreams, and despite such trance-like meditations, Giles had an aim in view. The caravan moved on. Four days more, and they had crossed the realm of dune-fields and salt lakes: *'We neared the spot from the west, where the Alfred and Marie Ranges lie – the first sight of which, from the east, had cost my former horse expedition in this region so dear.'*

The explorer gives, at this point, sardonic thanks to Providence for having denied his heart's wish, since he now realises he would have perished in the dune country. But a darker transaction was under way. In the first version of the journey, printed by the South Australian Parliament, Giles allows himself no more, and hurries on. By the time he published *Australia Twice Traversed*, thirteen years later, after long spells in the goldfields of Halls Creek, he could bring himself to recollect the scene. He looks at the reverse of love; he sees the other side of longing. The brief description that he gives veils his heart's loss beneath a wild contempt: The Alfred and Maries! Their Royal Highnesses!

*'Those hills were in reality much lower than they appeared to be, when looked at from the east; in fact, they were so low and uninteresting that I did not investigate them otherwise than with field-glasses. We passed by the northern end . . .'*

So he saw them at last as they were, those faint, notched indentations on the horizon line, upon which all the yearnings of his eyes had fixed. But which were the truer – the pale stone platforms, amidst the spinifex, or the dusty range-line, veiled, and shimmering in beauty and indistinct? I leaned forward; I bent over the page.

At which moment, the figure opposite me chose to reach across with one hand, and point to the book.

'You don't know a thing about him, unless you've been out there,' came a thin, hard voice.

I looked up, in some surprise. This individual was flamboyantly dressed: he wore cowboy boots, neat, faded blue jeans, a belt of heavy leather with a silver clasp, a black satin western shirt, its pockets picked out in bright red. He had removed his hat, which he was balancing on his knees, stroking it from time to time as if it was some kind of ritual head-dress. The face revealed was keen, and sun-tanned: there was something raw in it; his hair was long; his blue eyes glared into mine.

'But that's exactly where I'm going,' I said.

'And what gives you the right?' he shot back, smiling contemptuously. 'Who are you?'

I told him.

'You're not from round here, are you?'

'Round where?' I nodded to the window. We were overflying ridged, scarlet sand-dunes.

'I've been out there. I've been reading that country since I was a child. I've driven it. I've even walked it when I've had to. Esterline – David Esterline. Perhaps you've heard the name?'

He gazed at me, defiantly.

'Esterline – I don't know that I have.'

'You will! I'm a geophysical explorer.'

'A what?'

'A prospector.'

'And that's' – I looked at him again; I hesitated – 'that's what you do full-time?'

'Off-season,' he said, frowning. 'Rest of the year I work on station stock-camps, and I follow the circuit. I'm a rodeo rider.'

'Best there is?'

'Of course: bull-riding, buck-jumping; saddle-bronc, bareback. I ride anything, and everywhere. The Barkly, the Top End; across western Central Queensland; Tambo, Mount Isa, Katherine. I won first prize at Augathella last New Year's day.'

'I imagine it's a dangerous way of life.'

'You're not wrong! I've broken every bone you've heard of. I've got pins in my arm-joints, plates in my shoulders.'

'It's another world,' I answered, somewhat carelessly.

'I'm glad you said that!'

'Why?'

He gave a rueful smile.

'At least you recognise we've got a world! Let me show you something.'

He reached into his back pocket, from which he pulled out a torn, much-folded photograph. He handed it to me.

'What do you reckon?'

It was a portrait. It showed a young woman, wearing a fringed western jacket, staring into the sun, and smiling in a quiet, distracted way.

'She's lovely,' I said, in an appreciative voice.

'Bet you didn't think I could have a sort like that,' said Esterline.

'Girlfriend?'

'She lives in Lismore.'

'It must be hard for you to get down to see her.'

'It's been a while. She's married. Sometimes she writes.'

He glanced down at the cloud forms. I searched my mind for points of reference.

'Do you know Frankie Shadforth?' I asked.

This was an instant success.

'You know him? Why didn't you say so? The Aboriginal bloke – the champion rider?'

'The station manager at Seven Emu.'

'That's him. He set up the Borroloola Rodeo. I've ridden there myself. It's wonderful.'

His fierce, injured front subsided. Now he was quickness, light and charm.

'Come here.' He motioned to me. 'I'm going to tell you a secret.' He leaned forward, and whispered. 'I'm driving out tomorrow, from Hedland – to my ground, in the desert.'

'Your ground?'

'The ground I have under exploration licence – the prospect I've got pegged.' His voice dropped even lower. 'I've found something.'

'Is that right?' I said lightly, feeling the conversation was getting a little out of control. 'Lasseter's lost reef, perhaps?'

Esterline stared evenly back.

'You can laugh if you want. You think there's nothing out there? What about Telfer? What about the West Musgraves, and Murrin Murrin? The goldfields are out there, waiting. Uranium orebodies. Vast, deep-buried base metal deposits. It's virgin country. No one's been through, looking, really looking, using their eyes, not since the first explorers. But what would you know about it? I don't know why I even thought of telling you.'

This with the greatest scorn, and outrage.

'I'm sorry,' I said. 'You're right to be angry. I just couldn't resist. To me, the Sandy Desert's just an empty space upon the map. To you, it's something more.'

'Something very much more.'

'So, go on: what did you find?'

Esterline resumed, leaning across the little table, gesturing, staring into my eyes: the geology; the magnetics; the deep structure of Archaean rocks. He sketched the mineral basins for me; his words arranged themselves into complex theories; he became a man of science.

'And where is this prospect of yours?'

His eyes turned soft and hazy.

'It's far out, beyond where Giles went. Beyond Lake Dora; beyond the Stock Route. Out past Separation Well. I've been looking in that country for the last five years, on my own, each summer. Sometimes when you're driving in the sandhills, you come on outcrops, almost hidden. There's no clue to them, from the overflights, nothing – no way of finding them except being there, and no tracks out that way, except for mine.'

'And what led you there?'

The note from the aircraft's engines changed at that point. Our descent began.

'I can't tell you that,' said Esterline, with a derisive shake of the head. 'You don't believe any of this anyway.'

'Maybe I do,' I said. I kept my eyes on the window as I was speaking; through the clouds, the Pilbara landscape, a hard, oppressive purple, glowed. 'Why should that matter, anyhow? You've started telling me already, and it's not as if you're ever likely to see me again. I'm just someone you met on a plane flight.'

Esterline glared at me. He clenched his hands. He threw himself back in his seat.

'You don't understand,' he ground out at last. 'I'm not some loser from the bush. I know things. But if I tell you them, you'd think I was crazy.'

'I can handle that.'

'Well then,' said Esterline, his voice soft, 'I follow totemic birds.'

As he spoke, the plane tilted, and began to turn. Beneath us, stained deep red by the evening sun, Port Hedland's coastline came into view: dour plains, crisscrossed by roads and tracks and power lines. There was the town on its promontory, the iron-ore loaders, the bulk carriers out to sea; there were the shining towers of the HBI plant, surrounded by marsh and flood channel; the wrecking yards and salt-piles and ornate, square evaporation ponds.

'You what?' I murmured, gazing down.

'You heard me. I follow my totemic birds – they guide me.'

'And what birds are they,' I asked him, thinking how much Hedland, seen from that height, resembled the overprinted circuit lines upon a microchip, etched onto resistant silicon.

'What kind of bird could it be, out there? The kite-hawk of the desert, of course.'

I looked at him. He had my full attention.

'Don't laugh,' he snapped.

'I'm not laughing at all.'

He gauged my words; he made a quick, assessing, scornful noise.

'There are three kinds when you get to know them: three sub-species, almost indistinguishable, one from the other. They have little variations in their tail-shape, different feeding habits, different modulations in their calls. You can see them in the desert when the spinifex fires are burning, they're out there in hundreds, thousands. You can watch them circling high up in the sky, then diving down and swooping through the flames – and sometimes, when I see that, I think I love them more than life itself.'

'And how come they're your totem?'

'I grew up with them, for years, when we were on Meentheena station, east of Marble Bar. They keep watch over me in western Queensland; I see them in the gorges of the Sandy Desert.'

'They keep watch?'

'Can't you listen? I was up in Cape York once, mustering on a station there: Rutland Plains, close by the Mitchell River. We used to ride in to Kowanyama community. An old woman took me aside; she was the one who told me how the kite-hawks were following me. They were the emblem of my life: my bird; "*inurdj*", in Kunjun language.'

'And what happens when there are no kites in the sky? How can they guide you?'

'No one said they're always there.' He raised his hands in exasperation, and rolled his eyes. 'Are there higher powers always present in your life?'

The plane swooped in, touched down, taxied. Esterline and I walked together to the terminal. An anvil-cloud, with rain-veils adrift beneath it, covered half the sky.

'Isn't that majestic?' I said, wondering how to end this brief association.

'It's raining where I was born,' he said, looking at me with a sad, mistrustful smile.

We swept between the sliding doors. A knot of south-bound passengers stood waiting. Esterline took in the scene. He pointed; he nodded. I followed his gaze. Close by, half-turned from us, was a tall mine-worker, wearing a striking purple bomber jacket, with the silhouette of Mount Whaleback emblazoned on it, and the words: 'Layne Christensen Fontana – 550,000 Hours Without A Lost Time Accident'.

'A very Proustian thing to wear,' he said.

'Well, Esterline,' I laughed, 'you're certainly full of surprises!'

'What's wrong?' He wheeled round with an air of burning rage. 'Do you really think no one in remote Australia knows how to read?'

'Don't even try it on,' I interrupted. 'You can tell I take you seriously.'

He gave me a nod: he even blushed. He raised one hand to touch the brim of his dark, wide hat.

'That's not an "Honest John" you're wearing, by any chance?' I asked him.

'Might be,' said Esterline, with a sidelong glance. 'Might just be. And where are you going now?'

'Into town. I've got a friend here who works at the hospital – accident and emergency. His name's Gilbert Wallace. He's got some unconventional ideas about the North-West. You might find him quite interesting.'

Esterline looked dubious.

'Why don't you come along,' I hazarded.

'Well, why not,' said he, shrugging in the most offhand way. 'It's not as if I've got anything better to do, anyhow – not here, in Port Hedland.'

Together, through the dying light, we drove in. As we pulled onto the highway, and the loaders and cantilevers came into view, Esterline turned in his seat: 'If we're going to be friends like this, you might want to know a bit about me!'

'If you think it's really necessary . . .'

With the air of a man released from Trappist vows, he drew in a deep, decisive breath. The tale was striking. Esterline's recital gave it a sharp, spasmodic rhythm: the station childhood, the cyclones, rain and dust. Bush schools, and mines; helicopters, stock work. We were already crossing the bridge above the Newman railway when he brought his story to its close.

'That was quite a self-portrayal,' I said. I felt I had just been given the flavour of the man.

'And you,' he asked. 'What's your story?'

'Nothing so dramatic!' I laughed, and took the turning into town.

'I suppose, like everybody, you hate the Pilbara and Port Hedland?'

'Do you know,' I said, 'I can picture when I first drove in here, years ago, on the Karratha highway. It was blazing summer, the middle of the morning. There was red dust blowing everywhere. I came in along the scrub-lined causeway, past the iron ore plant, and stopped in that dead street where the post office is, and the banks, and union headquarters, and all the op-shops. I felt desolate: I had the sense of arriving at the entrance into Hell.'

'You see!' broke in Esterline, in triumph.

'But wait. Gradually, over time, my ideas changed. It began to speak to me. You know the way one's easiest, most convenient impressions so often seem to fade, and recompose themselves into their opposite. I found myself becoming intrigued by the place, by its light and colours, its buildings and their sounds. And my view of the landscape all around began to shift as well. I used to find it hideous, deformed, sterile; now I find it subtle, and dignified, and calm, and if there's anywhere in the world I'd like to spend more of my life, and plunge myself into, it would be here.'

'True?'

'Almost. That's not what Dr Wallace thinks, though. He can't stand Port Hedland – he finds it inhospitable and depressing. He wants the whole place shut down and evacuated: he says no one's ever had a creative thought in the Pilbara.'

'Typical!'

'Although I have detected signs in him of lessening hostility. Last time we spoke he said the shoreline of Nickol Bay, seen from a distance, looked like a cerebral cortex. And he's started climbing the peaks of the Hamersley Range, and walking through the river systems. He even said he wants to play the flute at the base of Joffre Gorge, and listen to the sounds reflected back to him. Here he is!' I pulled up outside the hospital. 'You can ask him yourself.'

Gilbert was standing in front of the after-hours entrance, his round, soft face picked out by the lights shining across the water.

'Listen,' he was saying in a patient voice into his mobile phone as we came up. 'There was nothing we could do. Her liver just exploded – absolutely – yes – it's all on the death certificate . . .' He snapped the phone shut. 'It's been another dreadful day.'

'This is Esterline,' I said.

Esterline glanced at me, a hurt look in his eyes.

'He's a friend of mine,' I went on, quickly. 'He's – he's a geological explorer. He comes from the Pilbara, from east of Marble Bar.'

'So you'll have noticed that it's getting hotter!' Gilbert launched in at once.

'Hotter?'

'Yes – last year was the hottest year on record. I estimate it's three degrees warmer now than when the Pilbara was first settled by Europeans. It's easy to die out here, even with litres of water by your side. You've only got to faint, or let your head come into contact with the ground. The moment your brain reaches 41.6 degrees, you're dead. And have you ever seen such miserable country,' he hurried on, with mounting descriptive lyricism, 'flat as the back of your hand, stunted vegetation, hardly any hills, and nothing in between. It reminds me of the effects of disseminated sclerosis, when patients lose their colour vision: all those bleached shades, the white sky, the pale sand, the grey sea.'

'We were just discussing how beautiful we thought it was,' I put in.

'Of course it's also beautiful,' said Gilbert, philosophically. 'In brief flashes, anyway. There's always beauty in the fury of the blast. I think that at the same time. In fact, I think it increasingly. One can think two things at once, you know – consistency's a much over-praised virtue. Now: are you going to invite me to dinner at the curious Mercure Hotel, with its curious foyer front-desk of tiger-iron, and its curious restaurant, curiously maintained at polar air temperatures?'

'I think,' I said, 'on balance, yes, we might opt for the Mercure, since the only time I've eaten at your house in Cooke Point, you served a single tin of crabmeat paste and a few slices of brown bread between the two of us, and you had, as I remember, very curiously, run out of mustard.'

'It's a hotel with a grandeur of its own, isn't it?' said Gilbert, ignoring this last remark. 'It almost has a mythic flavour, with its attendant bottle-shop, and the views across the shipping channel, and Cemetery Beach so close by. I'll meet you there in half an hour. I have to drive round to see the Coroner on the way.'

'Is that a regular thing?'

'Daily – if not hourly.'

I waited at a window table of the restaurant, shivering, and staring out to sea, thinking how mild the night-time sounds and shadows were, and how, in the Pilbara, contrary to every natural expectation, life seems sweet and soft. After some while, Gilbert appeared, a sheaf of papers underneath his arm. He sat down.

'Where's your friend?'

'He just went to pick up his supplies and his prospecting gear. He's driving out tomorrow morning, into the Sandy Desert.'

'Is that so?' said Gilbert reflectively. 'I thought he looked a little cracked. It's desperate out there, this time of year, like some medieval wilderness: nothing moves, except the flies, and taipans, and death adders, and king browns, and they're all in plague pro-portions, anywhere you camp.'

I took in this alarming judgement, and nodded.

'You're not thinking of going with him, are you?'

'Maybe, if he asks me.'

'And how long have you two been friends?'

'Actually, I just met him on the plane in from Kununurra.'

'Have you taken leave of your senses? He could be anyone – he doesn't look like a geologist. You have to be careful out this way. There are some real eccentrics wandering round here.'

'Surely not!'

'Political extremists, too! Just look at this place,' he gestured towards the lights of Finucane Island. 'It looks like Sakhalin – like the Gulag – like the House of the Dead!'

'It's an interesting comparison,' I murmured.

'Russian literature your specialty, is it?' said Esterline, sliding down into a seat beside us.

'In a sense, yes,' replied Gilbert, rather haughtily. 'It is. I speak the language. I've studied the country. I've translated two books from Russian.'

'You never told me that!' I broke in.

'You never asked me. You have to ask, and probe, if you want to fight your way through to the truth of life. You need to seek out what people are, the things they've done – have a sense of reality.'

'Well, maybe you could give us a few pointers, from all your dialectical experience, but tell us about the books first.'

Gilbert leaned against his chair. He interlaced his hands. His voice – high, elegant, sardonic – danced ahead. 'In my youth,' he began, 'I was a communist . . .'

'Almost a political extremist, in fact,' I interrupted.

'Do you want to hear the story?'

It was an intriguing tale: Gilbert, despite his exile in the Pilbara, was in love with ice, and snow, and alpine cloud. His sweetest years had been spent in Cooma, beneath the Snowy Mountains, where all through the winter months he would gaze up towards the distant whiteness of the slopes. The passions of his politics had, by his middle years, long since given way to a tranquil, distinctive blend of world-weariness. On a visit to Sydney – it was, he remembered, during the Soviet Union's final days – he found himself in Pitt Street, strolling by a Marxist bookshop, where a publication displayed in the window caught his eye. This was *Golden Rigma, the Siberian Tiger*, a bestseller of the Brezhnev years. So charmed was Gilbert by the story, and by the artistry of its painted illustrations, that he made a trip to Khabarovsk, the capital of west Siberia, where the book is set.

During his brief time there he was able to track down the author, Vsevolod Sysoyev. The two men discovered a shared fondness for the Sikhote-Alin mountains, home of Rigma, the tigress heroine.

'What a wonderful thing to do,' Esterline burst out at this point. 'To follow your instincts like that, right to the end.'

'Perhaps there is some hope for you,' declared Gilbert, tolerantly. 'And that was it. I received Sysoyev's permission. I set to work; and, here – the result.'

He pulled a typescript from beneath his chair, and, with a minor flourish, unfurled it on the table. Esterline leafed through.

'I did it,' Gilbert went on, 'while I was the doctor on an Antarctic expedition. We made a three-month trip to Heard Island, in late winter. There were some unusual challenges: I was working on an old Apple Mac, which I couldn't secure to the counter-top. It would fall about and smash to the cabin floor, whatever we did, in those high, gorgeous seas, and I would have to start afresh.'

He gazed out, as though lost once more amidst the wave-fronts of the Southern Ocean. There was a lull. The talk swept on, our voices intertwined. The evening gained its shape: the indigo-blue of Antarctic ice, the zodiacal light above the Pilbara, Giles and his impetuous forays.

'One last thing,' I said to Gilbert as we all stood up to leave. 'How can you object to Esterline's desert journey when you were prepared to follow your inclinations all the way to Khabarovsk?'

'Maybe I've changed my mind,' he said, 'on further reflection about your project. Seeking truth from the facts – that's the way we dialectical thinkers are, you know.'

I was left, in the foyer of tiger-stone, with Esterline beside me, inspecting the road bulletins and weather maps.

'"Marble Bar to Nullagine,"' I read out. '"Wash-outs at creek crossings – extreme caution advised. Skull Springs Road – closed to all traffic." Sounds like you'll have a rough ride.'

'They always say that. You don't have to stick to formed roads out there.'

He looked away slightly; he reached out a hand. 'So – see you, then: I'm heading off.'

I nodded.

'That's it, then?'

A pause.

'You want to come?'

'Well,' I said, with a shrug, 'I've got nothing better to do just now.'


Esterline appeared at daybreak in an ancient, dust-swathed four-wheel drive. Antennae quivered on its radiator grille. Swags protruded from the windows, spare tyres and jerry-cans had been lashed by guy-ropes to the rear. I surveyed it with extreme uneasiness. I had pictured us in some sleek turbo-diesel, gliding over sandhills beneath a hazy sky. My image of our desert journey underwent an abrupt shift.

'Grand enough for you?' called out Esterline. 'Still want to come? Brave the deserts?'

'Put like that, who could resist?'

'So jump in!'

We set off at speed down the straight road that leads inland to Marble Bar and Nullagine. It was a humid morning. Shafts of sunlight stabbed towards us through the clouds; they wavered, formed again, then vanished. Ranges gleamed in the distance. Plains of spinifex, pale yellow, stretched away.

'Bleak horizons!' I murmured, after a while, in an attempt at cheerfulness. 'Do you see those dust-storms, and the rain-veils up ahead? And what are those?'

A swarm of insects came spiralling towards us: moths; locusts.

They spattered on our windscreen, leaving turquoise smears in their wake. Esterline betrayed no awareness of these forbidding atmospherics. He stared ahead and clutched the wheel, frowning from time to time. I made a few more attempts at conversation. I half-shut my eyes. The country flowed on. The light shifted. The clouds changed. I glanced across. No words. Hours passed in this fashion: we were already at the Coongan River when Esterline leaned down, produced a tape, brandished it before me – 'Music?' – and slid it into the cassette deck.

'Slim Dusty,' he announced.

'Greatest Hits, Volume 23, or some such unsurprising compilation?'

He glanced combatively across.

'Is that a problem?'

'It's inevitable, I suppose,' I said.

'I'll tell you one thing for free,' he resumed, after several minutes. 'That mate of yours knows nothing about Russian literature.'

Was that what had been eating at him all the way from Hedland? I took care not to smile.

'And you do, of course?'

'In my own poor country way, yes. I may not have been to Khabarovsk, but I've had my moments.'

'And your favourite author, let me guess . . . would be Fyodor Mikhailovich Dostoyevsky!'

At this, Esterline laughed delightedly.

'Is it that obvious?'

'Your favourite book of his: *Karamazov*.'

'Of course – what else could it be?'

'Favourite scene: The Grand Inquisitor.'

'Wrong! You lose! I've got no time for all those Christian paradoxes. No: it's the scene when the Devil comes to Ivan Karamazov.'

'I don't know that I remember it,' I said. 'My Russian phase was a long time ago.'

'How can anyone not be in a Russian phase! It's close to the end of the book. Ivan's in a room, sick, hallucinating, and suddenly he sees someone sitting there on his sofa, someone who wasn't there a moment before: a shabby-looking gentleman. He's described very well. I could almost quote it to you word for word: his clothes are just out of style, threadbare, but respectable. He has a broad, frayed scarf around his neck; he has an opal ring on his finger. That's an interesting touch, I've always felt: to think some Quilpie opal could have found its way so far, out into the furthest reaches of the literary imagination! Ivan acknowledges his guest. They talk; they argue . . .'

'But,' I protested, 'no one could argue with the Devil.'

'You don't think so,' he said lightly. 'I find I'm arguing with him all the time. I sense his presence constantly, I half-thought you were him – maybe you are!'

'Me? What's devilish or demonic about me? That's a dreadful thing to say to someone.'

'Your openness to everything,' snapped Esterline. 'What else? Here you are, coasting through, watching, gazing into people's worlds. Look at the way you latched onto me, the way you want to hear everything, know everything, get me to confess all my secrets to you – and what are yours? What do I know about you? You're very careful to keep yourself to yourself. What's that but a devil's role? And what about how you're leading me on?'

'I'm what?'

I was by now quite sure some violent conclusion lay just ahead.

'You heard. I'd never be going out into this country at this time of year if you weren't with me.'

'So turn around. Go back. I don't care. Perhaps you've already forgotten: the truth is I'm only here because you told me you were going. You were driving deep into the Sandy Desert, where Giles had gone. That was the first thing you said when we started talking yesterday, when we were sitting opposite each other on the plane.

You were the one who leaned across and said you wanted to let me into a secret.'

'No,' breathed Esterline, ignoring this; sadly, reflectively. 'No – we can't stop now. We didn't fall in like that by chance. We're driving out because – because that's the shape before us.'

'But it's a bad idea?'

'Take a look.' He pointed ahead of us. 'Look at that sky. We're just as likely to get bogged, or flooded out, as get through. We were lucky at the Shaw; at the Oakover, who knows? But you can't call off a journey like this when you're on it. No.' He nodded, as though to himself. 'It's impossible. You have to go beyond.'

I turned things over: empty country; a deranged companion; a storm-front above. I reached for the volume control on the radio. Esterline cried out: 'Don't touch another man's dial!' He glared at me. 'Don't ever do that!'

'Why not? Is that some key point of prospectors' bush etiquette?'

'Don't you like these songs? This is the music of the Inland, if you really want to see this world! I mean really see it, not just pretend, and make little pin-pricks into it, and hide yourself away on the edges. I've met Slim Dusty myself. I've shaken hands with him. I was riding at the Dalby Show when he was there.'

'You move in exalted circles.'

'That's nothing compared to where we're headed now: Cotton Creek; Christmas Pool; the Talawanna; Georgia Bore . . .'

He wound down his window. He jabbed the music off. We drove on in even heavier silence, until the outliers of civilisation began to show: wrecked, rusted, upturned cars; abandoned huts of corrugated iron; sun-bleached, bullet-riddled business signs.

'We're getting close to Marble Bar,' I said, expecting at least some acknowledgment. No reply.

'Listen,' I turned to him, in mounting fury. 'You better let me off in town.'

He threw his head back, and began to laugh:

'What's the matter: haven't you ever driven out like this before? Don't you like a bit of edge, of jousting, sparring, in your friend-ships? That's how I run mine.'

'You call this friendship? It's like a war.'

'I wouldn't be taking you with me if you weren't my friend. Do you think I just pour my secrets out to anyone? I can't stand those insipid contacts people have in the cities. I want someone who'll fight with me; die with me. What's a friend but a kind of guardian angel, close above you, looking out for you all through your life?'

'And that's really what you're after? That's what we're driving out here for?'

'And you?' he parried. 'How about you? Don't you think you're always closer, just by being out here? Isn't that what you imagine the explorers knew? Isn't that what you're trying to prove to yourself?'

I said nothing for some minutes, and let these words of his sit with me, and took in the blood-red ranges all around. A junction loomed ahead of us. 'Telfer Mine Road', announced the sign. 'Impassable in Wet Conditions'.

We braked; we steered onto it.

'No turning back now!' called out Esterline. 'It doesn't matter, anyway. We're in my country at last: the Great Sandy. Dunes, and rocks, and corkwoods, and nothing else, for hundreds of kilometres. Might as well just relax; there's nothing more to say. We've had the great symbolic argument.'

'That was it?'

'Absolutely. We're like blood-brothers now, watching out for one another. Stretch back; shut those tired eyes.'

'And what about the totemic birds?'

'We'll see them, don't worry. I'll wake you as soon as we get near. There's something hypnotic about this country, despite all the jarring and the corrugations. In fact, I find I'm half-asleep myself, most of the time I'm on this road.'

'That's very encouraging.'

'I mean it. You'll drift off – just wait and see.'

'I doubt it.'

But so it proved. The landscape levelled out: quartz plains; sandstone mesas; the road a twist of white ahead, leading towards sandhills. It ran beside them; between them; they engulfed us. I gazed up. How worn they seemed, like the ruins of some kingdom, overthrown, and lost from history, the last traces of its splendour eroding, decaying, merging with the wilderness. I leaned back in my seat. Slowly, gently, I began slipping inside a dreamworld. Snatches of landscape, the Russian landscape, plants, green leaves, the flow of water, seemed to pass before me as I lay there drowsing, my head tilted back against the head-rest. How rough the road was; how harsh the sound of the engine: I swam up to consciousness. I woke. We were still in the sandhill country. The sun by now was low. Its shadows reached out like a mesh in front of us.

'Where are we?'

'You've been asleep for ages,' said Esterline. 'It's been raining. Look, in the rear-view mirror: you can see the cloud-front we just went through. And you missed everything: the mine-site, Rudall River, Watrara Pool.'

I reached for the map.

'You won't find us. We're a long way past there.'

I listened to the engine's pulse and hum; I settled back; I glanced over at him, and thought how strangely close to him I had come to feel, though I scarcely knew him; though we would, doubtless, never meet again.

Ahead, at that instant, something brown and ragged flapped up towards us. It hung, and hovered in our path: this moment had a regal, splendid slowness. Esterline, beside me, flung up his arm, and gave a brief, inhuman cry. We braked; we skidded, struck, came to a shuddering stop. Esterline went pale; he was trembling. He threw open the door, jumped out, ran back. I listened – to wind, and stillness. At last, I got out, looked round, and saw him: he was on his knees against the low sun, cradling in his arms a large brown bird, while above him, two more kite-hawks wheeled and looped and soared. Slowly, after a while, I walked towards him. I stood there, silent: he looked up at me. The hawk's wings drooped; blood oozed from its beak; its eyes were still.

'Esterline,' I said. 'It was an accident.'

I knelt beside him in the sand. He shook his head. I tried again. 'No one could have stopped – it was an accident.'

He said nothing. With great softness, he reached down to the kite-hawk's wing feathers, and ran his fingers along them, the way one might stroke a piano's keys. This scene of mourning went on for several minutes. At last – it is a gesture I think I shall always see him making – he raised the bird up to his face, he pressed it to him, and its blood smeared his cheeks and mingled with his tears.

## II

Weeks later, I flew in once more to Port Hedland, on the same flight, through the same storm-filled skies. I disembarked, and glanced round the little terminal, uncertain exactly what kind of face I was looking for, so cryptic were the telephonic self-descriptions Denis O'Meara, the prospector king of Marble Bar, had provided me with over the previous days, though since that first encounter his features, sheer, granitic, weathered, have become caught up in my mind with the rocks and ranges of the Pilbara. I find it hard to think of them and not of him: so much, indeed, is he part of my thoughts it sometimes seems to me our friendship could outlast life itself, and linger, like a trace, a hint of human closeness dispersed across the deserts.

That morning though, I waited for a stranger. I watched as my fellow-passengers claimed their bags, and left; the engineers and oil-rig workers gathered obediently at their departure gates. After a while I noticed a man, square-faced, broad-set, compact. He was seated, reading, wearing odd clothes: khaki shorts, thick boots, a work-shirt from the pockets of which dangled long strands of bright pink and yellow tape. A battered pilot's case was at his side. A silver magnifying glass hung from his neck. I nodded at this figure, in a brisk, non-committal way. He came up. He peered at me as though he was inspecting some exotic brand of merchandise – doubtless much as I was peering, then, at him.

We introduced ourselves. We went outside. I told him how grateful I was to be driving with him so deep into the desert.

'Yes . . . the desert,' he responded, rather edgily.

I was about to run through the sad tale of the last trip – I stopped short: 'That's not your four-wheel drive, is it?'

In front of us, parked between the hire cars and mine-trucks, was a Landcruiser, ochre-coloured, dilapidated, the same model, I could not help reflecting, as David Esterline's, though it seemed to be missing some important components: there were no side-mirrors; the winch on the front bull-bar had been snapped clean off.

'Don't let appearances fool you,' said Denis, in a breezy way. 'We've got everything we need in there: enough water for a week; tools, supplies, the trouble-box for emergencies, not that there'll be any, of course. It's got a lot of character, this vehicle. It's seventeen years old. It's on its third motor. It's done four hundred thousand kilometres on desert roads. The chassis's cracked; the axle once fused into a red-hot mass; it's been flooded, it's been on fire twice in one day – in fact, the second time we had to put the flames out with spurting jets from the beer-cans we had on board. It's a real survival machine, though: you'll always get through.'

'That's good to know.'

'Yes,' said Denis, as we drove off. 'Everything that happened in *The Gods Must Be Crazy* happened to this truck. These old four-wheel drives just never seem to die.'

We stopped at the highway junction. At that moment from beneath our feet there came a sharp, grinding noise.

'What on earth was that?'

'Oh, it's the first gear again. It fails sometimes. No problem at all. We'll just move off in second instead.'

And what if the other gears fail, I was about to ask, but Denis, with an air of great resolve, turned to the right, and set off at speed, switching on an elaborate UHF radio and a GPS receiver, which made a series of impressive electronic start-up sounds.

'You can navigate,' he offered, with an air of generosity.

'We're not actually on the Newman road, are we?' I said, after a few kilometres.

'You're absolutely right there, yes. Look, I was just about to mention to you: there's been a change of plan. We're going to call in at Marble Bar. It's Race Day. I couldn't forgive myself if I didn't show the place off. And you just can't go past the Marble Bar Races as a social event. Everyone who's anyone in the Pilbara will be there: mining magnates, doggers, geos, stockmen, the last of the old pastoral families, the aristocracy of the Aboriginal world – even a few old wildcards like myself mixed in.'

'What about the Sandy Desert?'

'We're still going there, don't you worry about that – just to a different part of it. I'm going to take you through Beyondie: Beyondie Bluff.' He spoke these words with dream-like softness. 'I've got a prospect there, one that's going to revolutionise the geological map of Western Australia. Sulphides; nickel; cobalt. I first went through that country ten years ago, and saw the rocks, and assayed them, and marked it out in the far corners of my mind. Even then I knew it was something. Now I know that landscape back to front. I've gone up every ravine and creek-bed. I only have to stand there, high on the slopes of the range, where the mineralisation comes pushing through, and I can feel it. I can tell there's a deposit – gold, copper, base metals – somewhere, far beneath me, three hundred metres down. It's just begging to be drilled. Another Telfer, maybe – maybe an Olympic Dam!'

'I don't suppose it's anywhere near where Giles's expedition went?' I asked.

'Giles? Are you interested in him? Is that what this journey was about? Why didn't you tell me? I've been following his trail for years. I'm a bit of a Giles expert, in a bush kind of a way. What a driven, friendless, troubled man! I've been along his exploration path, you know, tracking him. I feel I've come to know his habits very well. There's even a personal connection. Haven't I already told you the story of Giles's Lost Mallee?'

'His what?'

We hurtled on. Denis ran through the tale, which, impossible though it sounded in the telling, proved, like all the strangest Outback stories, to be true in every detail. On each of his inland journeys, the explorer, despite his lack of interest in the variations of the external world, would endeavour, if in rather desultory fashion, to collect specimens of the new plant life he came on for his Melbourne friend, Baron von Mueller. His last expedition, east from the Ophthalmias through the desert, produced a striking sample – a single eucalyptus branch, elegant, fine-leaved, pale of stem. Von Mueller, with his customary rapidity, catalogued it in the October 1876 issue of *Fragmenta Phytographiae Australiae*, a scientific journal of which he was virtually the sole author. He gave the new species an appealing name – *Eucalyptus Rameliana*, after a compliant Provençal botanist – but the descriptive note he added next was frustratingly vague, for its discoverer proved quite unable to remember exactly where he had come upon it. Giles, of course, had been intent, all through the trip, on his fateful desert ranges, and besides, for much of the return journey he was almost blind. As a result of these unusual circumstances, all botanical science knew, for a hundred years and more, was that the lost mallee had been encountered, once, by Europeans, beside a western desert watercourse.

'And that's how things stood,' said Denis, 'until a few years ago, when I came across a stand of them out on the Rabbit-Proof Fence, just south of where it crosses Savory Creek.'

'You mean it was you who rediscovered it?'

'Well . . . to tell the absolute truth, there was a scientist from the West Australian Museum who happened to find another cluster, just before me, in country quite close to where mine were. I actually grow them now, out on the block at Marble Bar. We've domesticated them. I'll show you one. They're delicate creatures. And we've got grevilleas, too, and desert corkwoods, and plenty of other rarities as well: the Goldfields Tree, the Halls Creek White Gum, the Ghost Gum from Nullagine. I think we had four hundred species last time we counted.'

'I wouldn't have imagined trees and rocks could go together.'

'Are you joking? Sometimes I think prospecting's just a way of spending time in nature. I love trees. I collect their seeds wherever I am. I plant them. I photograph them. I don't think there's anything on earth more beautiful than a white-trunked Snappy Gum, standing out from a deep red Pilbara ridge, caught by sunshine against dark wet-season clouds. I'm even writing a book about the native trees of Australia: my wife says if there's such a thing as reincarnation, I'll come back as one!'

'That might be a little inconvenient. For your prospecting work, I mean.'

'I don't know. Look at those beautiful bush almonds up there, so green, on the ranges – what they must know about geology! And the river gums, to the right of us, all along Doolina Gap . . .'

This exchange wound on, Denis exploring options for his arboreal future, until the race-track, marooned amidst the hills and spinifex, came into view, a scatter of trucks, coaches, four-wheel drives and horse-boxes lined up on both sides of its access road.

'Go through, Denis,' said the gate-man, reverentially.

'You're a celebrity out here!'

'Everyone's a celebrity of some kind or other in Marble Bar,' said Denis, modestly. 'But it's true I was a race judge at this meeting for twenty-five years – a very political kind of job. Sometimes it was a matter of survival to ensure the big races were all dead heats. Just take a look at this,' he breathed in. He spread his arms wide. 'Aren't you glad now that you came along? The Pilbara's laid out before you, all the grandeur and the sadness of the bush.'

I trailed behind him through the crowd: ringers in tight jeans and checked shirts; young families from Tom Price and Hedland, with elaborate baggage trains of picnic gear; jockeys in bright silks; Aboriginal children running through the enclosures, with their mothers giving chase.

'See,' said Denis, proudly, speaking into the middle distance, rather as if addressing some invisible documentary camera-crew. 'Grandstand, food-stalls, farriers, first-aid tent – we've got everything. You could almost be at Caulfield. And it's not a bad turn-out, either. Sometimes I think everyone in Australia comes to the Bar on race-day at least once in their life.'

He paused beside the stable-block. A handful of small, perspiring horses had taken refuge underneath a shade-cover of corrugated-iron.

'The best thoroughbreds in the North-West?'

'Of course! And that's Olive, at the podium, with the officials – she's the race-day vice-president. Used to be a champion gem-cutter.

I'll introduce you, if you like. And those are the big wheels, over there. But you'd recognise them all, wouldn't you?'

He nodded towards a collection of grave-faced individuals, standing close together, wearing somewhat studied versions of western gear: moleskins, riding boots, Akubras, polo shirts.

'No? That's the man from Stockdale, the exploration arm of De Beers.' He dropped his voice. 'They're looking for diamonds out here, in the hills round Nullagine; they've got an area the size of Tasmania under claim. And that's Gary Morgan beside him . . .'

'The pollster?'

'That's the one. He's a genuine Marble Bar eccentric. He runs the Kitchener Mine, just up the track at Bamboo Creek. By one of those strange coincidences in life, he always seems to peg the ground beside my prospects. And there's Larry Graham, the member for the Pilbara – he just got disendorsed by the Labor Party.'

'Why?'

'Oh, I think he was getting too close to his electorate. Politicians round here tend to take the locals seriously. There was Graeme Campbell, of course. Remember how he said no bill should become law until it had been passed by both Houses of the Parliament of Australia, and then thoroughly debated in the front bar of the Conglomerate Hotel at Nullagine?'

'Not much would get through then, would it?' said a wiry, hunched man, who had been hovering for some while on the fringes of this exchange.

'Alec! Now here's a real celebrity. Alec's forgotten more about Marble Bar than most of us have ever known.'

The recipient of this tribute beamed, and muttered a few words, which were drowned out by the race call. Denis left me in the celebrity's care. Some minutes passed.

'Big rains we're having at the moment,' ventured Alec. 'Not like eighteen years ago.'

'Really?'

Another pause. The crowd began surging past us towards the trackside and the winning post.

'That's right,' said he, slowly, dreamily, as if recollecting something from a previous life. 'It was a drought season; I was contract-pegging then. I was the only one doing that in those days, out near Corboy's, in the hills. There were dingoes in that country, by the hundred, marauding, hunting. They brought down a bullock in a creekbed thirty feet away from me one time. They even took down a horse on the main road. I used to sleep on the tray of my ute with my gun beside me. Once they tracked me up, twelve of them – they followed me all day, and just watched me. I shot two or three of them; the others ate the bodies. It wasn't the best sensation, sometimes, working out there, like that.'

'I've always thought they were magnificent animals,' I said, conscious this was not the ideal response to such a conversational opening.

'Magnificent?'

'Bold, self-reliant. Lovely coat. No smell.'

'I used to shoot them for the bounty, a long time back,' said Alec, in an even more reflective voice. 'At first the government inspectors only wanted the tails and tips of the ears, but then they started wanting the skin all the way back to the base of the skull, and the hind quarters too. You had to butcher them out there, and that didn't appeal to me so much. No one round here ever liked dingoes' – he lowered his voice – 'except, of course, that young bloke from the station on the road to Ripon Hills.'

'What station was that?'

'Meentheena – he kept wild dogs as if they were pets. He had a whole pack of them, black ones. But he's gone, now: took off without a trace. Most young people leave the desert country' – he shrugged – 'and of course they don't come back.'

He shook his head and began to drift away.

A tall man with long hair and pale sharp eyes came up.

'You didn't hit it off, you and Alec?' he said, with an air of amusement.

'On the contrary – I think he just told me something very interesting. Interesting to me, at least.'

'I can understand that. Old-timers like him know a lot. They've been out in this country for ever. It's as if it's entered into them; taken possession of them. But we know something, too.'

'We?'

He gave a mysterious smile.

'Who are "we"?'

'Can't you tell? I'm an exploration geologist. I've got my own ideas, though, about these rocks. I don't run with the corporates.'

'I suppose most people at this race-track are mavericks or free-thinkers of some kind or other. Isn't this part of the world a magnet for odd-balls?'

'Don't believe that for a moment. Look at all those types from De Beers and Rio Tinto,' he frowned, and almost spat out the words. 'Geology's probably the most conformist discipline in the whole world. They're all asleep, the men working for big companies. You don't seriously think they ever find anything, do you? They don't actually even see the rocks. They just let themselves be led by expectations and by prejudice. Now I – when I go out into the bush, I feel naked if I don't have a magnifying-glass in my hand.'

I looked round, despairingly, for Denis. A long exposition began: the diamond structures on the Skull Springs Road; the looming bankruptcy of the pub at Nullagine; the four hundred days my new companion had just spent field-mapping in the Strelley Hills.

'That sounds like hard work,' I said.

'Not at all!' He glared at me. 'You have to do that. Data is king; truth hides. I have a suspicious world-view. Distrust everything!

You need to be as careful as a secret agent. It all starts in the Archaean, in deep time, three billion years ago. Deep time, where theories have no weight, and patterns exceed what we know. My idea is that everything is wrong, every physical law is a mere approximation. The real history of the earth is written in galactic cycles. But conventional geology' – he gave, at this point, a pitying shrug – 'deals only in the story of the past hundred and fifty million years, in the phanerozoic, where the oil companies live!'

'Not you though?'

'I even make sure I camp on Archaean rocks! For me, the important cycles in rock formation come once every three hundred and fifty million years.'

'But that wouldn't be the majority view?'

'If they could hear me talking to you this way' – he glanced conspiratorially as he said this, towards the neat, marquee-like Stockdale Exploration tent – 'well, I think they'd have me locked up!'

We lapsed into silence. A race call began. The horses rounded the far bend, straightened, came towards us. Hooves drummed; the lead jockey, whipping his mount's neck with sinuous motions, flashed by. I detached myself from the geological revolutionary, and wound my way amidst the bookies' stalls, listening to their cries and to the hum of talk around me, feeling a sudden, pleasant distance from myself and all the usual urgencies of life. I drifted past a raucous Two-Up game, and lingered there watching, for several minutes. I made my way on through the crowd; it thinned. I fetched up beside the winners' enclosure: the jockeys from the last race were just coming in. The lead horse drew near in a slow, sideways canter, gleaming with sweat, tossing his head. His rider jumped off.

'He's pretty wild, boss,' he muttered to the owner.

'Of course he's wild, the way you used your stick, you idiot. There wasn't any danger he was going to lose against that pack of dead-beats.'

The horse, meanwhile, foamed, and pawed the ground, and stamped, and rolled its eyes. I walked up to them, and made as if to stroke the horse's neck. It backed away. The owner adjusted his large hat with great deliberation, once, twice, and gave me a hostile stare.

'He's beautiful,' I said.

'Beautiful! He's clapped-out, run-down, half lame – he's almost ready for the knacker's yard.'

With this he scowled, and waved at an Aboriginal stable-hand, who came running over and took the reins.

'Let him walk around a little,' barked the owner. 'Turn the hose on him. Let him shake his head a bit, scratch his balls if he wants, I don't care – they never calm down right away.'

The horse, neck arched, paced off into the ring, towards the stable-blocks. A jet of water played a moment on its back; spray danced and hovered in the air, and caught the sunshine, and each droplet glowed in rainbow colours, as if a halo had just touched the animal.

'What are you looking at with those big eyes?' snapped the owner. 'Haven't you ever been to the races before? You're in the Pilbara now, not in some bloody southern theme-park!'

'What's his name?'

'"Journey's End" – now piss off, or I'll have him put down tomorrow.'

The tall geologist had appeared at my shoulder:

'Denis and I were both looking for you,' he broke in. 'Let's take off!'

We retreated.

'Close enough for you?'

'In what sense?'

'I don't know that I'd be picking a quarrel with him, myself. He's bad news. The whole family's half-insane.'

'Who is he?'

'That was old man Esterline, of course. He's the biggest landholder left round here. Where did you tell me you two were driving out to tomorrow?'

'I didn't,' I said, and let his last sentence sink into my thoughts.

'So?' he pressed.

'South of Newman, and in from Kumarina roadhouse, towards the desert, and the Carnarvon Range.'

'At this time of year? You'll be lucky!'

'How come?'

'It's hot, and wet, and full of troubles out that way: good country for a slow, hard perish! Still, I suppose Denis is one of those rare prospectors who knows what he's doing, and he's always super-careful: at least he never seems to end up getting bogged.'

Those words came back to me some days later, close to the halfway point of our prospecting journey, as Denis, in mid-sentence of a geological lecture, turned the wheel and plunged us down into a steep-banked, rocky creekbed. There was a scraping, grating sound. We stopped; lurched forward; tilted towards the driver's side. The engine shuddered, and cut out.

'Interesting,' he said. 'Let's have a look.'

I jumped down. Far behind us, low against the horizon, grey-green, loomed the Beyondie Range. The survey cairn on its peak, where I had stood that morning and stared across the landscape, was no more than a shimmering, tiny speck. Black, burnt, tangled mulga-trees hemmed us in; the country fanned out in folds of charred-grey spinifex.

'Well, at least we're not bogged,' called out Denis, leaning down.

'We're not?'

The Landcruiser's front end was embedded in rock scree: one of its rear wheels was caught on the creek-bank, the other was suspended in mid-air.

'Not technically, no. Bogging incidents involve water, moistness; the sinking of entire vehicles, for example. They're the kinds of things an explorer really needs to be concerned about. This is more of a problem with the topography.'

'But we're stuck?'

'I wouldn't look at it that way. It's all part of the rhythm, the punctuation of the Bush. You simply have to react to it, the same way a prospector reacts when he comes upon an unfamiliar outcrop, or reads a new pattern in the minerals around him. I'd have to say a rear-end winch attachment could have been useful in this particular spot. We'll just have to dig our way out. It won't take long. Slide back in; reach over to the radio. We can listen to that tape again, the one we had on before, when we were up in the Gorge Range, sampling.'

'Not those opera duets by Freddie Mercury?' I said, with undisguised alarm.

'I think the Schubert Impromptus might fit better with Beyondie. It's still in the cassette.'

I reached for the switch, and turned it on. Nothing.

'It's dead.'

'Oh,' sighed Denis, 'that happens sometimes.'

'Does that mean the emergency two-way doesn't work either?'

'Afraid not.'

'Is there any feature of this truck that's going to last the whole trip?'

'I thought we were doing quite well,' said Denis, in an aggrieved voice. 'Don't worry so much – we can still walk our way out if everything else fails. We're only two days by foot from the road-house and the highway.'

We set to work. Six hours later the front grille of the vehicle was clear; the back wheels were almost level. Piles of rock and dirt were heaped up around us. I let down the jack. Denis drove up the far bank, at a steep angle, and out. I climbed back in, and looked across.

'That was a close call! Still, I suppose it's all part of a prospecting education.'

Denis gazed at me vacantly; he gave a little groan.

'Can you pass me over that strip of aspirin in the glovebox?'

I glanced at the package as I handed it to him.

'What on earth are you taking these for? They're extremely strong.'

'That's right. There's a good whack of codeine in them. I get migraines from time to time. When they're really bad, they often last for several days. I can feel one now, just starting to come on.'

'What are they like?'

'It's hard to capture in words. The edge of blackness; dull, nightmarish, heart-destroying pain.'

'You don't look that great, I have to tell you.'

His face was gaunt; his eyes were hollow. He grasped the aspirin foil in both hands, tore out several, and swallowed them.

'Thank God!' he said. 'It's really going to be a king-sized one.'

'That won't be enough to stop it?'

'Not at all, no. It's like a storm. It's still some way off, but you can feel it looming inside you. When it hits I usually just roll out my swag, and crawl inside, and lie there, and shiver for a while. Here' – he pointed at the wheel; his face had turned a sickly greenish colour – 'I think you better drive. Be careful of the clutch: it seems to be jamming at the moment. Make for the old homestead. There's a camping place I know past there – and watch out for the animals.'

'What animals?' I said, but Denis only leaned back in his seat, and let out a disturbing moan.

We set off. I struggled with the gears, and turned east, towards bleak country, the salt-lakes and the sinking sun. The track was faint and overgrown; it wound through dunes and over shale-beds, it disappeared in creeks and washaways. There were jolts and near-collisions. Ahead of us amidst the mulga, in the shadow of a bloodwood tree, something seemed to move. I shook my head, and peered through the windscreen, and sped on.

'That can't be a kangaroo,' I said to myself, out loud. 'It's huge, whatever it is!'

'Be careful,' muttered Denis, sighing. 'The big Reds here some-times stand their ground.'

'You're not serious,' I said, and accelerated. The kangaroo, by now quite close, jumped from the shadows, straight towards us. I braked, and swerved, and rode up the side bank, and round, almost overturning us in a side-dip, hurling Denis against the window, catching, as we ran past, a glimpse of deep-set, angled eyes, square red shoulders, a tight-clenched jaw.

'That was a near-miss,' I called out. 'Sorry. I believe you now! I'll be more careful next time.'

I pressed on, through rough, black, burned-out corkwood groves, between trailing, overhanging branches, until a further obstacle appeared: it was deep brown, and indistinct. This time I slowed at once. A donkey, large, white-muzzled, was standing, head lowered, in front of us on the track. I leaned out of the window, and shouted, and waved menacingly. Our adversary grunted, backed away as we crawled past, then gave chase, galloping, keeping level pace with us for several minutes, staring across at me with dark, envenomed eyes. Moments later, another set of shapes took form far ahead. They were high and irregular; their outline seemed to blur into the bush.

'More wildlife. It's like Fifth Avenue along here, Denis. I thought you said this was the loneliest track in all Western Australia.'

'That'll be the camels,' he groaned, and clutched the hand-grip above him, and turned away from me. And so it was. A group of worn, ragged beasts, their fur the dark dirt-shade of matted hessian, now blocked our path. I stopped.

'Just sound the horn and drive at them,' said Denis, his eyes closed. 'If it's not breeding season, they're usually quite timid. They'll run away.'

'Are you sure? They're enormous.'

I did as he said. The camels stared back contemptuously, then, one by one, with shambling steps, they turned and began to move ahead of us, keeping to the middle of the track and jogging wearily from side to side.

'They're certainly not going very fast,' I said, driving close up to the last camel, which glanced round, its mouth white with foaming spit.

A drop of this milky substance now flew through the air, and landed on the windscreen. I switched on the wipers. Nothing happened.

'Denis – what about the windscreen wipers?'

'I forgot to tell you – sometimes, on these long trips, they stop working.'

Another, larger, fleck of camel foam landed before my eyes, and then another.

'But I can't see a thing.'

'Stick your head out of the window, like everybody else,' he said, weakly. 'Be adaptive. You're in the Outback now.'

I crawled at camel speed, for several minutes, craning my head into the breeze, dodging the flying milky drops and ribbons, until the windscreen was encrusted with half-solidifying saliva smears.

'It's not as if there's a shortage of landscape for them,' I said, and swung out across country, steering between the mulga-stakes and winding creek-lines, but the camels, like some infuriating advance guard, veered with me, wide-eyed with terror, frothing and spitting as they cantered on. I swerved back. The camels did the same.

'I just don't believe this,' I said, almost under my breath.

'Don't be so unreasonable,' said Denis. 'They're lost, poor things.'

'Lost! They live here. We've been driving down their pads all afternoon.'

'But they don't belong here. They're in the wrong country. They always look lost, and lonely, and unhappy, whenever I see them. They're desperate, in fact: full of sadness, and grief, and fear.'

He lay back again. Like us, you mean, I thought, and drove on in silence some way further, through sandbeds, over corrugations, listening to my companion's slow drawn-out breaths and sighs, until the pain and gloom that held him seemed to reach out and take up station in my mind. At last the homestead and its outhouses came into view. I stopped beside its broken boundary fence.

'We're at Beyondie,' I whispered.

Denis failed to move.

'I might take a quick look round.'

'Make sure you don't go inside,' he called after me. 'It's always bad luck to cross the hearth of an abandoned home.'

I stepped through the rubble round the building: twisted strips of corrugated iron; wood panels, eaten half-away; a bedstead, creaking, rusted; cracked mirrors, tin plates thrown amidst the weeds and spinifex. I stayed for some while, watching the sun drop beneath the hills, listening to the wind's gusts, trying to picture the life that had once been there. At last I walked back, and started up the engine.

'Beyondie,' I repeated. 'It's a lovely name. It's hard to believe people lived this far out, once.'

'Not so long ago,' said Denis, opening his eyes, 'it was much busier in this country. There was a part-Aboriginal family living here, on this land, even in the sixties. I think they moved down to Meekatharra.'

'It's almost as if they're still here,' I answered, and drove on, until we had travelled far past the homestead. 'And what's that cleared line, ahead of us, running through those red sandhills?'

'Don't you know? If you followed that line far enough, it would take you right up past Savory Creek, all the way to Jigalong. That's the old Rabbit-Proof Fence, or what's left of it. Sometimes I think this is the secret heart of Australia, right here. I come out this way quite often, and camp along the line, where all the doggers and fence-runners used to work. Do you see those *Acacia Pruinocarpas*?'

'Those what?'

'The Gidgee Bush. Why don't you head for that rise, where they are?'

We camped. The dark came on. Much later, after hours sitting round the fire in silence, as the wood sang, and the reflections of the blaze lit up the bush around us, we began to talk: the desert country; the explorers' trails; the way the hills and dunes receded with such mystery from the eyes, and formed themselves into elusive, abstract shapes. After a few minutes of this, Denis hauled himself up.

'You still look fairly ordinary,' I said, rather startled by the thought that had just jumped into my head, for, on that low ridge-line, in the middle of that emptiness, suddenly my companion's well-being seemed to matter to me as much as my own.

'Yes,' he said, in a low voice. 'You're right. I had a bit of an instant back there, but I'll get over it. You can't keep a prospector down for long.'

There was a silence.

'I suppose,' I said at last, 'our journey out into the Sandy Desert isn't going to happen, is it?'

'Maybe not this time, mate – but we'll make it one day, I promise.'

'I'd like that.'

'I've always found, in life, the best way to get somewhere is not to want particularly to arrive. You can want things too much, you know.'

'Like Giles?'

'It's been a long while since I was on his trail,' said Denis. 'I've often felt you can imagine, when you're out here in exploration country, what it must have been like for them, on their camel-strings, riding through this silence, never knowing what lay ahead.'

'You feel them here?'

'Of course.'

'And have you ever seen anything, out in the desert?'

Denis looked at me sharply.

'I don't think you'll find anyone who spends long periods in the bush who hasn't seen something.'

'Go on.'

With an air of reluctance he told his story: how, long years before, he had been out prospecting with Eric Lockyer, his glamorous, bandana-wearing, one-eyed Aboriginal assistant. The two of them were in trackless country, far to the south-east of Marble Bar. It was night; they were at camp, surrounded by a swarm of chirping grasshoppers. Suddenly everything went quiet. The sky lit up, from horizon to horizon. It stayed bright for more than a minute. The lights that played above them seemed to have the shape of a vast sphere, dropping lower and lower, until, just as abruptly as they came, they vanished. The next morning the radio carried news reports of unknown objects far out to sea.

'And you said you only believed in natural phenomena!'

'I may not know the explanation, but I'm sure there is one. It's the same as gold dowsing. I took that very seriously. When I was young, in fact, I used to go on prospecting overflights, with my friend Bert Mitchell. Once we even went in search of Lasseter's Reef.'

I settled back: the tale unwound. Lewis Hubert Lasseter, as is well known, claimed to have come upon a mountain that was full of gold, in the course of a journey – almost certainly fictitious – made on horseback, in 1897, from Queensland, through Central Australia, and on, across the western deserts. Frequent attempts have been made since to find this outcrop. Lasseter himself died in the last days of 1930, during the unravelling of one of these expeditions, at a cave near Docker River.

'And he was a professional gold dowser, your friend?'

'Bert Mitchell! He was a builder and a carpenter, the best in the whole Pilbara. He's been a grader-driver on the Nullarbor; and he's the finest bush mechanic I ever came across. I first went out dowsing with him from Whim Creek, years ago. He'd been flying round in light planes for ages, with Lang Hancock, trying to find Lasseter's Reef. He had a theory that Lasseter himself had got it wrong, perhaps deliberately, to throw others off the track: that the reef wasn't out north of the Petermanns, and west of Alice, where everyone else had been searching for it, but somewhere much farther out, deep in the Sandy Desert. Bert used a single dowsing wire – that's all he had – and it would swing in his hand and point towards his targets.'

'Even from mid-air?'

'Especially from mid-air. Before we made our great search, he'd been out on a long reconnaissance flight, all the way north-west from Warburton, and picked out an area among the desert salt-lakes. They'd circled the plane around it, and watched the wire jumping. I looked at my records from back then the other day. His target's marked on the latest survey maps: it's called Lake Ryan. But if I went out, I'd be battling to find it again.'

Two months later, Denis, Bert Mitchell and a geologist friend of theirs had taken off from Port Hedland in a single-engine Cessna, flown by Max Frankston, the best-known exploration pilot in the far North-West. They staged through the Woodie Woodie landing strip; they cancelled the emergency watch.

'It was a secret mission?'

'It was a crazy time, when we were doing all kinds of weird things,' said Denis, a joyful tone coming into his voice. 'Remember, I was in my very early thirties in those days. It was the time of life when the journey still seems as important as the destination. We kept on, east-south-east, with Bert holding out his wire, hoping to intersect his flight-track from Warburton.'

'A kind of triangulation by dowsing?'

'Exactly. Long before we reached the salt-lakes, though, his wire began to turn and jump.'

'And that was Lasseter's Reef?'

He laughed: 'Who knows? We flew on, for two or three more hours, at eight thousand feet, against strong headwinds, through hazy, deceptive skies. We headed down; we landed on the hard pan, right beside the lake. Bert Mitchell and the geo walked about and collected samples round the salt-crust for most of the day. I stayed with Max, and together we cleared away the shrubs and salt-bush so the Cessna could take off again.'

'And did you find anything?'

'I think my life would be slightly different if we had! There was no outcrop or quartz reef; there was nothing in the rocks. We flew back towards Woodie Woodie. We must have used up more fuel than we planned – we ran out fifty miles south-east of the airstrip. We glided down.'

'You crashed?'

'It was a controlled landing without power – a very skilful piece of flying. We came down to ground-level. We clipped an anthill, and smashed up a wing. There was no radio contact with the mining camp. We walked our way back in.'

After this incident, Denis told me, his enthusiasm for airborne dowsing fell away. These events had taken place in August of 1970, at the very outset of the boom in desert exploration. Mid-way through the following year, at a deep-red outcrop between the Paterson Range and Lake Waukarlycarly, a set of intriguing surface gold intersections were made. These discoveries lay at the precise point on the map where Bert Mitchell's wire had turned during the flight out from Woodie Woodie. They were the first clues to the existence of Telfer, the richest gold-mine in the Australian North-West.

# III

A year passed. Giles and his journeys receded from my mind. I began working more and more in Alice Springs and the Aboriginal townships of the Western desert, and found myself returning to one community in particular, with which I had developed closer ties: Warburton, midway between Uluru and Kalgoorlie on the Great Central Road, the administrative centre of the Ngaanyatjarra lands. Warburton! Those low pink ranges; the storm-veils in the sunset, the horizons ringed with fire. Sometimes, even now, plunged in the life of cities, I still see myself there, the way one is always elsewhere in the mind's eye: walking through dry sandy creekbeds, beneath paperbarks and white gums; watching night-time softball games; heading down bush roads in half-disintegrated four-wheel drives. But most of all I see the country as I looked out on it for the first time, coming in low above the plains and patterned dune-fields, on the Aboriginal Air Services flight from Tjukurla and Alice Springs.

During those early visits, which were brief, and had the flavour of discovery about them, I would often find accommodation with a new acquaintance of mine, Esmé Vargas, in the low, cool buildings of the Arts Centre which she, almost single-handed, ran. This was an institution vital, as I soon saw, to the unfolding of the township's life, for it was here each morning that Warburton's painting men and women would gather. Here, on the floor of its dark, brick-blocked studio, they would sit cross-legged before their canvases and, with barely a nod to each other, resume their work, as if no pause or relaxation were permissible, as if their lives were being lived out only for the sake of those repeated, intricate designs. Sometimes I would sit beside them, for hours, following their even movements, wishing that I could summon up within myself such reserves of application and calm. In our midst, meanwhile, behind her desk, poised, grave as a Caryatid, Esmé would be caught up in telephonic dealings with museums or galleries, or some yet more bureaucratic engagements with the wider artistic world, even as she watched over the creation of these new paintings.

The Arts Centre also had at that time an informal second string: it served as a port of call for travellers from the desert's interlocking social realms, anthropologists, maybe, or native title lawyers, or architects, but in those harsh, wet months of summer, with all roads flooded, there were scarcely any of these chance arrivals. I spent many evenings there as the only guest, talking with Esmé, around the trestle table in her kitchen, while from the large, bare room next door came the sound of delighted laughter and cries of recognition as young Ngaanyatjarra families watched ethnographic films from their grandparents' days. In our reserved, and rather formal, conversations, Esmé and I, no matter what the starting point, would come circling back to the same themes: exile; memories of childhood; the crossed destinies that lead people to seek new, far-distant homes.

One evening the talk turned to the early days of the settlement, which was established as a Christian mission in the mid-1930s. It was odd, remarked Esmé, in an offhand manner, that the community had been named for the explorer Warburton although the first Europeans to see the hills were, in fact, Gosse and Giles. I laughed, and felt that strange pleasure which dawns when two distinct phases of one's life begin to touch. Cautiously, I told her something of the time when I first came back to Australia, and was rediscovering the country, and nothing had seemed more important to me than following in the footsteps of the great explorers. I had been full of longing then to drive out alone, across the Sandy Desert, or head west from the Rawlinsons, to reach the precise spot before the Alfred and Marie Range where Giles and Gibson had turned for home. Esmé smiled at this and said nothing.

'Of course,' I went on, 'they were defeated by lack of water. There wasn't any failure of resolve.'

'Lack of water? They were almost on top of the best permanent water supply in the whole desert, although it's probably a good thing that they didn't find it.'

'Where was that?'

'Perhaps,' said Esmé, thoughtfully, 'you should come up there with us some time, to Karilwara.'

'Where?'

'The waterhole, just beyond Patjarr to the west. You've been to Patjarr, haven't you? It's clustered round with important sites.'

'Patjarr. I've barely heard the name.'

'Is that right?' Esmé smiled. 'I'd have to say that's an extremely serious gap in your education.'


The settlement of Patjarr, though marked on hardly any maps and almost untouched by the wider world, can be reached with a degree of ease, two hundred kilometres to the north of Warburton, at the end of a corrugated desert track. It is inhabited by a group of Ngaanyatjarra and Pintupi families, whose members, perhaps fifty in all, come and go from as far afield as Tjirrkarli and Kiwirrkurra. Their community, which is no more, in truth, than a developed out-station, lies at the geographic centre of the Gibson, in unemphatic country, surrounded by rock-holes and breakaways. To the south is the salt-bed of Lake Newell, curved like a troubling question mark. Within view are the Clutterbuck Hills, christened by an aviator in survey times. All round is red dust, and the austere, metallic grey of corkwood. Yet since Europeans first stumbled on it, this confluence of creekbed, rock-fold and dune-field has drawn the western eye. Less than ten years had passed since Giles's second expedition and his broken return when subsidiary explorers armed with his maps, in search of minerals and pastoral territories, began their passage through. Mills, and Lindsay, and Carnegie all ventured amidst the

Gibson's sea of spinifex, tacking, in nervous style, from range to range. But, as often in the records of discovery, the most intriguing of the desert's travellers are those least known, and it was only after I had steeped myself in the Ngaanyatjarra world that I began to come upon their traces. I heard old, half-remembered stories; I saw carved, unfamiliar signatures on rock-hole walls or the backs of painted caves. This obscurity is far from accidental, for in its last phases exploration, like life, becomes a retreat, a silence, a turning in.

The pioneer of this near-secret tradition was the North Queensland pioneer, Frank Henry Hann. Hann was a celebrated prospector, who, in the 1890s, already at the mid-point of his long, gloom-struck career, abandoned Cape York, moved west and began a series of fruitless journeys into virgin desert. It was not the temptations of discovery that drew him, nor some quest for the vanishing unknown. He crossed and recrossed the same country, on different headings; the nature of the landscape, its mood and variation, passed him by. His journals give the portrait of a man voyaging towards self-dissolution, kept alive at each moment only by not staying still. The map records the tone of his experience. A bleak table-top bluff south of Yapupara bears his name; he christened Lake Disappointment, a vast salt-bed along the Canning, on the quite unreasonable grounds that it was dry.

Hann's travels were soon outdone by an even less heralded explorer, Sam Hazlett, the camel man, whose traverses remain unmatched to this day. His first attempt at inland adventuring, an eastward probe in 1904, from Laverton through the Jamieson and Tomkinson Ranges, went badly wrong, though the precise causes underlying his misfortune, like almost everything about his life, remain unclear. While encamped near Mount Davies he clashed with two Aboriginal warriors. A revenge party tracked Hazlett for a short distance, then, as a young man from Warburton once told me with great gusto on the very spot where this payback was accomplished, they filled their victim full of spears. Hazlett repelled these attackers; his travelling companion cut the spear-barbs from his back and chest. Gravely wounded, he was conveyed west to Leonora, and from there to his mother's house at Dalwallinu, where he lived for three decades a near-invalid. At last one morning he spat out the remains of a spearhead. He was restored to health. His taste for desert travel returned as well. Hazlett was particularly fond of his two dogs. He took them with him; there was a dedicated riding camel for each one. He set off on a journey from the Goldfields to the Rawlinsons, until he reached the spot where Warakurna stands today. Once there he decided to make directly north, through the Winnecke Hills, the Stansmore and the Kearney Ranges, across the harshest quadrant of the Centre. He came out at Halls Creek, and returned along the Canning Stock Route, a thousand more kilometres of hard stages south-west. The following year, as if to prove his feat had not been accidental, Hazlett made the round trip with his dogs and camels once again. His only memorial is the indistinct lake-bed not too far from Balgo which, on some charts, still bears his name. There are no romantic narratives of his progress; indeed written records barely mention him, though his name is still remembered, and still feared, in the Ngaanyatjarra lands.

He was the last in a lineage that, with its first step, had ensured its own eventual end, for in the world of appearances at least, the frontier had now been closed. There was nothing left to find. A decade or so passed. The Gibson gained a new utility. Roads were built across its sandhills; a diagonal line was drawn across its heart. This was the flight path for experimental rocket tests: it sliced elegantly through Pipalyatjara and Well 33, it reached from Woomera as far north-west as Talgarno, beside the Indian Ocean's shore. The Weapons Research Establishment dispatched a pair of bush patrollers to travel through the dune-fields and clear the line of native camps. These officers became custodians of lonely country. They spent their lives travelling across the landscape, and with them, often, would ride scientists, writers, ethnographers. Those times are recalled in *They Called Me Tjampu-Tjilpi*, the memoir, replete with instances of Aboriginal telepathy and magic, of Patrol Officer Bob Verburgt. Verburgt made visits regularly to Patjarr and Karilwara; this corner of the desert spoke to something in him. In the wider world, in consequence, it became known as a place of revelation, the remote heart of Australia. It even acquired a certain international fame, for in 1965, on the plains round Patjarr, Ian Dunlop of the Commonwealth Film Unit made *Desert People*, a celebrated documentary of the nomadic life. The following year a New York anthropologist named Richard Gould stayed nearby, and published a book revealing secrets from Karilwara, that remains outlawed in the desert communities to this day. A year more, and Patjarr served as camp-site for Verburgt and another free-tongued American, John Greenway, whose life's ambition was to come upon an uncontacted Aboriginal tribe. Multiplicit himself, Greenway admired the versatility of the Ngaanyatjarra people whom he met, and shared the sense of superstition that still hangs above their world. He struggled constantly to escape the trap of reason; he noted the unending coincidences that brought him, in his desert journeyings, to certain places 'on the anniversary of an early explorer's presence'. Above all other precursors, it was Giles who haunted him, and whose spectre pursued his steps.

At the end of several days marooned at Patjarr, in the summer of 1968, as Greenway recounts, Verburgt and he set off towards Mount Everard and the Gunbarrel's western arm. Near the end of their route, at Wrakina claypan, they pulled up to search for meteorites: '*I saw protruding from the brittle clay surface a half inch of something just the slightest bit too regular to be natural.*' Greenway had found a broad-hatchet, hand-forged, made in the late nineteenth century.

He linked it immediately to Ernest Giles: '*Capricious fate, who had dealt me so many cruel disappointments, had suddenly given me something, the best something, to balance the scale*' – just as the desert always gives those who search in its emptiness the dream, at least, of their desires.

After such a hectic European prehistory, it was inevitable that, when a community was at last set up, in 1990, close to the Patjarr hills, and Karilwara rockhole, the weight of the past would seem to press down upon it, and for some this settlement has the feel of an Athens or a Weimar. It does not lie completely within our world; lost time and antiquity form its present day.

Several months had passed already since our initial conversations when, together with Esmé and two painting women from Warburton, I drove north into the Gibson, on the road to Patjarr, across plains of yellowed spinifex and flame-red sand. After several days of slow travel, firing the country, and cleaning waterholes, we reached the junction at Mipultjarra, left the old track east, which runs towards the Rawlinsons, and headed into lush, park-like terrain. Soon the landscape had its effect upon us. Talk in the back of the truck had been unceasing throughout the journey. Now it ebbed. The old ladies began to sing, breaking off only to spot far-distant kangaroos and bush turkeys, and yearn for rifles with which to shoot them, or to comment on fine points of detail in the hills and breakaways. Around mid-morning we approached the settlement. Low ridges shimmered ahead of us; the white roofs of the buildings caught the sun and gleamed. We passed some broken sheds and water-tanks. The road crossed a creekbed, and branched in two. I slowed.

'So here we are,' said Esmé, smiling in her most beatific way.

I pulled up.

'This is it?' I asked, looking round, and trying not to sound too startled. 'The centre of the inland? The oasis in the desert?'

'Absolutely,' said Esmé. 'Karilwara. Where everything falls into place. Why? Were you expecting something different?'

We had stopped in a small, half-cleared rectangle, surrounded by a handful of sketchy dwellings, brown-painted, with cavernous, shaded rooms and concrete floors, their perimeters marked by tall posts and rails of iron. A few more houses, empty, formed an inner island block. Beside one of these a transport van with New South Wales registration plates and no windscreen, tyres or wheels, was stationed. We got out. A pack of dogs, barking frantically, surrounded us. There was movement; the locals gathered.

'Look at your face!' said Esmé, once the introductions and the first exchanges were all past. 'Don't tell me you're disappointed. I thought you knew enough not to judge from appearances.'

'And you're happy to be here?'

'Of course – always – or there's a part of me that is. When I lived here, before, when Patjarr was first set up as an outstation, and we were camping down near the creekbed, that was one of the happiest times of my life. Now every time I come here I'm afraid. I almost wish it didn't exist and I didn't have to live in fear of its being destroyed.'

'You sound as if you were talking about your home.'

'Not at all,' she said. 'I'm a guest here. I barely scratch the surface. You see that gentleman staring at us, over there, in the nearest house? You were looking at his paintings in the Warburton Collection: that's Mr Giles.'

'A lineal descendant?'

'Don't be like that. He's an important man.'

'In what way?'

'Think of a whole universe you know nothing about. Are you coming with me? I'm going to take a quick look in the community office.' She nodded at a wood-planked building. 'I'm curious about what's inside. They've started displaying local artworks. It's a big departure for a place like this.'

I followed her in. On a counter in the front room was a selection of reading material covered by a light coat of dust: there were road maps, brochures, travel tips, a guide to learning desert languages. I flicked through these, under the stern eyes of a pair of Patjarr women. After some moments I joined Esmé in the main room, where a ramshackle gallery had been installed: carved sticks, a coolamon or two, a row of small, square canvases. I was about to turn away when a wooden panel leaning against the wall in a corner caught my eye. It was a bright, blood-shaded red; upon this background a sheen of grey circles and radiating spokes had been lightly, swiftly sketched. What could I see there? The X-ray of a dazzling crown, the explosion of a distant star? I shivered as I looked at it. I walked over to Esmé, trying to maintain an air of calm. She was poised in front of the panel, hand to her chin, gazing down.

'What do you think?' she asked, in a professional voice.

I looked at the price-tag. It was ten dollars.

'I think you can risk splashing out.'

'It says on the back it's by Mr Giles.'

'But don't you see,' I said, suddenly uplifted by a violent tide of feeling: agitation; newness; joy. 'It's perfect – almost too much so. The explorer's landscape. We came out to Patjarr because you wanted to show me that, and here it is.'

'I don't think it can be by Mr Giles. It must be a mistake: it's not his style.'

I kept my eyes fixed on the painting. I had the sense, in those moments, of knowledge cascading, pouring into me.

'It doesn't matter,' I said, absurdly, 'what the style is – or whose. It's a beautiful thing. If you don't buy it, I'll buy it for you.'

'I don't know that we really want to unleash the Gibson Desert's first bidding war,' said Esmé, producing a ten dollar bill, which she deposited on the counter in front of one of the young women behind it, while, in the same fluid movement, lifting the panel and placing it in my hands. 'It's not that I don't think it's beautiful: it's too beautiful.'

'Because beauty's the deceptive surface of life?'

'Because in the desert,' she said, in a remote, sharp way, 'it means different things. You see that house over there, set apart? That's where Mr Stansfield lives, the community adviser. He's an unusual man; he knows a lot of things about this country, and Karilwara. Why don't you go and introduce yourself?'

'You don't mean that Ausco container, over there, with all the heavy fencing and the razor-wire around it?'

'That's the one. Here. You take the painting. Knock loudly – he sometimes falls asleep in the middle of the day.'

I did as Esmé suggested. After several minutes there was a scraping and a muttering, and the metal door swung open.

'Who are you?' said Mr Stansfield, in a broad, slow, ambling voice.

I told him.

'A visitor?'

'In a sense.'

There was a disconcerting pause.

'You'd better come in then. Take a look at this.'

He handed me a sheet of paper, which I gazed at for some while, without making much progress in my attempts at decipherment.

'What is it?'

Mr Stansfield stared at me sceptically. He had a strong face, a broad, high nose, and a desert veteran's seared and freckled skin.

'It's the future of Patjarr, that's what,' he said. 'It's been photo-copied over a few times, it's true, it's getting hard to read. See, that's where we are – latitude 24 degrees 36.8 minutes south. Landing fees nil. We've got the best airstrip in the Gibson desert – actually, to be strictly honest with you, it's the only one. All-weather. Gravel.

Eighteen hundred metres. Avgas. Free camping. That's our slogan, there. What do you think?'

I peered down again at the sheet of paper.

'That? – "The Middle of Nowhere, the Centre of Everywhere"?'

'I thought it up myself. I was giving flight instructions to a pilot friend of mine, and he said it was catchy. I've got a grand plan. I want to turn Patjarr into an essential node-point on the map of international light aviation tourism.'

His eyes strayed to the painted wooden panel, which I had put down beside my feet.

'Did you buy that? I thought it was worthless, myself.'

'I think it's one of the most magical, majestic things I've seen in my entire life.'

'Really? Maybe we should take it back and have another think about the price.'

'And how's your campaign going,' I said, hastily, picking the panel up. 'Many people flying in?'

'We had a few, the other month. I'm doing everything I can. I've just put up a viewing platform, at the airstrip – did you see it? I've got reflector lights, for night-time movements, and Aboriginal designs along the runway every ninety metres.'

'Is that really necessary?'

'You have to make a good first impression. If I don't do all this, Patjarr will die. We're only just struggling along as it is. I built this place up with my own sweat and blood; it's everything to me. I've started up other communities in the lands – Wanarn, and Tjirrkarli – but this one is the place I love.'

'So you'd like to be buried here?'

'You mean like old teacher Ruby, at Kiwirrkurra, who wanted to buy a plot of land on top of the big sandhill for her grave?' He laughed, and gave me a quizzical look. 'Is it that obvious that I'm sick? Do you think I'm dying?'

'Not at all,' I said, alarmed.

'It's true, of course. I have to get out of here: leave everything that matters in my heart. Since I came out to the desert, the odd thing is I've almost never gone anywhere. I might have had ten weekends in Alice in my ten years at Patjarr.'

He trailed off. There was a silence as he gazed out at the hills. I listened to the sounds coming from the community: a generator's hum; dogs barking; children's cries.

'How did you get here, anyway?' said Mr Stansfield, as though returning with great difficulty to his immediate surrounds. 'Unusual traffic we've been getting these last weeks: there was a road train with two buildings on that decided to go out this way to Carnegie station, even though that track's very much four-wheel drive. I had to do an aerial search. I found them at the junction of the Gunbarrel and the Gary Highway. It took them three weeks to get to Tjirrkarli: those buildings of theirs were in a very sorry state.'

'I can imagine.'

'Can you? What did you come here for – to buy paintings?'

'You might find it hard to believe,' I said, 'if I told you there was a time when I was very keen to retrace the expedition route of Ernest Giles.'

'Giles!' He shook his head, a touch dismissively. 'It's strange. I was interested in the explorers myself once. I suppose I needed people to follow, and admire. When I first came out here, I used to live and breathe them and their journals. These days, I've changed my mind. They just don't seem to suit the country. They all came through here, though, that's for sure. Some of the old people even think they've found the last signs of Leichhardt's desert trail.'

'That would be a story!'

'Yes,' said Mr Stansfield. 'They say he got close to the rock-holes at Tika Tika, near here, on the Warburton to Patjarr road, and carved his initials, and an arrow, on a tree which was burned down.

He had carts, and equipment, and buried treasure, which they still go out looking for. They think he might have been running away because he was German, and it was round the time of Maralinga, during the war.'

'And Giles?'

'With him, you're on firmer ground. You see those hills, out there, like a line of broken shells on the far horizon, above the plain?'

'Just.'

'Some people think that's the Alfred and Marie Range that the explorer could see at his furthest west.'

'Those? They're the Alfred and Maries?'

I stared out. There was no more than a vague discontinuity, a hint of uplift in the bush.

'Very likely, yes. It must have been round here, almost where Patjarr stands now, that Giles decided to turn back, on his second expedition, the one where Gibson was lost. Of course, in a way, you can't be sure: they don't really exist at all in a fixed and solid sense. Sometimes, when it's overcast, the range is too faint and indistinct to see from here; and then sometimes, when the heat haze gets strong, you make them out quite easily from much further away.'

'And do you get many people coming out here, in the tracks of Giles?'

'That's all died away now.' He shook his head, as if to lament the vicissitudes of popular taste, and shrugged. 'You've got no idea. It used to be different. They were like Cloncurry kite-hawks, once.'

'Like what?' I said, taken aback.

'It's just an expression.'

The day advanced. I got up to go in search of Esmé, and round up our friends for the return. As I was walking past the community store, a tall, graceful woman came drifting over to me.

'You bought my painting,' she said, and laughed, and pointed at the panel beneath my arm.

'It's by Mr Giles.'

'No, I painted it – for fun. He asked me. He said: "Paint me a snake one." That's the water-snake from Karilwara.'

I stopped, and stared at her.

'Are you sure?'

'Yes. I painted it in ten minutes.'

Her voice was soft, and had the dusty, smoke-impregnated tone one meets with often in the desert lands. She was wearing a black dress; her hair was long and wildly tangled. We strolled ahead. She began to tell me something of herself, and her work, and course in life.

'You speak very idiomatic English,' I said to her.

'And you could speak very whatever it was Ngaanyatjarra if you learned it. I studied proper English at school' – a little pause, here, of pride – 'when I was away, at Karalundi.'

'I don't think I know that school.'

'At Meekatharra. It's famous! Christian place. All the best people go there. My cousin Lizzie went there.'

'Well, that clinches it, then. And where have you just sprung from now?'

'Blackstone,' she answered, very seriously. 'You know that place – a long way south of here? I was down there to see my son.'

'You don't look old enough to have any children.'

She laughed again.

'I've got five – no, six,' and one by one she ticked them off: 'Griselda; Cosmo; Delilah, Cheyenne – my twins – and Jackson; and Florida Jane.'

'They're lovely names you chose.'

'They come from music, some of them. From jukeboxes, and radio. I play music, on radio, at Warburton. Heavy metal: AC /DC, Deep Purple. Seventies music, and Eighties.'

'Many listeners?'

She smiled, and looked down, as though to divulge the answer would be to break a code of commercial confidentiality.

'You like that painting I did?'

'Very much. Is that your usual style?'

'No. I paint skulls and bones. I made the design on the T-shirts for the softball team. Skulls and bones,' she said, meditatively. 'And broken hearts.'

'How do you paint them?'

She looked at me as though I was a simpleton, and, with one index finger, traced out the shape of a valentine, then, with the other hand, made a jagged, slashing movement.

'Like that!'

'And where does all the imagery come from – all those skulls, and bones?'

'Bikie gangs. They drove out to LA – to Laverton – when I was a young girl. I used to ride around with them.'

An involved story followed. She spoke swiftly, softly, almost whispering her adventures into my ear.

'And were you painting, then, already, when you were with the Hell's Angels?'

'Yes – but they weren't the Hell's Angels. Other ones.'

'Other ones? Another gang? The Coffin Cheaters?'

'You know them?'

'You could say that my path crossed with a Coffin Cheater's, once. Those must have been wild times.'

'Wild times,' she said, with emphasis. 'Different now. That fast life's all gone. I don't ride with anyone. I'm free – I've got no man – I go where I want. Sometimes Perth, sometimes Shark Bay.'

'You get around.'

'I like changing. I don't like to stay anywhere too long.'

'And what about when you're at home – apart, that is, from dashing off the odd unconsidered masterpiece?'

'I take the tourists around Patjarr, when they come, to our special sites, all those dreaming sites, where the white people want to be.' Her voice dropped; she began to whisper. 'Water-snake dreaming; porcupine dreaming . . .'

'Why are you whispering?'

'I do that sometimes – that's our way.'

'And where are all those special places?'

'Why? You like dreams or something? Over there – where the country's broken up.'

She pointed to the ridges on the far horizon.

'You don't mean the Alfred and Marie Range?'

'What?' – in tones of bafflement.

'That's the European name. It was very important, in European history, once.'

'We call that place Minna Minna.'

I turned the name over, silently, as if saying goodbye, in those moments, to the Alfred and Maries; goodbye to all that was vanishing and passing in my life.

'Easy to get there,' said my companion. 'Only you can't go self; I can take you. You have to be careful. Say your name to the country, to the rock-holes, so they know you – who you are.'

'Do many people go there alone?'

'One white man. That prospector – he went, last year, in a yellow truck.'

'Not Esterline!' I said, and laughed, somehow pleased to hear that name once more upon my lips. 'It wasn't him – out here. My God. My brother-spirit, David Esterline!'

'He's your friend?'

'In a way, yes, I suppose he is – if strangers from different worlds can ever really know each other.'

'We're very sorry for him,' she then answered, quietly.

'Why's that?'

Staring towards the horizon, or to its notched, mirage-like shadow, I listened calmly as she told me her brief, elusive tale: how Esterline had driven into Patjarr in his ancient Landcruiser, loaded with equipment and supplies; how he had spent some days prospecting round there, in the hills, before heading north towards a remote, dry tableland. Nothing had been heard of him until, months afterwards, a team from Conservation and Land Management on a botanical survey, deep in the Gibson, examining the regeneration of desert oaks, came on a vehicle, a khaki Landcruiser – abandoned, burned out.

She ran through these details, her voice faltered, and at last I realised that my friend, whom I knew so briefly, and who seemed to me so much like a bird in flight, aloft, wheeling on the highest thermals, was no more; he had stumbled, in the desert, bleak and harsh, which stretches away inside all of us. No longer would he be with me, as a guardian shadow – he had gone into the silence of the sky.